A TASTE OF TRUE BLOOD

A TASTE OF TRUE BLOOD

The Fangbanger's Guide

EDITED BY LEAH WILSON

BENBELLA BOOKS, INC.

Dallas, TX

Smart Pop is an Imprint of BenBella Books, Inc.
6440 N. Central Expressway, Suite 503
Dallas, TX 75206
www.benbellabooks.com
www.smartpopbooks.com
Send feedback to feedback@benbellabooks.com

Printed in the United States of America
10 9 8 7 6 5 4 3 2 1

Library of Congress Cataloging-in-Publication Data is available for this title.
ISBN 978-1-935251-96-5

Some copyediting by Oriana Leckert and Heather Butterfield
Proofreading by Erica Lovett and Gregory Teague
Cover design by Charles Brock, Faceout Books
Text design and composition by PerfecType, Nashville, TN
Printed by Bang Printing

Distributed by Perseus Distribution
http://www.perseusdistribution.com/

To place orders through Perseus Distribution:
Tel: (800) 343-4499
Fax: (800) 351-5073
E-mail: orderentry@perseusbooks.com

Significant discounts for bulk sales are available. Please contact Glenn Yeffeth at
glenn@benbellabooks.com or (214) 750-3628.

TABLE OF CONTENTS

INTRODUCTION

I was reading the first drafts of the essays collected here at a coffee shop when I ran into a friend who'd stopped in to grab an afternoon latte. She asked about the stack of papers and I explained that I was working on an essay anthology about *True Blood*.

Taking a surreptitious glance around, she lowered her voice, bent her head, and asked, "But isn't *True Blood* pretty much, like, *porn?*"

I could see where she was coming from. I could think of scenes—Sookie and Bill's season one graveyard rendezvous; the more attractive moments of some of Maryann's season two orgies; pretty much any scene involving Jason—that, if I were to come across them while flipping through cable channels, I might mistake for soft-core smut (with higher production values), too.

What you get out of *True Blood*, I think, depends on what you put in. (Granted, this is true of many things, both in life and on television.) If that's five minutes flipping through channels in a hotel room, it's probably porn. But if that's an hour, religiously, once a week (plus DVD re-watches, time on message boards, conversations with like-minded friends), it can be a whole lot more.

If you want to watch for the sex, you can. If you want to watch to ogle Eric ("Nordic, stoic, delicious Eric, with those bulging muscles, piercing blue eyes, penchant for T-strap tank tops," as Jonna Rubin sighs), or because you love Bill and Sookie's romance, the show rewards that. You can watch for the "complex social world . . . with an ever-expanding cast of interesting, engaging, and multidimensional characters," the way Karen Bethke does, or because "it's *fun*," the way her husband Bruce does. And if you watch for deeper themes (the "twining dance of abandon and repression" that Jacob Clifton sees in Tara and Jason's storylines), or watch to learn more about the human condition (the "terrors of intimacy" Carol Poole untangles in Sookie's relationship with Bill and with Bon Temps), *True Blood* has that, too.

It's a pretty impressive feat, to work so well on so many levels. And it's our goal to be a book that has something for all *True Blood* fans, no matter why they watch. We hope *A Taste of True Blood* will do just what its title says: give you a taste of what others see when they watch the show—and give you a few new reasons to watch, too.

Leah Wilson
April 2010

VAMPIRE PORN

DANIEL M. KIMMEL

Great opening credits do more than introduce characters. They act as a gateway from the real world to the world of the show, and give us a framework with which to better understand the events we're about to see. Daniel M. Kimmel dissects *True Blood*'s credits, reminding us what an opening sequence can and should do for a show—and stumbles onto a compelling and unexpected explanation for why its images unsettle us so much.

More than one person, told that I was writing an essay about the opening credits for *True Blood*, recoiled. It was something they had seen and now fast-forwarded through, unable to watch the montage of disturbing images. It was too "weird" or "upsetting." (Mind you, these were people who then sat back and enjoyed a show where the heroine has sex with a vampire and that was fine.) Even at the 2009 World Science Fiction Convention held in Montreal, the panel on *True Blood* began with a discussion of the opening. The sequence is a startling compendium of images that both sets the stage for the show and constitutes a story in itself. It was put together by a production house called Digital Kitchen, which has also done the openings for *Dexter* and *Six Feet Under*, the latter show created by Alan Ball, the person behind *True Blood*.

Rather than go through a shot-by-shot transcript, it's helpful to think of this sequence of seemingly random shots by its recurring motifs. (If you need to refresh your memory and don't have a DVD or an episode On Demand handy, the credit sequence is readily available as a standalone on YouTube and elsewhere on the Internet.) These motifs include the South, religion, bigotry, death, and sex.

Clearly these motifs are also the focus of the show. The location in rural Louisiana gives the show its particular small-town bayou flavor. Religion became a major subject in the second season, but right from the start the show was taken, in part, as a metaphor for the battle over—and religious opposition to—gay rights. In the credits we see a sign that declares, "God hates fangs," an obvious play on extremist religious protesters' claim that "God hates fags." Thus bigotry by humans toward vampires, even the good ones who drink Tru Blood instead of draining their mortal neighbors, is another obvious theme of the show. We also see bigotry from the opposite direction: by some vampires toward humanity. As for death, can you imagine a vampire story without it? From the undead vampires to the corpses of their victims—plus the bodies of those unfortunate enough to cross the paths of *True Blood*'s other killers, human or supernatural—the episodes are steeped in death. Finally, as for sex, it almost goes without saying that who's coupling with whom is one of the major forces driving the plot.

On a superficial level, therefore, the opening credits simply set the stage for the show. Yet if we removed the actual credits for cast and crew, the only thing that ties this sequence of images to the show is the appearance of the title *True Blood* in the latter part of the montage. None of the characters appear (as they do in the openings of such shows as *Dexter* and *The Sopranos*) and the scenes are not from past or future episodes (as with *The Wire*). So what is going on here and why does it creep us out to such an extent that some people can't watch the opening credits at all?

There seem to be three main reasons people find them disturbing. First off are those real images of unpleasant things that we usually don't think about. Whether it's the startling bigotry of a little boy in the regalia of the Ku Klux Klan or the high-speed consumption of an animal carcass by maggots, the images are shocking precisely because they're not fiction. Blatant hate and nature in the raw are disturbing.

A second level of creepiness is due to ambiguity, those images where we're not at all certain what's going on. We think we're reading the image properly and then something subverts it. At first glance the baptism toward the end of the credit sequence appears to be a statement of religious affirmation, but it also contains elements that make us question our initial impression. Why is it taking place at night? Why, after she is immersed, does the woman being baptized seem to be trying to escape and who are the two men pulling her back? We ought to be able to read this scene but we can't.

Finally there are images that are disturbing because they've been given new context: either how the image has been edited into the sequence or the appearance of the film itself. An example of the former is the image of the man in the rocking chair grinning at us. By itself it might or might not be disturbing. Coming immediately after the boy in the KKK outfit it becomes a statement about how things are different here in ways we may not like. ("A boy in a Klan outfit? You have a problem with that . . . Yankee?")The crumpling of the film in spots, and the drops of blood that appear not within the images but on top of them, are offered with no explanation at all, leaving us without a guidepost in a way that is particularly unsettling.

Taken together, we come to the end of what ought to be simply an introduction to the show, its cast, and above-the-line crew (producers, director, writer, etc.), instead feeling as if we've entered another world. It looks like our world, but there's an "otherness" to it that's hard to define. Part of the reason is that it goes by so fast— it only runs 90 seconds. We're taking in the information faster than we can process it. So let's slow down the credit sequence and take it apart and see if we can get at what makes it tick.

––––

ARGUABLY EVERY SHOT IN THE opening montage is there to communicate the show's rural Louisiana setting and to set the scene for us with some local color. For the viewer outside of the rural South, though, it's all weird even if there's nothing supernatural going on. The opening scenes take us from the swampy bayou, complete with alligator, to a series of houses. One is on poles above the water, another is a boarded up shack, another is an old but more stately structure. It is with this last image that we first see spots on the film, as if the footage is very old or damaged from overuse. We also start seeing signs that tell us we're in a bad part of town: "No Loitering," "The New Lucky Liquor." In *his* opening credits Tony Soprano got to drive through increasingly upscale neighborhoods before pulling into the driveway of his plush McMansion, demonstrating that he was moving on up, not only economically but in the hierarchy of the New Jersey mob. There will be no such

6

changes in economics or class in the images we see for *True Blood*. The two shots of an apparently abandoned car mired in the swamp let us know we're not in a place where such things would be safely and cleanly carted away.

Images of church steeples and cemeteries provide more local color, as well as touching on the themes of religion and death, while the times of day the shots depict—sunset, a full moon, and sunrise—are all markers for vampires being creatures of the night.

Of these "local color" shots there's only one that is disturbing, and if you're not paying close attention you might not even notice it, at least not on a conscious level. There are several shots of young boys that we'll examine below. However, there is one shot of a boy in a black shirt walking past a shuttered window on a brightly lit porch at night. We don't know who this boy is or, for that matter, where he is or where he's going. He could simply be joining his friends in some innocent pursuit. It's not the harsh lighting that makes the image disturbing, it's what happens to the boy. At the end of the shot the boy vanishes from the image, which then continues for another moment without him. What we see is an eerie little boy crossing the screen in a stark setting and suddenly disappearing. Given the context of the show, the boy might be a vampire, able to move faster than humans can detect, which turns this image into something quite different. Instead of an innocent boy going to collect fireflies, he may be an unnaturally young—even by vampire standards—predator looking for his next meal. It's the not knowing that's most disturbing.

———

THE IMAGES OF RELIGIOUS FERVOR may also seem strange to some, but they serve as a reminder that the show is firmly located in the Bible Belt. In many ways this, too, is part of the local color. The first such image is of people singing and clapping with joy at a black church. Our focus is a woman obviously in her "Sunday best," wearing a white dress and hat as well as a cross pendant. There are other people in the shot, including the only young girl seen in the credits sequence, but our focus is the woman. These are happy, prayerful people who would seem disturbing only to those whose idea of a religious service is stately decorum. What's unsettling is *where* the image appears in sequence: right between the boarded up shacks marked "No Loitering" and the New Lucky Liquor store. The context for these people who seem to be making a joyful noise is between decay and sin.

Indeed, these church images are used throughout in a way that either echoes or comments upon the images of sex and death. A series of shots set in a bar with a woman writhing against a man ends with a black minister doing an ecstatic leap into the air during a church service. More quick shots of people having real or simulated sex (see below) lead to a static shot of two church ladies, their heads bowed in fervid prayer. One appears to be crying while the other has her hands tightly clasped. They seem to be at the Church of Jesus (as identified on the name tag one wears) praying to be delivered from the depravity we—and they?—have witnessed in the previous shots.

Two later church shots, one of a black woman seeming to faint or fall into the arms of a white minister and another of possibly the same woman writhing in what one assumes is religious ecstasy, are intercut with increasingly frenetic images of sex. The series culminates in an extreme close up of a red lipsticked mouth inhaling smoke. This leads to what some viewers may assume are the final shots of the sequence, though they are not, in which a white woman is being ministered to by two white men in the middle of a pond at night. The garb and the gestures indicate that a baptism is taking place, although why it would be at night is not clear. Even stranger, after the woman is fully dunked as befitting a "total immersion" baptism, she seems to be trying to get away from the two men who pull her back. Did she panic, or is this not what it appears to be? We're given no further information, making what ought to be a moment of religious affirmation vaguely unsettling.

These particular images do give us some information about the show we're about to watch: we're in a community with an active church life; for some people the church may be a refuge or bulwark against the things they find degrading in the outside world; and there just may be some disturbing things going on in the churches as well. All of these ideas have been subsequently explored in the series so far, and there's no reason to think the show won't continue to do so.

———

ON INITIAL VIEWING IT IS the imagery of bigotry and death that may prove the most upsetting. On a superficial level *True Blood* uses its newly mainstreamed vampires as a way to explore civil rights issues, particularly, it would seem, that of gay rights. While Lafayette, the one openly gay character, seems to be well regarded, or at least accepted, by the other characters, that's because the newly outed vampires provide a fresh target for prejudice. The sign reading "God hates fangs" is simply the most obvious way the opening montage addresses the issue of bigotry, and it's more an example of sardonic humor than something that strikes us as viscerally evil. There are no actual vampires in reality to be discriminated against, after all. The sign's real-world inspiration—what the show's sign is, in effect, mocking—is much more deeply offensive.

There are three shots that touch on the earlier civil rights struggle in the South. The first is of white policemen carrying away a black protester by his arms and legs. The film appears to be news footage, possibly from a sit-in, and informs us about the history of where the story is set. Although the show's characters seem largely free of racial prejudice, the shot of the protester being carted off is followed by a similar shot, presumably from the same event, of passive white onlookers witnessing it with approval. There is certainly no indication that they are shocked by what they are seeing or in any way object to it. It's part of the history of the region, to be sure, but the credits are primarily focused on the present day, so this use of historic footage stands out. As we see below, there's an open question as to just how much the "New" South has changed.

The image likely to shock here comes a few moments later. It is that shot of an adorable young boy, maybe four years old, dressed up in Ku Klux Klan regalia complete with white hood. He looks out at us with an expression that's hard to read. He is clearly at an age too young to comprehend the meaning of his garb, but it is also clear he is being brought up to hate, especially when we notice the baby bottle in the hand of the adult standing behind the boy. He has been imbibing bigotry with his mother's milk. This image disturbs not only because it depicts the corruption of innocents by adults who know exactly what they're doing. It disturbs because it seems real. This black and white footage, too, appears to come from a news report or documentary, not something created for the show. If we assume the reality of that image, it is more horrifying than any vampire because it reflects an evil of *our* world, one that won't disappear when the episode ends. The only solace we can take is that the image seems to be from the past, probably decades ago, and we can tell ourselves that such things are not happening today, at least not out in the open and as blatantly as that.

Or can we? The very next image we see is of a middle-aged man in a rocking chair, greeting us with a mocking grin. His appearance and clothes suggest "backwoods," and we might ask if this is that boy grown up, at least in the context of the montage. Where the viewer is appalled at the image of the child Klansman, the rocking man seems to find it, and our reaction to it, amusing. This gives way to a series of shots of two young boys, obviously in the present day, sharing some sort of snack that leaves their lower faces covered with juice the color of blood. It is only a few moments later that the boy in the black shirt "disappears" from the porch. The cumulative effect of this sequence completely subverts the image of children as innocent: they wear Klan outfits, they eat something that makes them a bloody mess, they vanish into thin air. All of this is anchored by that grinning man in the rocking chair, which at least subtly, raises the specter of child abuse and even molestation.[1] The sequence as a whole leaves us in a dark place, that nighttime porch with limited light.

We see one final image along this theme: a cross ignited in flames. The burning cross is, of course, an image of the Klan. It's not clear where this color footage is from, whether it, too, is archival or was created for this sequence. However, given the default assumption that the color footage is all taking place "now," we're left with the inescapable notion that this organized hate continues in the New South and that it's not just the vampires who need to keep looking over their shoulders.

---

[1] Please note: This is a comment on the image in the context of the credit montage and not at all of the actual person in the rocker who was reportedly a very friendly fellow who invited the film crew into his home.

AS ALREADY NOTED, ANY TELEVISION series about vampires will, inevitably, focus on death. Vampires themselves are "undead" and those who are not fastidious in how they feed will leave a trail of bodies in their wake. Anyone squeamish about such things likely wouldn't be watching *True Blood* in the first place. What makes the credits sequence creepy is what images have been selected to represent death. The first is a cemetery, a familiar locale in horror, especially when dealing with vampires who sleep in coffins by day and emerge at night. The first is a cemetery, a familiar locale in horror, especially when dealing with vampires who sleep in coffins by day and emerge at night.

Instead of dead people we get images of animals as predators and prey. Like a nature film run amok, these are things that frighten us. First we see an image of a snake baring its fangs and rearing back to strike. Visually the fangs link the snake to the vampires of the show, but this is an all-too-real image that most of us hope never to see in person. For those of us who are city dwellers and can't tell one snake from another, this is a life-threatening image. Is this a venomous snake? Is its poison deadly? Fast-acting? Wouldn't I rather be getting a cup of coffee instead? A few shots later, another predator becomes prey when we see what appears to be an alligator skull hanging from a porch, its jaws opened as wide apart as possible.

The film's editors keep upping the ante. The next death image is of road kill, a possum or similar creature lying bloody and quite obviously dead in the road. We want to look away, as we might in real life, but that's not the nature of television viewing where, unless the television is simply serving as background noise, we are focused on the screen. Still, dead animals on the road is a fact of life anywhere wildlife and civilization share the same environment, and for locals this would not be shocking but merely something for the local road crews to clean up. The young frog or lizard caught in some sort of Venus Fly Trap–style predatory plant is also disturbing but, again, this is simply nature at work. There's a food chain that humans rarely think about because we're at the top of it, but for much of nature life is eat or be eaten. The image may bother us both because we're not used to confronting such things in our modern lives and also because the arrival, or outing, of vampires means that we may *not* be the top of the food chain anymore. Given the illegal market for vampire's blood, who's consuming whom has certainly gotten more complicated.

This leads to what may be the most upsetting image of all: high-speed photography of a dead fox being consumed by maggots. This, too, is perfectly natural and this, too, is something we don't really want to see, particularly every week at the start of a new episode. It is an "ew" moment, where we may want to look away from the screen in disgust.

One final nature shot is more ambiguous. Something—a locust?—is emerging from a cocoon. Besides the general ickiness of any birth process (even when the result is a much desired and loved baby), it's not automatically clear what's being born here. Is it is dangerous or benign? This, too, fits in with the theme of the show, where the emergence of the "vampire community" has led to societal debate on whether vampires as citizens is a good or bad thing. Much as we like Bill Compton, whether we'd welcome the other vampires we meet on the show into our neighborhood is an open question.

AS WE TURN TO OUR final theme, mention must be made of the song that plays throughout the opening sequence, a hauntingly discordant number by Jace Everett called "Bad Things." Its lyrics are about obsession and power games ("I don't know who you think you are/But before this night is through/I want to do bad things with you"). Played over images of hate and death, and people seemingly praying about such things, it would be eerie enough. However, when the sequence's creators add a complex layer of sexual imagery, the song cannot help but be read in that context. The "bad" things the lyrics reference may, in fact, be earnestly desired by the participants—as with vampires and "fangbangers"—and seem depraved only to those on the outside who disapprove.

It is in the sexual imagery that the series tips its hand, making explicit what is mostly only implied: that the tolerance *True Blood* asks for vampires is, in reality, a plea for tolerance for human sexual expression in all its forms. Though some of these images are shown long enough to register, others are on screen so briefly that they border on the subliminal. It is only by pausing and going through the sequence shot by shot that all of the images become clear. Indeed, it is during the opening location shots, just before the "No Loitering" shacks, that we get our first quick flash of sex: two naked women, with drops of blood not on the women but on the image itself. (We will return to those drops shortly.) Meanwhile the first clear sexual image we see is a woman dancing or writhing in her underwear in what appears to be a motel room. It's not clear who, if anyone, she is performing for, but her movements are unmistakably provocative and sexual. After the sequence with the young boys described previously, there is a clearly visible shot of a woman covering her bare breasts as she dances.

This leads to a bar sequence that reveals several layers when examined closely. First there's a heterosexual couple going hot and heavy, clearly getting as close to sex as they can while remaining fully clothed. The woman is in cut-off shorts and a top that consists of little more than a front piece and some ties. As they grind together she lifts her legs—she's seated—and puts them around the man as he pushes into her. Other men nearby seem not to be paying attention. There's a quick insert of an unidentified naked woman with blood on the image, and then a cut to the same scene from another angle, where we can see that the woman is sitting on a pool table. For those with long memories this image might evoke the setting of not only a notorious 1983 New Bedford, Massachusetts, rape case but *The Accused*, the 1988 Jodie Foster movie loosely inspired by the real-life incident.

Now we shift to another bar scene. Whether it's at the same bar or a different one isn't clear and may not make a difference. What is different is that we now see two men in conversation, each with their left arms up and next to the other, one of them leaning against the wall and boxing the other in so it seems like a partial embrace. Reading that as homoerotic may be a stretch, but not when it's juxtaposed with a fleeting image, also with blood drops, of two naked men, with one holding the other closely from behind.

Returning to the couple at the bar—assuming it is the same couple—we see them now on the dance floor, and the film "stutters" so we can't miss her shaking her booty at him. He then embraces her from behind and they continue to dance, cheek to cheek, as more blood drops appear on the film. As with the two men, this image is followed by a quick shot of a naked male and female coupling, with the woman being taken from behind. This, too, is accompanied by blood drops. From here on out there are several hetero- and homoerotic images mixed together. Some, like a red-lit woman undulating on all fours on a barroom dance floor, are easy to make out. Some, like the male couple where you can actually detect pubic hair and part of the penis of one of the participants, occur so quickly that they register as undifferentiated naked flesh. The shot of a woman seemingly possessed at a church service quickly leads to the dancer writhing on the floor, linking these two kinds of ecstasy in ways neither would ever imagine.

When we now encounter the red painted lips seductively inhaling the smoke it can be read as a fetishistic moment where the smoke stands for the life force (i.e., the blood) vampires suck in. After the appearance of the *True Blood* title card, this is made explicit with a shot of a female couple, a brunette holding back the head of her blonde partner (victim?) to expose her throat. Is this a moment of passion, of vampiric feeding, or both? The contrast and confusion of death and sex has been widely commented upon. On the one hand, sex, since it can potentially lead to new life, is the opposite of death. It is an affirmation of being alive and creating life. On the other hand, the moment of orgasm, of losing one's self in the other, has been called *le petit mort* or "the little death." Briefly, lost in sensation, one ceases to be. So this confluence of sex and death in a vampire story can evoke all sorts of feelings.

The credit sequence concludes with the previously mentioned baptism, followed by a final rapid-fire montage: the neon cross seen earlier, various naked bodies, the sun rising, the woman dancer, and daylight. Some more blood drops appear on the images. Where are the blood drops from and why are they there? They are not *in* the images; the dancer, for example, is not being splattered with blood. Instead the blood is on the film itself. This implies someone outside the credit sequence who is watching it with us, and whose reaction to the images leads to drops of blood flecking the screen.

In watching this short film we're constantly given indications it is old and beat up, possibly watched repeatedly over a long period of time. The images fade or crumple, and spots (other than blood) appear. It seems like nothing so much as an old pre-video stag reel that would appear at bachelor parties or other all-male occasions and that may have been utilized as a solo sex aid as well. In spite of the sexiness of some of the images, their mixture with death, bigotry, religious fervor, and violence (as in a quick shot of a man shoving another, in what we imagine could turn into a barroom brawl) is not something a normal person would find arousing. Indeed, it's hard to think of any *mortal* man who would see this as anything but memorably weird and creepy.

Ah, but a vampire? To a vampire humans at their most vulnerable—whether consumed by lust, hate, or religious ecstasy—must be especially enticing. This sequence is disturbing in the same way stumbling upon another person's private collection of pornography would be: it gives us a peek into someone else's psyche that we would just as soon not have. How much more depraved it is to discover what excites one of the undead.

Those blood drops may represent the splatter of a victim enticed back to the vampire's lair for a promised video treat. Or they may represent the sort of vampiric release that would truly make this uncomfortable to watch. For the folks at Digital Kitchen who created the credit sequence, all this may be just a collection of images that sets the scene for *True Blood*, as their openings for *Six Feet Under* and *Dexter* do for those shows. No one is claiming they intended to create vampire porn. However, when so many people have such a visceral reaction, there's clearly something more going on.

It is the cumulative power of the real and the ambiguous and unknown that takes us from our living rooms and into the world of *True Blood*. The result is that some people will continue to fast-forward through the show's opening credits, for reasons they can't fully explain to themselves or to anyone else.

DANIEL M. KIMMEL is past president of the Boston Society of Film Critics and reviewed for the *Worcester* (Massachusetts) *Telegram* and *Gazette* for twenty-five years. His reviews currently appear at NorthShoreMovies.net. He has been a contributor to *Artemis, The Internet Review of Science Fiction,* and *ClarkesWorld.* His essay "The Batman We Deserve" appeared in SmartPop's *Batman Unauthorized.* The author of several books, he is currently working on a collection of his writings on science fiction films.

SOOKEH! BEE-ILL! AND THE DOWNFALL OF WILLIAM T. COMPTON

How Vampire Bill Went From Sex Symbol to Sad Punchline

JONNA RUBIN

When it comes to TV, love can be fickle. And it's not just the characters we see on screen whose loyalties change with the direction of the wind— ours do, too. Characters that thrill us one week can bore us the next. Take Bill Compton . . . please. Jonna Rubin charts how over the course of two seasons Vampire Bill won then lost our hearts, and speculates on how he might—*might*—be able to make it up to us.

Everyone loves a bad boy, especially if he's a vampire. I mean, isn't that why vampires are experiencing such a renaissance in pop culture? Isn't that why an alarming number of my contemporaries—thirtysomething women, *ahem*—have a life size cutout of Edward Cullen in their possession?

Don't get me wrong—nice guys have their place. In fact, it is my opinion that everyone *should* choose the nice guy when it comes to a life partner. The heady, dangerous guy isn't going to pick you up on time, bring you flowers, or be the loving father you've always dreamed of; I get that. I married the good guy, and am extraordinarily happy about it. True story.

But that's in reality, folks, and if there's anything *True Blood* isn't, it's reality.

The vampire's very nature—requiring human blood or a reasonable facsimile for sustenance—makes being a good guy a tenuous possibility at best. And isn't that the point? *True Blood* is fraught with sex, nudity, and inherently dangerous characters, from shapeshifters to maenads to vampires. Whatever creature they serve up for us to fall for, one would hope that there would be an element of sexy, sexy danger involved. It's fantasy, after all.

Sadly, at the end of season one, when it comes to our lead vampire, it seems hope is a futile thing indeed.

Let me be more direct: Can Alan Ball and Stephen Moyer stop making Bill into a perpetual, wet, limp noodle and turn him back into the *al dente* bite of deliciousness we enjoyed in the first season? Is Bill Compton even worth watching anymore, or has he reached the comically weak point of no return?

From the minute he first walked into Merlotte's, the lights went dim, time slowed down, and his—look, I'm sorry, there's no other way to say this—*smoldering gaze* captured Sookie's attention, I was smitten. Well, maybe not *smitten*, but all aflutter with something less wholesome-sounding and more than a little inappropriate and, uh, lusty-tasting.

He's dangerous—even as she saved him from certain death at the hands of the Rattrays, he reminded her that vampires, including him, could turn on her at any moment. Yet it only added to his allure. During his second visit to the bar, he beckoned her closer with little more than a look, and she strode over to him, fueled entirely by animal attraction. He was sex, personified—from the way he tilted his head, to the position of his hips as he slid the chair out for her to join him. By the time he offered his hand, palm open, it was no longer an innuendo. It was the full monty, baby, and we were all in it, knee-deep and panting for more. She closed her eyes, twisted her body in pleasure, and breathed deeply. So did I.

Before you knew it, we were panting heavily, slamming our hands against the table, yelling, "Yes! Yes! YES!"

Meg Ryan's fake deli orgasm had nothing on this. That Vampire Bill—well, Bill 1.0, anyway—was a hot one, oh yes he was. In fact, it seemed there was little he could do to dissuade us that he wasn't the hottest vampire in pop culture history.

We were wrong.

Let's compare this above scene to that of one toward the end of season two. Picture, if you will, a church sanctuary full of suicidal soldiers of God and a bevy of angry vampires about to wage a modern version of a centuries-old war. The entire room is about to erupt in a murderous melee, and most of the room is angling to kill Sookie. For all Bill's talk of how desperately Sookie must be protected, he is nowhere to be found.

And then suddenly, there he is, barging into the room, a day late and more than a fang short, screeching, "SOOKEH!" in a Southern accent that would make Paula Deen move to New Jersey. By the time he reaches her, the conflict has been defused— by her dimwitted brother Jason, no less—and she falls into him with more drama than Scarlett O'Hara as he croons, "It's okay, you're sayfe nayow!" ("Timebomb," 2-8).

And with that, an entire legion of would-be fangbangers headed to the mall to trade in their Bill Compton poster for a life-size cutout of Edward Cullen. The defection was complete.

Most of us saw this coming—we read the subtle signs that while Bill was purporting to move further toward a humane existence, what he was really becoming was an impotent vampire and, worse, an unattractive, impotent *man*. The scene in the sanctuary was merely the final nail in the coffin where Bill Compton, Sex Symbol lays. Fans everywhere mourned, but only for a moment. After all, there is still Eric. Nordic, stoic, delicious Eric, with those bulging muscles, piercing blue eyes, penchant for T-strap tank tops, and that voice! Oh, it's low and sexy and . . .

I'm sorry, where was I?

Oh yes. Bill. Right. The two Bills are so divergent that it is as though they are played or written by two entirely different people. So, what happened? Why do so many viewers—well, this one anyway, but you can't tell me I'm alone—now put their proverbial pants back on the moment Bill steps onto the screen? Is it the hair? The accent? His insistence on returning to a very lame version of humanity?

Let's start with looks, shall we?

While one could certainly argue that Bill's fall from grace as a sex symbol can be traced back almost entirely to personality changes, it's hard to deny that on closer viewing, there were subtle aesthetic changes taking place as well. If we take a look at Bill's first appearance in "Strange Love" (1-1), he little resembles the Bill who so foolishly bursts into the Fellowship of the Sun church during his ill-fated fall from grace. Everything about him is rough around the edges—from his slightly rumpled hair parted haplessly to the side, to his worn army jacket, very likely carried over from his days as a soldier during the Civil War. He exudes casual confidence, harkening back to a time well before metrosexuals came onto the scene, when a man getting a pedicure was an action punishable by death. (I'm pretty sure a hairbrush, too, was considered a prohibitively feminine object back then.)

Perhaps most mysteriously, however, he is unshaven, sporting a delicious little five o'clock shadow along with that mussed hair. (Not to run too far afield here, but I can't quite get a grip on the hair growth patterns of vampires. If hymens grow back to their original condition, why doesn't hair? Eric's facial hair is nearly gone in season two, and Bill's stubble meets a similar fate. And if Eric is naturally blond, as his heritage and backstory would suggest, why does he need highlights?)

Over the course of the season, his clothes become slightly more tailored, but always appropriate for a southern gentleman—never too namby-pamby, yet occasionally fitted and belted just enough to show off his enviable backside. Then there's the henley. Mmm, the henley, wardrobe staple of sexy, murderous men. I'm not sure when or how it happened, but the henley has become the go-to shirt for men up to no good. Michael C. Hall's Dexter Morgan—the only serial killer who's safe to marry—wears a waffle-weave henley as part of his killing uniform, and Bill often leverages its body-hugging qualities to enhance his vampire allure. Form-fitting and open just enough at the collar to give a sneak peek of what's underneath, the henley is a surprisingly mundane, yet effective, wardrobe tool for men of the dangerous, blood-letting persuasion. Viva la henley, I say!

His accent is present, but still sexy. He's too gentlemanly to have the boyish, good-old-boy allure of Josh Holloway's Sawyer in ABC's *Lost*, but he evokes just enough of Rhett Butler to be charming.

One hot dude, right?

Season two's Bill is a little more groomed, but instead of working for him, the look is so buttoned up, it's almost stifling. You'd be hard-pressed to find a scene where Bill isn't wearing a belt, and there is far too much shoe-clicking going on for my liking. In nearly every scene, he's clacking around all over the place, like a secretary in high heels. And bangs! When did Bill get bangs? Oh heavens, they're almost wispy, and yet unfortunately blunt, like he did them himself in the bathroom on a whim.

And look, I don't even know where to start with the changes taking place in his accent. Once subtle and strangely exotic, Bill 2.0's accent is . . . well, it's awful. Instead of feeling authentic, it's all I hear when he speaks—it's so conspicuous, it nearly drowns out the meaning of the simplest of words. What I find most surprising about this is that actors usually improve their accent as they grow more comfortable playing their characters. Sadly, someone seemed to decide that what Bill really needed were more impotent cries of "SOOKEH!" and less, uh, subtlety. Or maybe a near-constant outpouring of absurd emotion just doesn't sound good with an accent. It could go either way.

A little humanity is irony. This is . . . something else.

Intellectually, I like to think I get what the show was aiming for here. Yes, Bill is regaining his humanity after countless decades spent losing it to the ways of the vampire. I believe that's probably a bit of a struggle. And yes, yes, I could see how it would be difficult to reconcile the need to live off of human blood with the desire to be, uh, human in spirit. Frankly, though, I'd have been happy if his homage to humanity had primarily consisted of subsisting on Tru Blood, while he continued to be menacing as hell for the fun of it. Unfortunately, if you're Bill Compton, a key component to becoming more human is morphing slowly into a combination of Felix Unger and Andy Rooney.

Bill 1.0 is human enough to be appealing, but there's no denying he's a vampire. He acts on impulse, and the results aren't always pretty. Take, for example, "Escape from Dragon House" (1-4), where, irritated at the harassment from the police officer who stopped him and Sookie after the raid on Fangtasia, he toyed with the cop like prey, glamouring him, taking his gun and leaving the officer to stew, quite literally, in a puddle of his own urine.

Okay, maybe that wasn't the sexiest of scenes, but you get my point. Bill 1.0 was a force to be reckoned with, while the updated version . . . well, not so much.

Frankly, I'm not even sure Bill 2.0's version of humanity is something I, as an actual human, am particularly interested in. In "Nothing But the Blood" (2-1), instead of focusing on new vampire daughter Jessica's survival in her new form, he was awkward, bumbling, and helpful as a salve of lemon juice on a razor burn. When she cried, she was shocked to see that her tears had been replaced with blood, a key detail he never shared with her. Not only was he completely unable to be any sort of commanding presence at a time when she needed it most, but his lessons for her were giant, steaming piles of buzzkill. No hunting or killing, a rigid, early bedtime, and a useless demonstration of which bins paper and glass products go in. Yes, in the important facts to know about becoming a vampire, Bill Compton-style, recycling ranks in the top three.

It seems that being human, at least according to this vampire, means having absolutely no idea how to man up and mentor the next generation without sounding like an old fart. Think I'm exaggerating? In the same conversation, he grumpily instructed her to clean herself up and remove her makeup, announcing, "I will not have you looking like a slattern." By which, he awkwardly explained, he meant a lady of the evening.

It's no wonder that Jessica, in her petulant teenage frustration while trying in vain to find her preferred cocktail of Tru Blood, announced, "You are soooo not Eric."

No, he most certainly isn't Eric. Which brings me to . . .

It's raining sexy supes, Bill, but you're too busy playing Wii to put up a damn umbrella.

While the character of Bill Compton was circling the drain, one of the best things to come out of season two was the intense character development of secondary, and even tertiary, characters. It was a pleasure watching Tara Thornton—and by association, the gifted Rutina Wesley—have her own storyline independent of Sookie and Bill; and Lafayette, and even Terry Bellefleur, became some of the most talked-about characters after nearly every episode. And though it was distasteful to book purists, I was transfixed by the Maryann Forrester storyline and fell hard for Michelle Forbes as a result.

However, the real standouts were Sam Merlotte and Eric Northman. Relegated to supporting roles in season one, the two moved from background noise to viable competitors for the audience's affections, if not Sookie's.

In fact, it's almost as though Sam and Bill switched roles sometime in the off-season. Though rakishly handsome and rugged, season one's Sam was awkward, pleading, and a little too desperate for Sookie's attention to be considered appealing. Even his sexual relationship with Tara felt forced and inauthentic, like he was playing the role of someone who could handle a casual relationship—you got the feeling that Sam liked to be in love for the sex to count, and even then, it only counted if it was with Sookie. Excuse me while I grab my barf bag.

In season two, however, Sam really came into his own. From growing comfortable in his own skin through an ill-fated dalliance with a fellow shifter, to repeatedly putting his own life on the line to protect the integrity of the town he loves, Sam Merlotte became one stand-up hunk of a dog—err, man. The plaid shirts, cowboy boots, and Texas-sized belt buckles only added to his allure.

And then there is Eric. Oh, Eric. Who else can make track pants and flip flops so sexy? Sure, the guy might sport foils and lament that Pam, his longtime partner and progeny, is going to kill him for getting blood in his famously blond locks, but no mind. Consider the fact that he sullied them while ripping the limbs off of a man during an angry snack, and the situation is significantly less wimpy than it appears. Highlights: the new instruments of masculinity? Well, hardly, but on Eric Northman, *everything* is manly.

While Sam's affections were directed elsewhere and his love for Sookie appeared to gravitate toward safer, more platonic ground, Eric's sights appeared laser-focused on Miss Stackhouse alone, putting Bill in a precarious position, and with good reason. From his preternatural calm to his gravelly voice and command of multiple languages, Eric is the anti-Bill. I'm not sure anyone considered Swedish to be sexy, but we learn something new every day, now, don't we?

Eric, too, rose to the occasion when Bill failed. Diabolical and manipulative, in season two he repeatedly abused his power as sheriff to subvert Bill, and brought in Bill's maker, Lorena, to divert his attention. A little weasely, yes, but remarkably effective, considering it was Eric, not Bill, who ultimately arrived to rescue Sookie from certain doom in the basement of the Fellowship of the Sun in "Release Me." It was during this rescue, too, that we—and Sookie—first got a glimpse of Eric's sexual magnetism as he leaned in ever-so-closely and whispered, "Trust me," in a come-hither voice, just before guiding her through legions of religious zealots bearing stakes and silver. (Incidentally, this was the same episode where Bill made his humiliating "SOOKEH!" proclamation. Coincidence? Doubtful.)

Later, too, his machinations proved effective, as he managed to get Sookie to drink his blood, thus making him more attractive to her to the tune of one very gratuitous, very satisfying, between-the-sheets fantasy involving his naked backside. He also showed her real emotion as he mourned for his maker in Godric's final moments. And Bill's impotence was never more apparent than when he confronted Eric for his transgressions, only to be met with a derisive, "Are you picking a fight?" accompanied by an amused grin.

It is rumored that Eric has more screen time than Bill in season three, and no one, least of all Sookie, should be complaining. And as for Bill, he'd better put down the Wii golf (see? Even his video games are old-mannish) and start focusing on what matters, before it's too late. That is, if it isn't already.

(Oh please, please, let it be too late. Please.)

Alone, he's merely annoying. Together, they're intolerable.

The real tragedy here is not the simple downfall of Bill Compton as a sex symbol or even his slow descent into recycling-induced madness. ("Glass or paper? GLASS OR PAPER?") No, the most imminent crisis is the position he's put Sookie in, which is that of a simpering, manipulative, intensely irritating partner in a treacly Nicholas Sparks film. Not even the original novel—the inevitably bad *movie*.

Admittedly, Sookie Stackhouse is a tough character to bring to the screen. Good to the very core, she is constantly dancing on the edge of a knife, one sanctimonious deed away from becoming diced into cloying little bits. Unlike the novels, which are written in first-person narrative from Sookie's perspective, the TV show doesn't make us privy to her thoughts. As written, though she is still the quintessential good girl, her observations are not as black and white as they appear in the series. And while Anna Paquin's portrayal of Sookie is plenty nuanced on its own, the complexities of Sookie's nature play much better off of characters whose essential natures are a bit darker.

In the beginning, Bill was the perfect foil for Sookie's inherent goodness. Surrounded by worthy men who desire her—Sam Merlotte, and even Hoyt Fortenberry—Sookie was instinctively drawn to him, both by his inner silence and outsider status. Though she later claimed to have been naïve about the nature of vampires, her ignorance was no doubt willful, for though Sookie may be many things, she has proven on many occasions that she is not stupid.

Their early relationship was charming and sexy, if simplistic. She giggled; he brooded. She was brave and unyielding in his presence, even as he reminded her of his animal nature. During their second encounter ("Strange Love"), he taunted her with his craving for an artery in her groin, and repeatedly admonished her that vampires cannot be trusted—and yet, she remained undaunted and full of her trademark grit. Even as he was behaving gentlemanly on the surface by asking her for dates and begging her permission for a kiss, his body language was predatory, and he manhandled her a bit. There was little doubt that he was all man, albeit a dead one.

When, after a startlingly brief courtship, they finally hit the sheets, it was a little romantic, sure, but it was also desperate, dangerous, and deliciously ill-advised. The woman's grandmother had just died, for heaven's sake, and what, she's tooling through the woods in a white Stevie Nicks nightie on her way to have sex—for the first time ever, I might add—with a vampire? It's incredibly stupid, but incredibly hot at the same time. And while the sex itself was tender and unfortunately a bit campy (a fireplace? Candles? Really?), when she finally offered him her neck, it was almost as though Sookie had been lost down the rabbit hole of evil forever.

Oh, but we *wish*. Sookie and Bill have their last moment of tolerable interaction in the form of dirty—literally—sex in the cemetery after Bill is discovered alive ("The Fourth Man in the Fire," 1-8). From there, it was a downhill journey on a plastic slip 'n slide coated in heavy corn syrup.

"Do you need me?" Bill crooned at the beginning of "Nothing But the Blood."

"I always need you," Sookie singsonged in return.

And oh, it only gets worse. The two of them appear to be on a private journey in a Kathie Lee Gifford-inspired romantic cruise for two, led almost entirely by Sookie. At this point Bill has, despite his position of extreme physical power, handed the reins of their relationship over to Sookie, no questions asked. From begging for her approval and acceptance of Jessica, to pleading her forgiveness for what he did to her Uncle Bartlett, it's amazing Sookie has any respect left for him at all. In fact, it's becoming increasingly apparent that she doesn't, and one can hardly blame her.

It is Sookie who insisted that she put herself in danger for the sake of the greater good by going undercover in the Fellowship of the Sun, while Bill pleaded with her to go home. Well, actually, he did more than plead. He took a giant leap into the realm of absurdity with some *Thorn Birds* dialogue, was what he did.

"Let's slip away to Bon Temps right now. Let them devour each other and leave us alone!"

In the same breath, he suggested they cuddle in lieu of sex. *Cuddle.* Unsurprisingly, it was Sookie who insisted they have sex, as he begged for her affections and demanded that she placate him by telling him aloud how much she wanted him.

Ultimately, it was Bill himself who said it best in "Never Let Me Go" (2-5): "Here I am, responsible for you and Jessica . . .

and yet no decisions are mine," he whined, sporting puppy dog eyes. "It makes me feel . . . "

"Like a human?" Sookie helpfully suggested.

"Like a waitress," he sighed.

Oh, Bill. Break out the Dr. Scholl's, because I'm sorry to say, the shoe fits.

Can this vampire be saved? Maybe if he grows a pair . . . of fangs, that is.

With season three looming just around the corner and the future of Sookie and Bill hanging in the balance, it's hard not to wonder if there is any redemption for our fallen hero. Fortunately, Sookie's ladies' room hesitation over Bill's marriage proposal led to his cliffhanger abduction (never have I been so grateful to see someone be captured) and an inevitable split, however temporary. Mercifully, this provides an opportunity for them to reset, perhaps even terminate, their relationship. With their saccharine love story hitting the skids, Eric or Sam could have an opportunity to strike up a fling with Sookie and bring back a little much-needed sexual tension to the series.

The sad truth is that it's just not that interesting to watch a happy, committed couple go at it, swooning merrily all the way. A healthy, boring sex life, while fulfilling in reality, does not a good fantasy make—if it did, then most porn would be about thirty-year marriages, not random encounters with sexy strangers. Fantasies thrive on intense, fleeting chemistry, and a committed Bill Compton offers nothing of the sort.

Breaking up Sookie and Bill won't solve everything—not by a long shot—but it's a small step in a winding road to recovering the loss of one of the sexiest vampires ever to grace the small screen. Perhaps, too, in Bill's heartache, he will find himself enough to have a one-night stand with the first woman who strikes his fancy—and while he's at it, maybe he'll commit a few senseless killings to bring back his taste for human blood.

It's time Bill learned a valuable lesson—one that Dr. Phil has espoused to heartsick women for decades—no relationship is worth changing who you are. So sack up, old sport. You're a *vampire*. Act like one.

And if none of that works, I, for one, would appreciate it if he would at least resurrect his enviable collection of henleys. It's not going to fix everything, but it's a start.

———

JONNA RUBIN spends her days writing, child-wrangling, and drinking far too much caffeine while daydreaming of a world where vampires, werewolves, and other supernatural creatures actually exist. A former newspaper editor and publicist, she developed an unhealthy obsession with vampires at the age of thirteen, when she began checking out books about Vlad Tepes and Elizabeth Bathory from the local library; surprisingly, her mother did not send her into counseling. Since departing the high-powered world of small-town community journalism, she ekes out a living writing and blogging about motherhood, pop culture, and life in New England at www.jonniker.com.

HOME IS WHERE THE BAR IS

MARIA LIMA

It's hard to imagine *True Blood* without Merlotte's. Where would Bill and Sookie have met? How would we know what was going on with Lafayette, or Sam, or the rest of the town? Maria Lima looks at Merlotte's role in Bon Temps and in *True Blood*, and shows us what we can learn about them both from our favorite bar and grill.

> SAM: Damn it, Maryann. This is my bar. These are my people.
>
> —"Keep this Party Going" (2-2)

Every TV show has one: that place that when you go there, you're part of the club, one of the gang, an insider—a home away from house, a place where you feel comfortable, whether diner, bar, or pool hall. *Cheers*, the popular 1990s comedy, revolved around a Boston bar, while *Friends* characters hung out at Central Perk, a coffee house. On *Star Trek: Deep Space*

Nine, you'd often find the officers, residents, and visiting aliens at Quark's, and on *Star Trek: The Next Generation*, the place to be was Ten Forward. In *True Blood*, that homey place is Merlotte's, the local neighborhood family-oriented bar where the food is fabulous (as is the cook), the staff is amazing (in more than one way), and the customers? Well, depending on the night, it's either feast, famine, or war. And don't forget—at Merlotte's, everybody knows your name . . . and what you've been up to.

TV hangouts like Merlotte's or Cheers act as a sort of focused lens for an ongoing series, particularly those with ensemble casts. They concentrate the events, the characters, and their reactions, growth, and change. Not only do we, the audience, experience the lives of the primary characters, we also get a chance to spend time with the "other guys" (Lafayette, Terry, Andy, Arlene, Hoyt). Perhaps one of the most fascinating roles that Merlotte's plays is as Sookie's window to the world—because of her ability, she's isolated in Bon Temps, born and bred in a town where she knows everyone and everything. Merlotte's, through its patrons, allows her, and us through her, to expand our horizons. As a public establishment, Merlotte's serves (pun intended) as a means for her, and us, to encounter the outside world. This is the attraction of a place like Merlotte's, and the reason this watering hole has established a life of its own—a following and focus just as if it were a character in and of itself. Merlotte's is the representation of Bon Temps, in all its Southern glory and much of its shame.

Merlotte's plays a lot of roles in the series. First, it functions as a location—the quintessential small town fry-bar patronized by the locals, perfect for showing viewers what Bon Temps is all about. Second, Merlotte's helps reveal the characters: from the owner and workers to the patrons who hang out there. Finally, Merlotte's reflects and encapsulates the emotional arc of the show. In season one, it's all about getting to know the people, the situations, and where folks fit in. In season two, the happenings at the bar reflect the breaking down of those established roles and expectations.

Location, Location, Location

> SAM: We're a long way from Fallujah.
>
> —"The Fourth Man In The Fire" (1-8)

In shows set in the 1950s, Merlotte's might have been a roller-skate-wearing-waitress drive-in or a local burger joint. In the twenty-first century, everyone's at the bar: women and men go there for happy hour, to let down their hair after work or look for love, and possible meat market, and kids go there with their families for a meal. Since a TV series rarely has the budget to show all the various locations that a real town would have, the neighborhood bar/hang-out becomes the stand-in.

In Starpulse.com's "Favorite Fictional TV Hangouts," the author asks: "What would our favorite shows be without a common ground, a 'hang-out' if you will, to bring all of our favorite characters together?" The author then states (about *Cheers*): " . . . the viewer cared about the characters that spent (most of, it would seem) their time at this bar." That's the key, isn't it? The important thing about the TV hangout is not the place itself, but that the place frames the characters and the action. Where else can you gather residents and strangers alike without crossing the invisible line of threshold? In a vampire-themed series, this threshold line is more than just a socio-cultural understanding—a vampire can't enter a dwelling without its owner's express permission. As Bill says to Sookie: "You have to invite me in. Otherwise it's physically impossible for me to enter a mortal's home" ("The First Taste," 1-2). In order to make the stories work, the series needs a central location where we—the audience—can see both residents and outsiders interact, to show us the pulse of the people. Where else but Merlotte's? Sure, I suppose it could have been a laundromat or a Starbucks, but a bar is more than just a place to congregate—a neighborhood bar evokes comfort (food), excitement (liquor), along with the ubiquitous gossip that is endemic to small and fairly closed communities. It's often the center of the action, the place where stories begin. Just like Lorelei and Rory went to Luke's for a coffee, breakfast, and gossip, the residents of Bon Temps come to Merlotte's for much of the same.

Would the series work without Merlotte's? Could all of the action have taken place elsewhere—say at Fangtasia (the vampire bar in Shreveport)? I can't imagine that it would. If *True Blood*'s action were set in Fangtasia viewers would lose the sense of Bon Temps—of small-town northern Louisiana, so dissimilar to what most non-Louisianans know of the state. Bon Temps is a small conservative town; it's not New Orleans, and its vampires aren't Anne Rice's vampires. Compared to Lestat's world, Fangtasia is tiny, and also a bit lame—vampires dressed to impress, goth wannabes in crazy makeup and clothing. But compared to the rural Bon Temps, Fangtasia is Big City, Sexy Shreveport, and everything that implies to a person from a small town. It's lights, flash, glamor, temptation, and things that go bump in the night. It's attractive, yet dangerous—something that perhaps draws a person out for a night or two. But it's not Bon Temps, not home. Merlotte's is a haven, a place to hang out, a place to feel like a part of the community while downing a couple of cold ones and shooting the shit with Sam or Tara.

In good times, Sookie, Arlene, Daphne, Sam, and even Tara and Lafayette work together in fun and contentment. Other times, the bar is no more than a hotbed of discontent, with red-necks and frat boys harassing either the waitresses or Lafayette, Shreveport vampires creating a ruckus, or maenads inciting orgies. What does this say about Merlotte's? To me, it's nothing that isn't normal for most neighborhood bars—well, normal if they were frequented by vampires and shapeshifters, that is. The small-town bar exemplifies the complex microcosm of society, and that includes both the good and the bad.

Julie Lindquist comments in her book *A Place To Stand*: "At best, the bar is a place that offers, in its communal spirit and rituals of solidarity, a real sense of relief from social imperatives that exist 'outside'; at worst, it is a fertile ground in which the worst cultural manifestations of working class alienation and despair can germinate and thrive." We see this dichotomy again and again in *True Blood*. Merlotte's is the place we, and *True Blood*'s characters, continue to return—whether for good or ill.

A Vampire Walks Into a Roadhouse . . .

> BOY: Who are these people and what the hell is this music? I feel like I'm trapped in some hillbilly's Oxy-Contin nightmare.
>
> —"Strange Love" (1-1)

Good shows tend to be about the characters, and *True Blood* is no exception. Both as a framing device for our characters and as the jumping off point for action, Merlotte's in its role as second home and hangout helps to reveal who's who in Bon Temps. It's at Merlotte's that we first met Vampire Bill Compton: dark, mysterious, brooding—and exactly what our primary character, Sookie Stackhouse, has been looking for all her life.

Merlotte's is a place of comfort for Sookie, and a place of success. It's where she feels wanted and useful. Being a waitress at a small town bar may not impress city folk, but for Sookie, it's a job that she can do, despite her "handicap." For Bill, hanging out at Merlotte's reminds him of what it is to be human and demonstrates his commitment to mainstreaming. Bill's initial entrance, sitting alone, quietly brooding in the midst of all the bustle, starkly highlighted his utter separation, his loneliness. He could have chosen Fangtasia and drunk with others of his kind; instead, he chose Merlotte's, a place that's never seen a vampire, because he wants to reconnect. After all, these are his people, too—just several generations removed.

Sam Merlotte treats his bar as a way to belong. But instead of silent angst, Sam's emotions about Merlotte's are more positive. He built Merlotte's as a place to call home, built a "family" there—the waitresses, his customers. Instead of sitting apart from the people of Bon Temps, he has become one of them. He's taken in strays—Terry Bellefleur, suffering from his own internal battle; Lafayette Reynolds, a true outsider, though a native son; Tara Thornton, another of the walking wounded. Even Sookie's a stray in her own way. Sam acts as a big brother figure, a protector, offering his home (the bar) as a place of comfort and neutrality. As much as he obviously dislikes having Bill around, Sam lets him be, because Sookie's chosen him.

Tara comes to Merlotte's to escape her drunken and abusive mother. Hoyt Fortenberry often goes there with the other guys on the road crew to hang out after work, and it's not a far stretch to imagine that Hoyt's avoiding his own mother, not a drunk like Tara's, but controlling and overbearing. At Merlotte's, Hoyt can just be one of the boys, relaxed, enjoying a beer and hoping to connect with a nice girl. Merlotte's regular Jane Bodehouse drowns herself in drink at the bar, yet is safe in the knowledge that someone there will take care of her. Detective Andy Belle-fleur and Sheriff Bud Dearborne can often be found in one of the booths, even when there isn't a case to be solved. Jason Stack-house, Sookie's brother, treats it like his own personal hook-up joint, dropping in for a few beers with the boys, and scouring the place for his next female conquest . . . or perhaps an encore round with a previous one.

For all of these characters and many others, Merlotte's serves as a refuge. If home is the place where, when you go there, they have to take you in, Merlotte's can be seen as a substitute for home: a safe haven, especially when home isn't so safe. And why Bill, Sookie, Jason, and the rest need a safe haven is usually key to their characters. The reason each of them keeps returning to Merlotte's tells us who they are. In season one, as the viewers are introduced to each of the characters and their story-arcs, their stories often begin—and end—at Merlotte's.

For Everything, There Is a Season

> SOOKIE: Every time I think I know what's what, turns out, I don't know anything.
>
> —"Nothing But the Blood" (2-1)

Merlotte's is also where we begin to see each season's stories unfold. In season one, not only did the main storyline begin in Merlotte's, it's where it culminated, as Sookie realized the identity of the killer and fought off Rene (a.k.a. Drew Marshall). Then, the writers end the first season and kick off the second in the Merlotte's parking lot, as Sookie discovers Miss Jeannette's dead body in Andy Bellefleur's car. Though each season is about the same people, the underlying mood and atmosphere is wildly different from one to the other—and the setting of Merlotte's not only reflects this change, but concentrates these effects as only a local hangout can.

WHERE EVERYBODY KNOWS YOUR NAME (SEASON ONE)

In the first season, the roles of the customers were clearly defined. If characters were locals (i.e., longtime residents), the waitresses knew their regular orders, Sam always seemed to have a nod for them, and Lafayette or Terry Bellefleur knew how to cook their burgers. More than likely, they even had a favorite table, booth, or chair at the bar. But when outsiders entered, everyone's hackles immediately went up. In the first episode, when the Rattrays were on scene, Sookie immediately put on her dumb waitress mask. Even if the viewer hadn't read the books, between Sookie's attitude and the dialogue, the viewer just knew these two were Big Trouble. But the Rattrays are just the tip of this complex iceberg. The overarching stories of season one were all about learning Bon Temps, getting used to who's who, what's what, and how everyone fit into the town's character map. Though there were disruptions in the normal flow of things (the Rattrays; the visiting Shreveport vampires; Jason being accused of murder), they were only small blips and things quickly returned to normal. Even the murders of Maudette and Dawn, and of Rene, once simple good ol' boy and later stranger, only hinted at the deeper fault lying beneath the recently destabilized foundation of Bon Temps. The town's corruption remained hidden, underground—nothing in plain sight. Jason and newcomer Amy's abduction of the vampire Eddie took place in Jason's basement; Lettie Mae and Tara's exorcisms with the "psychic" Miss Jeannette happened deep in the woods; even the most important moments in Sookie's relationship with Bill happened mostly elsewhere (he courted her at her home, bedded her at his). Through most of the season, Merlotte's remained stable, steady, and a comfortable place for Bon Temps' residents to be. It wasn't until the season's end that all stops were pulled out and the place that was once as complacent and comforting as Cheers, Perks, or even Al's Drive-in began to disintegrate.

SHAKE, BABY, SHAKE (SEASON TWO)

If season one was about learning about the seemingly solid foundation of Merlotte's, season two was about destroying it, exposing secrets and lies, tearing apart the comfortable façade, and revealing the shaky underpinnings—the dark underbelly that lies beneath. From the beginning of the season, when Miss Jeanette's body was found in the parking lot, her heart torn out (a graphic reflection of how Merlotte's own heart is ripped out during this volatile story arc), the writers systematically took the sense of comfort and stability we'd come to associate with Merlotte's apart. By the end of the first episode, Maryann's influence had begun to affect all the people of Bon Temps, especially some of *True Blood*'s main characters. By the end of the season, we had seen things break: the foundations of beliefs (Jason's), of normality (Maryann), of relationships (Sookie and Bill). Intruders gained ground (Eric in Sookie's dreams; Maryann at Merlotte's), and things and people we thought stable became lost or began to fall apart (Godric, Andy Bellefleur). These themes were reflected in the changes at the bar itself.

After Amy's death, Sam hired Daphne, a pretty yet absolutely incompetent waitress who disrupted the even, easy flow of the bar's business. Daphne inserted a level of discomfort; she was a cog that didn't quite work in Merlotte's well-oiled machine. She got orders wrong, and couldn't learn. She couldn't write orders, spilled trays of drinks, and got in the way, frustrating Arlene,

Sookie, and even Sam, whose previously stable temper frayed much more easily this season. Although it was not until later that Daphne's true allegiance was discovered, her presence set the season's tone from the very first episode.

Lafayette, who once could be counted on for sassy, humorous wisecracks at every turn, was diminished due to his incarceration in Eric's basement, and became a shadow of the confident man he once was. Quiet, shy Hoyt Fortenberry took up with his complete opposite, the volatile Jessica—Bill's vampire child and a teenager with raging hormones and blood lust. Not a single person remained untouched as the very fabric of what was once reliable unraveled.

The entire atmosphere of Merlotte's changed as the season progressed. Instead of quiet country music in the background, the patrons were treated to Maryann's own brand of wild 'n crazy melodies, volume blasting, her magic spurring them on to behaviors they'd later regret. Merlotte's was no longer a comfort—not to the townsfolk, not to Sookie (who because of her work for Eric was out of touch, out of reach), or to Sam, whose history with Maryann led him to consider leaving the place that was once safe. He was so out of sorts that he took to running through the woods with Daphne, a return to the wild he once hid so carefully. All of season two, in fact, seems to undermine the complacency of Bon Temps; it was a shakeup, if you will, of everything the town and townsfolk had long known as safe and familiar. In "Scratches" (2-3), the idea that Sam himself might even consider leaving freaked Tara out. It was not until the very end of the season, with the unveiling of Maryann's twisted plan and its subsequent foiling, that Merlotte's and, by extension, Bon Temps and its residents, returned to normal . . . for whatever values of normal still existed after everything that happened. Like the residents of Bon Temps, Merlotte's will never be the same. Order has been restored, yet too many secrets were revealed, too many lives upended for Merlotte's to continue to be the same homey, comforting place it was before.

———

STILL, NO MATTER HOW DESTRUCTIVE the season, or how much upheaval the town's norms and values suffered, Merlotte's remains. The building stands solid on its ground, a symbol of Bon Temps' ability to rebuild. Sam's still behind the bar (at least as season three begins). Sookie and Arlene will still serve drinks, and Lafayette and Terry will continue to provide the patrons with great food. As an article on WomansDay.com about TV's favorite hangouts explains: "We tend to get drawn into our favorite TV shows, we know what the characters do for a living and are privy to their groups of friends. But in order to really love a sitcom or dramatic series, it must be set to perfection—in other words, it's all about the hangout spots. From the *Three's Company* bar, Regal Beagle, to Beverly Hills, 90210's diner, the Peach Pit, these renowned places—where our favorite small-screen characters gathered—ignite big memories for those of us who loyally tuned in." TV hangouts are where we get to know the characters, and these places become part of viewers' vocabularies. If you say "Cheers" to a TV fan, they'll immediately think of the show and the eponymous bar. Ten Forward will always be the place where Whoopi Goldberg served drinks in a funky purple hat.

Whatever changes are in store for *True Blood*, I can't help hoping that Merlotte's will remain the central place to see and be seen, the place where your favorite chair is waiting—where Sam's drawn up your usual draft and, as always, where everybody knows your name. Some days, despite the insanity there, I wish I could sit at the bar and down a cold one, too.

MARIA LIMA is a writing geek with one foot in the real world and the other in make-believe. Her Blood Lines series (Pocket/Juno) is set in the Texas Hill Country—a fabulous place for things that go bump in the night. Maria loves to read, write, and watch genre TV and feels very lucky that people actually pay her to do one of these things. Her role models include all the amazing kick-ass women who write urban fantasy. Find her at www.thelima.com or at her blog: www.chickwriter.com.

TO LIVE AND LIVE IN DIXIE

Magical Creatures and Traditional Southern Culture

PAULA ROGERS

In a literary and television landscape growing more and more crowded with vampire stories, *True Blood* stands out in part because of its setting. Let those other vampires sparkle in the American northwest; the South, and specifically rural Louisiana, is the perfect place to tell a story about vampires' integration into our society. Paula Rogers, no stranger to the South herself, explains why.

Let's be honest—the South certainly has some skeletons in its closet. Slavery, segregation, struggles to fit into a modern economy—the list is long and uncomfortable. But for all the negative associations, there has always been plenty that is wonderful about the culture. A lot of incredible people have called the South home, and still do. As a native Texan, I proudly accept whatever part of being Southern that entitles me to. Especially the biscuits.

Part of what makes *True Blood* so compelling is how the show develops in its Southern setting. Imagine if *True Blood*

weren't set in Bon Temps. First and foremost, how would fans—
true fans—identify one another without first imitating Bill's
impossibly syllabled "Suugh-kie"? Much would be lost in that
instance alone. And let's not linger on the thought of the same
vampire storyline set in California. *Hella Blood* hits at an entirely
different emotion. "Welcome to the B.T., bitch"? New York vampires would be far too preoccupied with their rents, careers, and
making quips over Tru Blood martinis to spend perfectly good
nights slowly wooing sweet-natured human lovers. *True Blood*
set anywhere else just wouldn't be *True Blood*.

Despite and because of its past, the South offers a ripe setting for magic. For as much as old Southern ways were challenged by the developments of the twentieth century, such
drawing-room rules must be flummoxed entirely by vampires.
Or are they? From the way the show takes advantage of rural
Louisiana to make room for the supernatural, to the way that
vampires coming out of the closet awakens the tension between
the old and new South, *True Blood* takes full advantage of Southern geography, history, and culture.

The Middle of Nowhere

Even though *True Blood* does fold in woefully plausible reactions to vampires from the world at large, the emotional core
of the story comes from developing extraordinary relationships within a secluded location. This means Bon Temps can
only have one resident sexy vampire to flaunt the taboo, and
Sookie can't pal around with any other humans who've fallen
in love with a bloodsucker. It means no wave of earnest vampire singles to slowly swell the Bon Temps dating pool, and no
OMG texts to other vamp girlfriends about what to do when he
almost combusts in the sunshine while trying to save your life.

No well-lit billboards to illuminate shadowy woodlands, and no community dense enough that heading out for a secret voodoo exorcism is an activity the neighbors would notice. *True Blood* has to happen in a place small enough to allow its drama to become huge.

Although we're hooked by relating to that drama, *True Blood* also gets real mileage out of how little we're allowed to relate to the locale. The suspension of disbelief required for a vampire story thrives in a setting removed from the vanity culture of reality TV, the DIY taste-making of bloggers, and the whole house of mirrors to this collective condition called reality. The spot has to be far away from the scrutiny of our everyday thoughts, and reasonably capable of mystery.

So what crawl space of American culture has yet to be overexposed? Or perhaps the more accurate question is: What part of American culture could we reasonably *believe* has yet to be overexposed? Look no further than a region whose fiction and nonfiction identities are as swampy as its landscape. As we watch the show, lurking in the backs of our minds is the feeling that all this vampire/shapeshifter/maenad stuff really *could* be going on somewhere within the humid mists and dusty old plantation houses of rural Louisiana. Who's to say what happens there? As inelegant as it seems, a smattering of modest wooden houses along dirt roads is today's remote castle in a dark, stormy, and hard-to-pronounce land. Insert joke about unintelligible Cajun accents here, but even that touch point doesn't apply, because Bon Temps isn't in Cajun country, or nearby New Orleans; it's in northern Louisiana. Both Rene's muddled lilt and Miss Jeanette's voodoo turned out to be false associations with New Orleans culture. There's really no established pop-culture frame of reference for what goes on in a place like Bon Temps, beyond the usual small-town storyline.

This is not to suggest that the rest of America dismisses the South, but it is a place within our country that still holds a certain mystery, and also a certain fear and darkness. With twenty-three Civil War battles having taken place within the small space of Louisiana alone, any given spot within the state could be a place where blood was shed. Racial lynchings were widespread throughout the South, well into the civil rights era, and Louisiana was no exception. And what of the even earlier days, and their scores of slave and Native American deaths lost to recorded history? Louisiana is a place crowded with ghosts, and the only ones who could have seen exactly what happened are also likely to have been responsible for some of that bloodshed themselves—the vampires. For human viewers, the image of century-old vampires still roaming the plantation fields that humans abandoned long ago begs macabre questions about who actually had the more successful harvest in the history of the rural South.

Any road trip through the nonfiction South will show that if there's a town below the Mason-Dixon Line whose landscape doesn't include the neon logos of Wal-Mart, Chili's, and Krispy Kreme, it's probably just as likely to have vampires. Merlotte's, the locally owned center of Bon Temps, defies real estate gravity by not pulling a vast mini-mall of nail salons and dry cleaners into its orbit. The parish's romantic maze of misty green spaces provides room for both shapeshifters and imaginations to roam. What fan hasn't wondered how delicious it must feel to transform into a dog and run through the lush, dewy woods that shroud Merlotte's? It certainly beats the city life. No super-highways slice the town in half, and no subdivisions full of McMansions dot the fields—surely property bargains. Bon Temps is the fantasy version of the Southern landscape, both commercially and geographically.

Even if Bon Temps is largely an invention, as fantastical as an immortal lover, it echoes the actual South just closely enough to support the unreality of the show. Like the characters caught between accepting the supernatural and trying to get on with life as they knew it, the modern South struggles with choices of identity. The place is stuck in between its real and mythologized past, unsure how to reconcile the cruel source of its former glory with its nostalgia for the honor of the old ways. Even more to their consternation, Southerners have become pop-culture caricatures, symbolic of being left behind by the modern world and economy. *True Blood* mirrors this identity crisis by creating a version of the South that is an impression, not a documentary. Bon Temps is a collection of types—the bumbling sheriff, the flamboyant African American cross-dressing drug dealer, and the sweet grandmother in her plantation home. These types contradict each other, letting viewers choose whatever version of the South they want to accept at various points in the show. This variety dramatizes the distance between how the South sees itself, how it really is, and how we want to see it. This gap is exactly what provides room for the magical. Supernatural beings would stand out as absurd against a setting that was too closely tied to reality. In an imagined landscape of the South, a population made of imagination seems all the easier to believe.

Separate but Superior

Vampires are walking time capsules. And nothing takes the tidiness out of history like the truth. With these immortal creatures out in the open, the Southern past is no longer relegated to history books or grizzled defenders of hand-me-down glory. The good ol' days suddenly have walking, talking witnesses. And now that vamps have surfaced in Bon Temps, it makes sense that they would bring history's demons along with them.

Though the South may waver in finding its modern direction, one element of its past will forever be chained to the place. The tragic racial history of the South still looms large in our perception of the area, and *True Blood* certainly does not sidestep this influence. Unlike in reality, however, *True Blood*'s social struggle is not between groups of people who are actually equal beneath something as arbitrary as the color of their skin. Instead, the group fighting for equal rights is legitimately Other (as in *dead*), and in this case, they are verifiably superior to humans, at least in terms of physical stamina. Also unique in the show's world is the fact that the dominant group, the humans, can justify repressing vampires out of fear, since vampires naturally tend to view humanity as less of a race and more of a menu. The struggle in human–vampire relations is not simply about a distribution of earthly power, as it was with the South's racial conflict. For humans, it is about accepting that there are superior beings, and killing machines at that, walking among them. This requires not an act of tolerance, but one of faith. It is less about extending or even sharing power than it is about giving it up. Accepting vampires means swallowing the idea that a creature who is naturally equipped to kill you, and in fact greatly benefits from doing so, chooses not to purely because of selfless morality. That's a bit like asking a fat, juicy pig to cozy up to a hungry, knife-wielding human who swears to be a vegetarian.

Still, humans also know a little something about guilt and regrettable cruelty, and so mentions of the vampire issue on *True Blood* cannot be separated from the racial history of the South. Sookie first tried to shame Tara into accepting Bill by equating vampire wariness with discrimination, and accusing her, of all people, of prejudice. This, of course, backfired on a woman as smart as Tara, and she (characteristically) had plenty to say on the issue. When, during his first official meet-and-greet, Tara brazenly asked the 174-year-old Bill if his family owned slaves, she was both stepping outside of her Southern conditioning and invoking it directly. She knew she was breaking the social code simply by being rude, especially to an older man, yet she also knew that the brutal history of the region, as well as her race, entitled her to answers. Though Adele and Sookie were eager to avoid conflict and the question, Bill was, so far as we know, forthcoming and admitted to having had slaves in his family, though he didn't own them directly himself.

Convenient. But what if Bill *had* been a slave owner? Should he be held to twenty-first-century standards for a nineteenth-century act? Slavery was legal in his day, and practiced by men in much more prominent and authoritative roles than an ordinary civilian family man. And what about other vampires who lived through the antebellum South? It's totally plausible that ex-slaveholders carry on side-by-side with citizens of this more racially sensitive era. Maybe some of them voted for Obama (wait, can vampires even vote?), but chances are that not all of the old Southern vamps are reformed. But, like the grandparent who serves up side helpings of political incorrectness during holiday meals, are they just the products of their times? Reparations were famously paid by the government to help mend the fractures in society left by slavery. Should Washington now demand reimbursement from vampires?

In literature and pop culture, vampires have always symbolized humanity's inherent darkness. But in *True Blood*'s Southern setting, that darkness refers to both what's on the inside and how we look on the outside. As a minority group, the vamps provide a safe way to explore past racial tensions that still exist in the South. Though it's impossible in real life to tell what prejudices lurk inside someone's mind, in the world of *True Blood*, Sookie Stackhouse can do exactly that. When her vampire suitor appeared at Merlotte's to see her, she knew exactly what unspoken judgments about her and her date were being made. Bill, too, noticed that everyone in the restaurant was staring at them. We saw the panorama of disapproving faces glaring at the smitten couple, echoing the paranoia that bubbled up around interracial relationships in the South. Since history has taught us that keeping minorities from assimilation is wrong, we instinctively cheer Sookie's decision to flaunt social codes and date her vampire. We immediately associate Bill with the discrimination we know was a major part of the region's not-too-distant past, and we see him as a victim—whether or not he used to own slaves, or be an aggressor in other ways. This softens our remembrance of just how dangerous he can actually be.

Bill is also different from the other vampires because he wants to mainstream, even after being hunted for his blood in episode one. Eric and his crew at Fangtasia are separate by choice. Bill's desire and efforts to assimilate recall other acts of social rebellion in the South. In the shadow of civil rights pioneers, Bill is seen as more approachable not just because of his interest in humans, but also because of his implied bravery. By playing on Southern racial history, *True Blood* gets us to sympathize with a killer just because he is an outcast, no matter how justified the townspeople may be in making him so.

But vampires are not the only magical creatures that provide a way for *True Blood* to use racial tension to dramatic effect. Maryann the maenad captured the entire town in her spell, and no one (except Sam and Sookie) was immune to the sway of her sinister influence. Though Maryann manipulated all of Bon Temps to do her bidding, she pushed two particular people furthest into her raptures: Tara and Eggs. Both characters are African American, and in a Southern context, Maryann's possession of them takes on the added tinge of enslavement. If she had a white man out killing on her behalf, it would definitely seem twisted, but the fact that she snared Eggs plays on our instinctive discomfort at seeing a white woman forcing a black man to do her dirty work. This reference plays expertly on Southern history to deepen our sense of Maryann's cruelty and make her defeat feel like a defeat of Southern demons in general.

What Makes a Man?

For many of us born with the double X, there are certain words that are always accompanied by a little gasp of bliss, a little flutter of the heart. Cupcakes. Puppies. And, perhaps most "ooh"-worthy of all, Southern gentleman. No matter where you live, this notion of a man who is impeccably polite *and* vigorously masculine is catnip to many women. In classic form, the Southern gent is well-to-do, charming, and dashing. Honor is his highest virtue, and he is ready to protect his lady and his land at a moment's notice. He is modest. He rides a beautiful horse. And his accent is as sticky sweet as melting honey on a hot day.

Of course, modern women of the South and beyond have had to accept that this type of man is simply no longer around. Today, a formal inquiry as to whether he may call on you has been replaced with the casual vagueness of "I'll call you." Or maybe he'll just send a text, whatever. In the age of Facebook snooping and tough-minded calculations of whether or not he's that into you, the sense of romance the Southern gentleman once embodied has gone extinct. But what if one day a bona-fide Southern gent showed up right in front of you, all smooth mannerisms and smoldering glances, ready to come a-callin'?

I'm referring, of course, to Vampire Bill. There goes the heart flutter. In the show, Bill earns the coveted title, if only on the technicality that he was actually around for the heyday of the ideal itself. But we, as viewers, know that being a gentleman takes more than simply defying death for centuries. Even if we accept him as more of a victim than a vampire, Bill is still strangely comfortable toeing the line between controlling and abusing his power. We've seen instances where his outbursts aligned with Sookie's best interests, such as glamouring the unlucky cop after a raid at Fangtasia. We cheered his decision to break vampire codes in order to protect Sookie when he killed Longshadow. Although a Southern gentleman would do whatever was needed to defend that which he holds dear, he would never be cruel for sport. Bill, unfortunately, has done exactly that. While embracing his vampire nature, he spent many decades draining humans for nothing more than hedonistic pleasure. He was completely detached from his humanity, no matter how virtuous that spirit may once have been. Though Bill seems to have found redemption in Sookie, he is, at the very least, a lapsed gentleman.

Yet this is the objective view from the sofa, not the South. Even for the most vanilla of vampire men (I'm referring to a certain creature of the night prone to sparkles and sulks), their allure always plays on nostalgia for a simpler, better past, now on offer in handsome, oh-so-handsome, form. It's a best-of-both-worlds scenario—the modern man with (literally) old-fashioned values. And as far as Southern-man credentials go, it's hard to beat having fought for the homeland in the Civil War. So powerful is this feat that it still makes good, proper ladies swoon, even if it does technically mean being dead and walking the earth only because of decades of feasting on human blood. Take note, aspiring gents: adorably outdated notions of "courting" and self-deprecating mentions of being out of practice go a very long way in the charm department.

Loyalty to Southern heritage is strong enough that Bill's Dixie roots make him "one of us," despite being a vampire. It's hard to imagine that being true in any other part of the country. It's another reason why Adele so readily accepted Sookie dating Bill, and why speaking to the Descendants of the Glorious Dead was the best thing Bill could have done to gain Bon Temps' acceptance. When Bill spoke about the area's past, the townspeople were as rapt as if Bill were telling them about themselves. And that's because in the South, the past is still hugely alive in the present's identity. Despite all the darkness it has put behind it, the modern South has never reclaimed the former grandeur that all Southerners claim as their birthright. Though twenty-first-century Southerners surely reject some aspects of the old ways, they also yearn for its comforts. A speaker from that era, even a vampire, would do more than offer a good story; he or she would be seen as holding the key to returning the South to its hallowed past. As an ambassador of Dixie, Vampire Bill holds an authority for modern Southerners that lets him mainstream in Bon Temps more easily than any other place in the country.

Belles of Bon Temps

Beyond the grits, grease, and gators, the South is synonymous with a particular brand of good old-fashioned charm that still lingers amid the cicadas and cottonwood trees of yore. From personal experience, I simplify this social phenomenon as Love Her to Death Syndrome. As in, "Love her to death, but she's just *got* to stop dressing like a woman half her age!" (I would also accept the condition's other moniker, Bless Her Heart-itis.) I honestly adore this about Southern culture, and my life outside of Texas has shown me that it's just much easier to continue chatting with someone over hors d'oeuvres when they have at least made the effort to judge you politely. Southern hospitality holds that strangers are met with smiling faces and invitations to come on over for sweet tea and pie, even if they are simultaneously being held to centuries-old codes of race, class, and gender.

The Southern belle is the keeper of the region's characteristic manners, and Adele Stackhouse sets a powerful example of proper Southern femininity. While providing both Sookie and Jason with a rotating supply of freshly made comfort food, Adele mysteriously withheld judgment on the lives of her grandchildren. For a woman always on the phone about the latest gossip, it must have taken quite an act of will for her to seem so blissfully unaware of Jason's exploits and greet him as a conquering hero (with no mention of just what, or whom, he may have conquered) each time he surfaced for a meal. But when Jason landed himself in serious trouble, Adele revealed herself to be more aware of his true character than her cheerful façade let on. She urged Sookie to act on her brother's behalf. But she didn't just ask Sookie to go flirt with Sheriff Dearborne in a fancy dress à la Scarlett O'Hara. No, this sweet little old lady asked her granddaughter to use her telepathic powers to spy on the thoughts of all the unsuspecting people of Bon Temps in order to discover the real killer.

This isn't the only instance where Adele seamlessly folded the supernatural into her routine of cooking and cleaning and library societies. She revealed to Sookie that her late husband, Sookie's grandfather, also "knew things." She politely skirted direct references to the psychic elephant in the room, but helped Sookie infer that Adele knew, and accepted, that the world was full of such unusual gifts, with the simple, conservative statement, "There's a purpose for everything God creates." Perhaps because of that belief, Adele also seemed more than happy to accept the magical creatures who had suddenly revealed themselves in her hometown, including the one who wanted to date her granddaughter. Instead of warning Sookie against venturing out with a vampire, Adele wondered if Bill might come and speak to her historical group. She welcomed Bill into her home, reeled at her social faux pas of offering him sandwiches, and admonished her grandson to be polite. Adele was the ultimate gracious Southern hostess, whether her guests were human or not.

Such tireless manners are where Adele's Southern conditioning came through. As a white woman from a good family, the social mores of the South would have been good to her. Yet as a modern Southern woman, she must also have at least recognized that the good ol' days were not nearly so kind to everyone. Adele thus carried on the traditional Southern theater of serving up plentiful helpings of the good in a carefully constructed cover for the bad. A true Southern lady must lead her family by example rather than actual authority, for fear of overstepping her place. Her best weapon in this struggle is to be unfailingly pleasant and upbeat, and that means ostensibly ignoring what's wrong, while secretly keeping an eye on how to fix it, by any means necessary.

So what happens when a young, up-and-coming Southern belle is also a telepath who falls in love with a vampire? Adele was Sookie's model of the Southern woman, and Sookie follows her example even into the uncharted territory of the supernatural. Although Sookie has the ability to read minds, her sense of propriety keeps her from outright snooping. Her method for getting the information she wanted out of Longshadow, Pam, and Eric during her first visit to Fangtasia was unrelenting Southern sweetness, much to Bill's increasing discomfort. She ventured to Dallas to help find Godric out of a sense of duty, and she refused to turn her back on her social responsibilities, even to non-humans. Like her grandmother, Sookie uses manners as her compass in society, no matter where she finds herself.

But taking Adele's example further, Sookie's boldness embodies one of the Southern woman's secret weapons: the unwavering belief that she can get things done. In popular parlance, this is known as *grit*. We can't help but admire a young woman who believes in herself, even in the face of stronger and more powerful institutions, or, in this case, creatures. As a citizen of the twenty-first century, Sookie has more social and political power than Southern women of previous generations. As a telepath, she also wields considerably more metaphysical power than her peers. Yet, despite her abilities, she refuses to be anything but a lady. Sookie proves that a modern Southern belle can still flourish, even when the rules of the game have changed dramatically.

So, Whose South Is It?

Maenads, vampires, and other supernatural surprises have shaken up the traditions of the South within the microcosm of Bon Temps. The suspension of disbelief required to support a vampire story sheds light on contradictions within the landscape itself. As a minority, magical beings of the South can't escape the region's cruel history of racism, and the show exposes this hidden tension to great effect. The longing among Southerners for a return to Dixie dominance provides a convenient cover for handsome, antebellum vampires to assimilate where they might not be so lucky elsewhere. Finally, the stalwart smiles of Southern hospitality have greeted the unexpected vampires who've shown up for dinner, and a seemingly average woman with beyond-average abilities proves that Southern charm can work on a variety of creatures.

So, as it turned out in *True Blood*, the South has weathered the initial shock, and absorbed the presence of magical creatures surprisingly well. The fact that a Southern vampire is still most at home among Southerners, even human ones, means that there is room for these beings within the culture's identity. Average people of the South seem to fare best by continuing with their patterns as much as they can, and applying the same old rules and lessons of history to their newest neighbors.

So between the humans and the supernaturals, who can truly claim the South as their own? It certainly isn't Jefferson Davis anymore, and maybe that's the most specific answer available. Once vampires exposed their existence, it's as if they, ahem, re-vamped the South itself. With the creatures of our imagination surfacing, there also comes a challenge to the culture of our imagination. In places like Bon Temps, this means confronting how much the mythical Old South, demons and traditions alike, ever really existed. Vampires have rewritten the rules of what it means to be Southern for both humans and magical beings, and the answer turns out to be more broad than either history or modern culture would have ever suggested. And to think, these true-blooded Southerners have been there all along, just below the surface.

PAULA ROGERS is a writer and illustrator based in San Francisco. Her work in print and radio has been featured by San Francisco's KQED Public Radio, National Public Radio, the Third Coast International Audio Festival, and Salon. She worked as a copywriter and editor for *Show Me How*, an infographic guide to life published by HarperCollins, and currently illustrates new titles in the series. When not deepening her relationship with her computer, she enjoys painting, opining, and nurturing an unhealthy interest in numerous fictional characters.

WORKING CLASS HEROES

The Blue-Collar Politics of *True Blood*

NICK MAMATAS

We know *True Blood* has political overtones; vampires' ongoing struggle for rights, seen largely via television news, keeps them at the edge of our awareness. But there's another political struggle being acted out on our screens. Nick Mamatas summons up the ghost of Karl Marx and casts Sookie as the newest hero of the proletarian revolution.

> Capital is dead labour, that, vampire-like, only lives by sucking living labour, and lives the more, the more labour it sucks.
>
> —Karl Marx, *Capital*, Vol. 1, Chapter 10

What do television characters do for a living? There are plenty of doctors, more police than even a police state would deploy, corporate lawyers and brave prosecutors, spies and super-heroes, and in old sitcoms, the very many men in gray suits who kept their occupations a secret even from their children. There are also store owners, and a few members of the cast might be cabbies or waitresses, but all of them will be portrayed as little more than broad types. And today we have *The Office*. TV is white-collar. When there are working class people on television, they are often portrayed as socially backward, politically retrograde, and more than a little stupid—the abusive loudmouth Ralph Kramden, cranky racist Archie Bunker, Slobbo-American Al Bundy. There are more starship captains than longshoremen on television. *True Blood*'s depiction of working class characters is refreshing, and that's even though some of them are malcontents, or drug addicts, or just not very bright. Because as bad as some of the working class people are, *True Blood*'s ruling class of vampires is so much worse.

One of the great secrets of modern society, according to the anarchists, socialists, and other working class radicals is this: workers don't need the bosses. We could organize our own labor and reorder society itself, if only we could take power. Workers' power is a secret power, one obscured by daily life under capitalism. "Every cook can govern," as C. L. R. James once put it.[1] The first two seasons of *True Blood* are all about Sookie realizing her secret power and her ultimate superiority over the forces—sometimes hidden and sometimes deceptively attractive—that would rule over her and all of us. One can track the ability of the human characters to navigate the supernatural and social challenges they face with their place in the working class. There are plenty of pitfalls for workers—that opium of the people, religion; the nanny state; the police and military (class traitors, if the bellowing Reds on Berkeley street corners are to be believed); and various lumpen criminal activities—to fall

---

[1] "Every Cook Can Govern: A Study of Democracy in Ancient Greece, Its Meaning for Today."

into. And indeed, in *True Blood* we have the Fellowship of the Sun, do-gooder "social worker" Maryann, and the underground market for V to bedevil the working characters. Sookie Stackhouse, though, has avoided these traps and thus discovered not just her magical abilities, but worker's power.

Sookie Stackhouse is a waitress . . . and so much more. She remains, however, a worker to be exploited. The joke of her name—Sookie sounds just like "sucky"—makes her ripe as a target for the newly emergent vampire community. Sookie exists to be fed upon, to have her labor sucked out of her by the "dead capital" of vampires such as Bill and Eric. But Sookie is a tough cookie. Her special talent for telepathy makes her both an asset to the vampires and also too valuable to be sucked dry and left in a ditch. As a waitress, Sookie is just another conscientious server with a ready smile; as a psychic she is skilled labor, able to do what even thousand-year-old vampires cannot. That makes her valuable, and thus fuels the conflict between Bill and Eric over the right to own Sookie's labor-power. Eric, an old vampire from the era of feudal relationships and Viking raids, feels that he can simply claim Sookie for his own. Bill, famous for his growling proclamation, "Sookie is mine!" has a fair amount of trouble resisting Eric's demands. For her part, though, Sookie doesn't need the vampires. She not only saved Bill at the beginning of the series from a pair of criminals, she saved herself from Rene after both her "owner" Bill and her workaday boss, Sam the werecollie (a herding dog, sort of a metalepsis for how small businesspeople deal with their employees), tried and failed. The vampires of Bon Temps and environs depend on her. Sookie's life, despite its romantic failures, was better before the vampires came out of the coffin.

Class politics is nothing new to vampire fiction. From *Dracula* on, the vampire has often represented the old and dying aristocracy of Europe. Violent and powerful, these symbols of older pre-capitalist regimes weren't put down by fearful peasants but defeated by modern men of ability and reason. In the classic novels and stories, middle class heroes were the traditional enemy of the vampire. However, as the political power of the aristocracy receded into history, vampire aristocrats lost their lands and peasant herds and joined the modern ruling and middle classes. Lestat was just another immigrant who made good by becoming a vulgar rock star, and the vampires of the new urban fantasy novels have more in common with *Sex and the City*'s Mr. Big than they do with the royal Vlad the Impaler. Vampires are the new middle class—powerful but also trapped between the demands of the supernatural world on one hand and the mass of workaday humanity on the other.

True Blood's vampires are more than a little pathetic, despite their "glamour"—(both supernatural and material). Bill Compton came from a family of slave owners, which tells us that his social position was superior to, say, the average Confederate conscript during the Civil War. But upon his return to Bon Temps in the modern era, he sleeps in a hole in a crumbling house. Eric, over one thousand years old and the local vampire sheriff, has the fashion sense of a babygoth and owns the ridiculously named and appointed vampire bar Fangtasia. Even country girl Sookie—who in season two is excited about continental breakfasts—knows what a stupid name that is. Bill had to explain, "Vampires are very old. Puns used to be the highest form of humor." One can only think of middle class businessmen who buy fancy cars to deal with their midlife crises, or suburbanites who take photos of their in-ground pools to show them off. Even Sophie, the vampire queen of all Louisiana, can think of little better to do with her power and prestige than to hang out in a home that looks like a Barbie Dream House® and play Yahtzee® with her bored harem. These aren't aristocrats; these are the *nouveau riche* trying to play at royalty. Poor Bill can't even pretend to be more than he is—he literally beds down in the refuse bin of history moments before every dawn.

Sookie can be read as a "feminist" hero in the way many of the new breed of post-Buffy/Anita Blake "kick-ass" heroines are. Some viewers may declare Sookie a feminist simply because of her politics: working class whites are generally considered to be so conservative that they'll vote against their own economic interests in order to express "lifestyle politics." Every conservative movement from the "Reagan Democrats" to the current Tea Party movement was supposedly chock-full of angry white working men and women. If Sookie has any sort of progressive ideas, according to this reading, it's because she *must be* a feminist symbol. After all, she's not like all the other rednecks, hicks, and religious nuts in Bon Temps. But in the end, Sookie just isn't much of a feminist.

Sookie believes that she does need a man more than a fish needs a bicycle. She wants a happy fantasy life with Bill; her man completes her. She lives out her small-town values with little conflict, despite being a cultural outsider and now a "fang-banger." (The sex scenes between Bill and Sookie are also a bit more romance novel cover than they are empowered egalitarian pleasure exchanges, blood aside.) Sookie's also not much on traditional feminist independence. She lived with her grandmother well into her twenties. Sookie is much more a Southern proletarian progressive than she is a middle-class feminist, and that's not something we get to see on television very often these days. Like most women in poor areas she works because she has to, not because she is pursuing a white-collar career. If Sookie has progressive ideas, as represented by her friendship with Tara and her support of vampire rights, this is also best seen as an artifact of her blue-collar lifestyle.

There is a huge income gap between white workers and black workers in the South thanks to the legacy of Jim Crow and to so-called "right-to-work" legislation that drastically limited the union movement. The racist system of the South was top-down, designed to drive a wedge between black and white workers, sharecroppers, and small farmers. Indeed, the history of racialized slavery in the U.S. can be traced all the way back to Bacon's Rebellion in 1676—in which poor whites and blacks united to temporarily gain control of the Jamestown colony. Bursts of interracial solidarity among poor whites and blacks in the South during the early days of Reconstruction, during the Populist movement of the late 1890s, and during the Congress of Industrial Organization's years of the union movement (which opened up membership for blacks in most industrial unions, leading to an organizing boom) had to be put down violently by the white ruling class of the South—with the help of apartheid-style legislation and even Klan terror tactics.[2] If the white working class were really so organically racist, would any segregation laws or other "divide and conquer" techniques even be necessary?

That's the social history from which Sookie Stackhouse emerges. If Sookie has black friends—most white people in Bon Temps don't appear to—and can see some vampires as oppressed victims of human society, it's thanks to her real-world elbow-to-elbow interaction with her friends and family, and her own life as an outsider and poor working girl. If she can

---

[2] There is an enormous literature on the subject of racism and race in a U.S. context. To start, there is no better place than Theodore W. Allen, *The Invention of the White Race*, vols. 1 & 2.

see the difference between Bill and Eric, why that's just more class politics. Vampires aren't all evil exploiters; the ruling class vampires are! Poor Bill is just a member of the vampiric middle class, caught between Sookie and the working class community of Bon Temps on the one hand and the hungry hierarchy of his vampire superiors on the other.

Sookie's not the only worker on *True Blood*. There are few *bon temps* in Bon Temps. Brother Jason works for the highway department, a rough job that is also handy for explaining away his bodybuilder physique. But Jason, in season two, ended up being suckered by the Fellowship of the Sun into joining their paramilitary/religious leadership program. The Fellowship is interesting not only because it is a religious movement, but because it is clearly a parody of the sort of "prosperity gospel"[3] that has convinced so many working people that Jesus Christ, a poor carpenter, wants everyone to be a wealthy American with a big house and three SUVs. Perhaps needless to say, for the Newlins, religion was only a way to gain power—power they feared having to share with vampires—but for Jason it initially seemed like so much more.

Jason's experience in the Fellowship mirrored the sort of social climbing the prosperity gospel encourages, and also reflected the rise of far-right paramilitary groups who feel that the Constitution and the U.S. government have been hijacked by minorities. Though vampires in *True Blood* are often "coded" as gays (they "came out of the coffin"; the issues of equal

---

[3] See Hanna Rosin's "Did Christianity Cause the Crash?" in December 2009's *Atlantic Monthly*. Therese Odell noted the similarities between the Newlins and real-life prosperity gospel peddlers Joel and Victoria Osteen in 2009 in "*True Blood*: Meet the Osteens Newlins" in *Tubular* (online: http://blogs.chron.com/tubular/archives/2009/06/true_blood_meet_2.html).

rights and marriage are prominent), in season two they were essentially coded as the anti-Semite fantasy of Jews: they kill Christians (Theodore Newlin), they are a small minority with immense power, they have distorted physical features, and their cosmopolitanism and decadence are a threat to traditional values. Jason even hit bottom after his affair with Amy, played by Jewish actress Lizzy Caplan. Amy was from Connecticut! She studied philosophy!

German social democrat August Bebel once called anti-Semitism "the socialism of fools"—Jews across Europe, and especially in Germany, were scapegoated for economic and cultural disaster in the nineteenth and early twentieth centuries, and fascists were thus able to outflank both the social democrats and the communists by tapping into widespread discontent with the industrial and financial order of the post-World War I era. In *True Blood*, anti-vampirism is the *Americanism* of fools— vampires are the traditional scapegoats (gays, Jews, decadent outsiders, secret societies) made dead flesh. And what is the American Dream for boys like Jason but success, a hot blonde girlfriend (the married Sarah Newlin will do), and the ability to shoot lots of people while being entirely righteous in doing so? As with most dreams, though, eventually one has to wake up. Thanks to his connection with his more thoroughly grounded sister Sookie, Jason managed to escape the Fellowship before it was too late.

Then there's Tara, who cannot really keep a job. Indeed, who could blame her? Working class jobs in the post-industrial South generally are awful—long hours, low pay, no respect (especially for an African-American woman in a white-majority area), and, in a town like Bon Temps, few prospects for advancement. When Tara ended up in the clink overnight at the end of season one, she was bailed out by Maryann Forrester, whom we were told is a type of "social worker" when she was first introduced. While the Fellowship of the Sun storyline was played largely for laughs and cheesecake appeal, the Maryann plot was much more subtle (well, until the wedding scenes). Working class people are, thanks to exploitation and the constant demands for more profits, always on the edge of the social welfare system. (Indeed, they're sometimes over the edge, even when employed. The *New York Times* reported in 2005 that more than 50 percent of Wal-Mart employees receive no employer-based health insurance, and that 46 percent of the employees' children are either uninsured or depend on Medicaid.[4])

As a social phenomenon, social work came out of the nineteenth century reform movement, which accomplished many wonderful things. Child labor laws, compulsory education, public sanitation . . . all wonderful. However, these same reformers were often champions of prohibition and eugenics. Anti-drug sentiment about the use of opium fueled the Asian Exclusion Act of 1924, for example, and cocaine and marijuana were criminalized thanks in part to wild stories about the violence of blacks and Latinos under the influence of these drugs. Also, social workers can have a fair amount of power over their charges. In 1960, the state of Louisiana cut welfare benefits for over 20,000 children as they were not living in "suitable homes" (i.e., their adult guardians were having extramarital sex)[5] and welfare workers often conducted midnight raids in order to make sure that there were no men in residence in recipient homes. In

---

[4] Michael Barbaro's "Wal-Mart Memo Suggests Ways to Cut Employee Benefit Costs."

[5] Taryn Lindhorst and Leslie Leighninger's 2003 article "'Ending Welfare as We Know It' in 1960: Louisiana's Suitable Home Law" in *Social Service Review.*

the 1990s, even families applying for assistance could expect to undergo a period of surveillance and have their friends, relatives, landlords, and employers interviewed by state officials. Since the mid-1990s, law enforcement and welfare agencies have worked together on "Operation Talon." Food stamp recipients with outstanding warrants are called into a welfare office having been told either that they are receiving some bonus entitlements or that there is some problem with their entitlement . . . but when they arrive, they are arrested by local police. Even aid recipients with no legal issues can expect to be photographed and fingerprinted today when applying for benefits in a procedure all but identical to being booked after an arrest.[6]

The Maryann plot in season two was a clever inversion of the moralism that limns the institutions of social work and the welfare state even today. Tara, virtually unemployable, prone to alcohol abuse, and from a "broken home" with an alcoholic mother, was taken in to learn survival skills and proper behavior thanks to the generosity of Nice White Middle Class Lady and the cooperation of local law enforcement. Tara is practically the poster girl for the "tangle of pathology" that Patrick Moynihan said in 1965 described "the fundamental weakness of the Negro."[7] (Despite—or perhaps due to—this sort of racist formulation, Moynihan enjoyed a career as a Democratic Party New York senator.) Luckily, this racist narrative is subverted in *True Blood*—the show's paternalistic welfare state doesn't exist to trade government cheese for mandatory moral instruction, but is a vehicle for decadence, terror, and the destruction of free will.

---

[6] Kaaryn Gustafson's "The Criminalization of Poverty" in *The Journal of Criminal Law and Criminology*.
[7] *The Negro Family: The Case For National Action*.

What Tara learned from our Nice White Middle Class Lady, instead of the usual sort of "moral hygiene," were the benefits of embracing a horrifying and violent hedonism of the sort not even the vampires can match. Even Maryann's Greco-Roman origins were clever—what led to the collapse of Rome but decadence and corruption at the very *top* of society? Tara as disgruntled worker has some problems, to be sure. Many of the problems even come from the fact that good jobs are few and far between in Bon Temps—it is pretty much working for Sam Merlotte or the state somehow (as a cop, on the roads). But Tara in the hands of the social welfare system, having fallen from proletarian to foundling and ward, ended up more pathological than the late New York State senator could have ever imagined. Eating hearts, blacking out, nearly murdering others, betraying her friends . . . Tara could get a job with Blackwater. She should have stuck with working at the big box store where we first met her at the beginning of season one.

Ditto Lafayette, the short-order cook (and Jason's co-worker on the road crew), webcam boy, and drug peddler. He's also a prostitute, and one of his clients is a right-wing state senator who makes both anti-vampire and anti-gay speeches. Lafayette is hard-working, but in the weak economy of Bon Temps even his many jobs and, uh, "business endeavors" don't offer a good standard of living. And no wonder, given the artificial scarcities and anti-market policies of the vampire overlords. Lafayette runs afoul of Eric and vampire law for selling the ultra-addictive V—a precious resource that vampires, perversely, wish to give away for free in order to better ensorcell their human servants. Lafayette, in his attempt to break the vampire monopoly on blood, is imprisoned in Fangtasia and virtually enslaved by Eric.

The V plot is no mere anti-drug parable. Clearly, vampire blood is considered a wonderful thing by the vampires of *True*

Blood, and they are eager to harness it for their own ends and their own power. Bill used it to heal Sookie, and their lovemaking is rather more bloodsplattered than the sex scenes in other HBO programs. Eric also happily contrived to have Sookie do some sucky-ing in a scene that was played for comic effect when Eric mugged for the camera. Vampire blood is only portrayed as a dangerous drug—with tense close-ups, no incidental music, and down-market set dressing—in the hands of humans who dare take for themselves the means of vampire (re)production. Power is a drug, but drugs are power, too, as the history of the Opium Wars and Air America show us. V is the perfect symbol of capital itself—it's made from human blood (you are what you eat) and, owned entirely by vampires, it is the source of their power over humans. If war ever breaks out between vampires and humans, perhaps the vampire anti-war slogan will be "No oil for blood!"

True Blood inverts most of the narratives we see of working class people on television: religion is a trap rather than a sign of superior morality, middle-class reformers are evil hedonists, and the whole bit with vampire blood gives a whole new meaning to the term "commodity fetishism." Sookie, instead of being weak and subservient, is strong and independent because of her proletarian background, not despite it. If only her friends and family would take Sookie's example seriously in subsequent seasons, we could have a new slogan for the show. Rather than the vampires declaring, "I wanna do bad things with you," perhaps the humans can declare, "Workers of Bon Temps, unite. You have nothing to lose but those fangs!"

―――

NICK MAMATAS is the Bram Stoker and International Horror Guild–nominated author of three and a half novels, including the forthcoming *Sensation* (PM Press, 2011) and *The Damned Highway* (with Brian Keene, Dark Horse Books, 2011), and over sixty short stories that have appeared on Tor.com, *Lovecraft Unbound*, *Weird Tales*, and many other magazines and anthologies. As editor of *Clarkesworld* he was nominated for the Hugo and World Fantasy awards and with Ellen Datlow he edited *Haunted Legends* (Tor, 2010). Currently, Nick edits novels for Haikasoru, an imprint of Japanese science fiction and fantasy in translation, for VIZ Media and reviews books and films for SciFi Wire.

THE EGO, THE ID, AND SOOKIE STACKHOUSE

True Blood's Freudian Analysis of Intimacy

CAROL POOLE

When we think of romantic intimacy, we think of laying ourselves bare to another person, physically and emotionally, and having that other person expose their innermost self in return. Being able to hear another person's thoughts is as intimate as it gets. For Sookie Stackhouse, though, that kind of knowledge is messy and hurtful—a barrier to intimacy, not a shortcut. Love, in *True Blood*, seems to be a state that can only be achieved through ignorance. Not a particularly optimistic view of human nature . . . but, as Carol Poole points out, one Sigmund Freud would appreciate.

What's a nice girl like Sookie Stackhouse doing in a place like Bon Temps, where the vampires are depraved and insatiable, and the humans are really no different?

Though Sookie, the heroine of *True Blood*, bears a passing resemblance to Buffy the Vampire Slayer—both are young, blonde, and quick-witted—the fictional Louisiana town where Sookie lives is no Sunnydale. Bon Temps is not a uniquely wicked or supernatural place, not a Hellmouth. It's just an ordinary town full of ordinary human nature, and that's what makes it so dangerous.

Fans of *True Blood* creator Alan Ball's previous HBO series, *Six Feet Under*, a realistic drama about a family of morticians in L.A., might have wondered how he would approach such different territory. Given how achingly repressed his WASP-y *Six Feet Under* characters were—people who moved as though their bodies harbored undetonated mines—how would Ball handle a supernaturally themed show set in a working class, Bible-belt bayou? Would he let the *bon temps rouler*? Let it all hang out?

As it happens, that is exactly what he has done in *True Blood*, and the result is astonishingly gross, violent, and messy. In *True Blood*, not only vampires feed on blood. Humans greedily suck vampires' blood for the rush of potency it gives. When vampires die, they don't tidily expire in puffs of dust; they ooze, gurgle, and gush, spraying the room red. Lovers bruise, bleed, drug, and save each other over and over. The mind of each Jane and Joe in the local tavern seethes with invisible drama. Envious, spiteful, predatory thoughts pervade the town like secondhand smoke, making it impossible to say whether the vampires represent humankind's shadow, or vice versa.

In the world of *True Blood*, vampires and humans alike are dangerous to themselves and to each other. Contact is explosive— sometimes literally. And yet, *True Blood* is basically the story of a young woman's search for true love. Sookie Stackhouse is the counterpoint to Bon Temps, the heroine who balances the town's amoral anarchy with her own stubborn integrity. If anyone in Bon Temps can find a way to survive love in such a place, it's Sookie.

––––––––

IN THE DVD COMMENTARY ON the show's first episode, Alan Ball said that *True Blood* is about the terrors of intimacy, which raises the question, *whose* terrors? Presumably, Ball was thinking about fears that are universal, yet what we see in *True Blood* seems to express a personal vision of intimacy as a wildly intrusive, deadly, and uncontrollable kind of experience. The way sex and death collide in *True Blood* brings *Six Feet Under* vividly to mind. Watching the townsfolk of Bon Temps having one of their frenzied, relentless orgies under the influence of the maenad Maryann, I feel that I understand why *Six Feet Under*'s Fishers were always so repressed. They must have felt in their bones that if they ever really relaxed, *this* is the kind of thing that they would do!

Why is intimacy so scary in Bon Temps? One reason might be that *True Blood* reflects some of the particular terrors faced by gay American men of Ball's generation. Ball was born in 1957, and came of age as a gay man in a time period heavily impacted by two equally virulent and mindless threats to survival, homophobia and AIDS. *True Blood* refers to both of these threats in various ways. There is a literary history of vampire imagery representing homosexuality, a tradition that Ball flagrantly enjoys in touches such as vampires' "coming out of the coffin." But the show clearly aims to do more than signify the American gay male experience of the late twentieth century. In *True Blood*, Ball wants to say something more about human nature.

In fact, in that pilot commentary he says that he wants *True Blood* to portray the supernatural not as something outside of nature, but as a deeper and more primal manifestation of it. This makes his use of vampires and other supernatural themes in *True Blood* deliberately psychological, and Ball's idea of nature appears to be thoroughly Freudian. More than any other contemporary television show I can think of, *True Blood* revives the pessimism and yet also the artistic appeal of Freud's original ideas about human desire and instinct. It is a gorgeously grim vision in which each person is embattled not only by the external world but also by chaotic, unconscious impulses from within.[1]

Freudian psychology might seem like an odd choice for a politically and socially progressive race- and gender-conscious storyteller to use today. But it makes a lot of sense in the world of *True Blood*, where every worst stereotype about sex and intimacy is blown up to supernatural proportions. It is as if Alan Ball were saying to the audience, "All right, let's say that everything the homophobic right says about gay people is true. We are amoral, sex-craving predators—at least, that is one dimension of who we are. But if so it is because we are human, not because we are gay." If Freud gave us a vision of sexual desire as an almost superhumanly dangerous and all-powerful force, he was also the one who created the philosophical framework through which we can imagine such a thing as sexual liberation.

---

[1] Anyone wanting to get a feel for the basic difference between a Freudian and a Jungian orientation to depth psychology (arguably the two most influential branches of psychoanalytic thought in American psychology) could do worse than to compare *True Blood* with *Buffy the Vampire Slayer*. One telling difference is that in *Buffy*, the unconscious dimension of the world is inherently ordered and meaningful; it links people to each other via shared visions and missions. The demons are knowable from the books Giles keeps in his library, and as the good guys use this knowledge to fight the demons together, their separate struggles to become better people converge to the benefit of all. In *True Blood* people are fundamentally alone, threatened by chaotic and conflicting instincts. There is no one remotely like a Giles in their lives—no wise and entirely benign teacher or source of knowledge. (The character who came closest to playing a Giles-like role, Sookie's Gran, made a dramatic exit early in the show's first season.) In *True Blood*, even the imaginary creatures like Maryann suffer from existential uncertainty, and oneness is nothing but a dangerous illusion.

By positioning sexuality at the center of human psychology, Freud sought to free people from crippling guilt and fear about their basically animal natures. Yet his own vision of that nature was darkly ambivalent, informed by the very Victorian fears he hoped to cure. In *True Blood*, Ball has fun with both sides of Freud: the pessimist and the champion of freedom.

Late in his career as he was summing up some of his most important ideas, Freud described the individual in "The Ego and the Id" as "a psychical id, unknown and unconscious, upon which surface rests the ego." In Freudian theory, the id[2] is the part of the psyche, vast and chaotic, that is made up of impersonal natural instincts, desires, and passions. The ego[3] is the conscious part of the psyche that has the ability to be aware and to choose. Where id lacks any consciousness of limits or of responsibilities, ego acknowledges the demands of the real world and works hard to adapt to them. The id sees only what it wants; the ego perceives external reality. Ego is what gets us out of bed in the morning to go to our jobs; id is what longs to stay in bed eating chocolates all day.

In the same essay, Freud made it clear—here is one of the tragic parts—that he saw the ego as being much smaller and weaker than the id. The ego, said Freud, sits on the surface of the id, like the tiny collection of germinal cells that forms a little disc on the surface of an egg yolk. This humbling image expresses Freud's pessimistic conviction that all of humanity's efforts to be reasonable and moral can never hope to equal the forces of blind, impulsive nature that drive us—forces we can never directly see in ourselves, but can only hope to learn about gradually and incrementally.

---

[2] In the original German, the term Freud used was literally "the it."

[3] In Freud's original German, this term was literally "I."

Since Freud's time, neuroscience has greatly altered our models of how the mind works. One of the most fundamental changes is that today's science is not nearly so dualistic. Instead of seeing humans as being tragically divided between anarchic nature and the striving to be civilized, contemporary neuroscience has a more positive and nuanced appreciation of nature's tendencies toward order and cooperation. But a Freudian vision of intimacy in *True Blood* seems wonderfully right, with its wry insistence that terror has a place in intimate relationships.

Closeness is terrifying in *True Blood* because it involves being open and vulnerable to unknown, unknowable, irrational, and potentially violent impulses. A mother's caress may swerve without warning into a beating, because even mothers can be possessed by demons, which are not really demons at all but just a jumble of rage and alcoholism. A night of recreational sex between buddies can end in death. A reasonably decent guy can find himself as an almost accidental kidnapper and share a surprising moment of empathy with his vampire victim, before participating in (and being traumatized by) the vampire's horrific death. In one way or another, Hunter's Soufflé is always on the menu in Bon Temps. Relationships between all the characters in *True Blood* are fraught with the ever-present danger of some catastrophically murderous or just misguided impulse overthrowing everyone's plans.

"The id," wrote Freud, "has no means of showing the ego either love or hate. It cannot say what it wants; it has achieved no unified will." Without a unified will, the id, in Freud's conception, is the site of continual, mindless struggle. Freud theorized that the id not only contains desires for sex and all the "mischief" it entails, but also deep, "mute but powerful" wishes to avoid the pain and struggle life brings. He speculated that satisfying sexual desire might actually have the effect of ridding oneself (temporarily) of that desire, leaving one open to the instinct to seek death's peaceful relief.

In *True Blood*, it is often hard to tell which instinct, sex or death, predominates. Humans desire vampires, and vice versa, sometimes for blood and sometimes for sex or love. Intimacy is dangerous, ultimately, because one never knows whether it leads toward new life or toward a seductively pleasurable death.

———

OF ALL THE CHARACTERS IN *True Blood*, it is Sookie who best embodies the role of the ego fighting its never-ending battle to hold its own in relation to the id. (The whole town of Bon Temps—French for "good times"—seems to stand for the id.) It is telling that things go to hell in Bon Temps when Sookie leaves in season two on a trip to Dallas; in her absence, the maenad Maryann takes over and the town plunges into an orgy of sex and death, and it takes Sookie's return to end it and restore the peace. Like Jimmy Stewart in *It's a Wonderful Life*, Sookie is an unwilling champion for her town's moral integrity.

Sookie has more reason than anyone else in the show to feel like an embattled ego struggling not to be engulfed by the id's chaos. She is a telepath, someone who has to work hard not to be continually hearing a barrage of other people's seething, urge-laden thoughts.

When Sookie first appeared in the show's pilot episode, she seemed both prim and willfully innocent. She scolded her friends for joking about sex, and seemed not to want to know that her boss Sam found her attractive. It was understandable that her friends liked her anyway, because the viewer is given some extended samples of the kind of mental noise Sookie is continually having to try to block out of her awareness. She has good reason for being a little standoffish, if not vigilant.

But things began to change for Sookie right away, when a handsome vampire walked into the bar where she was working as a waitress. When she met Bill, of the antiquated manners and prosaic name—the first vampire Sookie had seen in person—she was anything but wary. After a long, mesmerized look at him, she turned to her friends and gushed: "Can you believe it? Right here in Bon Temps? I've been waiting for this to happen since they came out of the coffin two years ago" ("Strange Love," 1-1).

As Freud might say, mischievous Eros had come into Sookie's life. Literally within minutes, she risked her own life to save his and was well on her way to being in love. It wasn't enthrallment. While vampires in *True Blood* have the ability to control human minds, Sookie is immune to their charisma. There were layers and layers to her initial attraction to Bill—he was irresistibly strong yet in need of her, he shared her old-fashioned morals, and he was both smart and gorgeous—but the key to unlocking her heart was that Bill's mind did not intrude on hers. She couldn't read his thoughts.

Twenty-odd years of telepathy had left Sookie lonely and disillusioned. From childhood on she had been an unwilling witness to the most disturbing thoughts hidden in others' minds. Sookie knew what the sheriff and his deputy thought when they saw a murder victim's naked body or stopped for a beer after work. And dating had been nothing but a disaster. Invaded by other people's unfiltered desires, Sookie felt disgust for most of her fellow humans most of the time. Her standards for her own behavior rose accordingly; other people might be "nasty," but Sookie was different. Until she met Bill, she never met a temptation she couldn't conquer.

After saving Bill's life in the pilot episode, Sookie tried to read his thoughts and discovered, to her wonderment, that she could not. "Oh, my stars," she breathed, gazing at him with a new kind of intensity. Here at last was someone she could touch without mental intrusion. She could do with Bill some of the things people in love get to do: yearn for him, even idealize him, project her fears and fantasies onto the blank screen of his strangeness and unknowability.

Falling in love brought Sookie into contact with her own irrational desires for the first time. Having the whole town's collective id funneling through her consciousness had not left Sookie much room to encounter her own. In fact, before meeting Bill she seemed like the only one in Bon Temps without an id—a hero moved only by her notions of right and wrong.

Her seeming fearlessness led Bill to marvel at her in turn. In a world where vampires drank manufactured blood at bars tended by shapeshifters, Sookie stood out as something enigmatic and fascinating. "What *are* you?" is a question Sookie heard again and again, from Bill and, in later episodes, from other supernatural beings, and her usual answer—"I'm a waitress"—convinced no one.

In fact, Sookie doesn't entirely know what she is, and neither does the audience, but one thing seems clear: whatever her powers are and wherever they come from, we are all hoping that they are enough to help her survive the terrors of intimacy, unlikely as this hope might seem in Bon Temps. Wrestling with her desires, fighting for her integrity, Sookie seems to represent the ego battling to survive the continual pressures from the id—and this makes her a hero to root for.

———

THE NIGHT OF HER FIRST meeting with Bill, Sookie dreamed. In her dream, she woke in her bedroom and went to the window. Looking out into the night she saw Bill standing on her lawn, so she put on a robe and went down to meet him. He vanished and then reappeared as she kept turning to find him. Their eyes met and he began to unbutton his shirt.

"I never thought I would be having sex with you," she said. "At least, not so fast."

Bill gave her an evil leer, tonguing his fangs suggestively. "Who said anything about sex?" he said ("The First Taste," 1-2).

In her dream, Sookie faced terror about opening herself to intimacy with Bill. Would she be devoured by him? Bill vanished, eluding her attempts to find him, before then reappearing, and she made no attempt to defend herself from him. These aspects of her dream showed her trying to digest the experience of being unable to read his thoughts, and wondering whether her desire for Bill had more to do with the id's desire for life and sex or death.

Bill, who is a very decent sort for a vampire—brooding, possessive, violent, but working hard to resurrect his humanity—kept trying to remind Sookie that he was more dead than alive. "Vampires," he told her, "often turn on those who trust them . . . We don't have human values like you" (1-1). Sookie only gradually seemed to take in the signs that Bill was more complicated and darker than a knight in shining armor. But even after a series of disappointments her desire for him survived.

Both Sookie and Bill share an understandable tendency toward boundarylessness when it comes to love. Bill's natural bent is to thirst for blood more than for sex. Freud might say that the death instinct dominates Bill's id. Through her telepathy, Sookie has not so much a desire as an involuntary, innate way of connecting with others as if there were no skin separating them, as if they shared one nervous system. Their mutual attraction was immediate and intense. There was no build-up, no getting-to-know-you phase. Sookie and Bill came together in a heady plunge into the unknown.

After saving her life and tending to her wounds, Bill asked Sookie, "May I ask you a personal question?"

Sookie replied, "Bill, you were just licking blood out of my head. I don't think it gets much more personal than that."

She had a point, but one could also say that blood-licking is an odd or at least ambiguous way to be intimate with another person.

The kind of intimacy Sookie seems most adept at happens via fighting—not violently, but in a kind of affectionate-but-mad tussling she does with everyone she loves. Fighting, we can assume, gives her a way of having contact without being flooded by the others' private thoughts. For her, thought-reading is often traumatic. At best it can be useful for detecting threats, but it is never a mode of intimacy.

With Bill, for the first time Sookie can bask in another's presence and let her guard down. This is such an unknown feeling for Sookie that it's not surprising if she can't easily tell the difference between intimacy and an emotional merger that equals death. Sookie's need for an unguarded closeness opens her up to intensely primal feelings that, as Freud would say, she cannot possibly understand or even know about—yet these unconscious passions make her reckless. In her dream, she did not seem to feel she had a choice about allowing Bill to take her in whatever way he wanted. Or was she the one who wanted to be devoured and taken out of the struggle of her life? Her dream seemed to foreshadow the potential for both love and death in Sookie's relationship with Bill.

It is a complicated relationship. As she gets to know him, her view of him continues to darken. She sees him toying sadistically with a human. He has creepy vampire friends. Sookie claims that it is only because of Bill's remaining human-ity that she can be with him. But in season two, this belief of hers was undercut by her growing attraction to Eric, a vampire who makes no pretense of morality. The uneasy question of whether Sookie is actually attracted to Bill's vampirism remains unanswered.

For his part, Bill has often told Sookie that their relationship is a miracle that enables him to feel again. But the more he believes he needs Sookie in order to feel his own feelings, or even in order to *have* feelings to feel, the more vampirically possessive and controlling he becomes in relation to her.

On the other hand, their relationship is nothing if not lively, and Sookie never seems to be in danger of being controlled by Bill. The lovers fight, make up, and grow increasingly close by working through all kinds of difficulties together, from Gran's death to numerous assaults made by various human and vampire antagonists. Bill and Sookie even have a kind of child together, the teenaged vampire Jessica, who has brought a very sweet pathos, as well as a lot of trouble, into their lives.

In fact, as the story of *True Blood* moves along, shy hopes peer out from behind the scary imagery. Sookie's intimacy with Bill literally drains her lifeblood, but *True Blood* has a remedy for that—B vitamin supplements. Unlike traditional vampire stories in which Dracula's bite always heralds death, *True Blood* offers a hope that maybe, just maybe, a girl can survive the heady rush of life and death instincts colliding, and find true love with a vampire.

AS OF THE END OF season two, Bill and Sookie's future is very uncertain. But both are surviving, arguably even thriving in, their dangerous relationship. They are doing better, at least, than most of their friends.

In general, major characters' romances in *True Blood* tend to go very badly. Sam's girlfriend tried to have him killed by a mob before her heart was ripped out and fed to enthralled lovers Tara and Eggs—whose inability to deal with his guilt for everything he did while enthralled led to his death. Sookie's brother Jason has had a disastrous string of relationships with women who end up dead. In their different ways, *True Blood*'s characters all ache for intimacy but not all of them survive the attempt.

Arguably, Freud's pessimism about human relationships errs in overemphasizing people's separateness from each other—in seeing people as fundamentally alone. Freud's model of the ego in relation to the id suggests that people's relationships can only take place in the precariously managed interface of their egos, both of them struggling not to be overwhelmed by their own ids or damaged by attack from the other's. This model helps explain why people might fear intimacy, but doesn't offer much hope that intimacy could be a safe or even natural state to achieve.

In his DVD commentary Alan Ball says that *True Blood* explores the human longing for a way to transcend individual boundaries. His vision of this longing seems to share Freud's basic premise that separateness is the reality, and transcendence is a dangerous illusion. Sookie and Bill each suffer from a fundamental loneliness that makes their hunger to dive into each other all the more compelling. Bon Temps is full of people who ache to share themselves deeply with someone, but when they try to do so, the result is often a bloodbath. Ball wisely takes a playful, ironic approach to these dark themes, and by doing so leaves some room for hope, however irrational it may seem.

If intimacy is too dangerous for the show's ordinary mortals, Sookie may have the heart and the strength to survive it—or at least it seems to be her unique job in Bon Temps to try. What makes Sookie *True Blood*'s heroine is that she does things no other human has to do, or can. She has larger-than-human powers and immunities. When Bon Temps loses its mind, Sookie has a way of keeping hers, though the price is a continual struggle against the chaos of instinct. If her romance with Bill is subject to all kinds of hazards, it has at least survived longer than love usually does in Bon Temps, and that may already be a heroic achievement.

———

CAROL POOLE is a psychotherapist practicing in Seattle. In addition to her clinical work she enjoys psychoanalyzing stories, from ancient myth to pop culture. She has contributed essays to two other Smart Pop anthologies—*The Psychology of Joss Whedon* and *In the Hunt*—and presented "A Small Bundle of Shivers: Imagery of the True Self in *Great Expectations*" to the International Forum for Psychoanalytic Education's 2009 conference.

COMMUNION OF BLOOD

A New Gospel?

PETER B. LLOYD

Can you be both Christian and a vampire? The Fellowship of the Sun would say no. They believe that God hates fangs, and a cursory search of the Bible seems to support them; in Leviticus 17:10, for instance, God says, "I will even set my face against that soul that eats blood." But Christian doctrine is known for being a little . . . flexible. Here, Peter B. Lloyd presents a new version of the gospel as suggested by *True Blood*: Christian vampirism.

One thing is clear: a living God is full of surprises. Some people put their trust in dead idols that belong in dusty museums or heritage trails. But we Christians place our faith in the hands of a God who is pulsing with life and vitality, who walks with us day by day, and throws us new challenges to help us grow in grace.

Jesus never held back from bringing us new ways of living. He threw down the gauntlet to the whole human race when he said "Love your enemy!" The people of the time said, "Away with you! God Himself told us to take an eye for an eye!" But Jesus stuck with this new way of life, the path of loving your neighbor as yourself. And to underline his authority, he showed us all his supremacy over death. He raised Lazarus from the dead, and he even allowed himself to be crucified and then came back to life. Believe me, you don't want to mess with people who come back from the dead! If Jesus says "Love your enemy!", then, really, you should be loving your enemies.

Have you thought of what Jesus' next big surprise might be? You can be sure it won't be anything that any of us can foretell with our puny human imaginations. This living God of ours may already be posing a new challenge to us. When you hear it, I know a lot of you are going to think like the Philistines of old and tell me, "Away with you! This can't be right!" Believe me, I felt the same resistance when I first heard the rumors of what might be a new gospel in the pipeline. I thought, "Jesus is telling us to do *what*?!" But a still, quiet voice in my head said, "Yes! Maybe this is what you've known all along! It's right there in the Bible but you just didn't see it! The new gospel would be an unfolding of what was already in the divine plan!" And my heart was filled with joy, as yours will be! And my blood tingled with excitement in my veins and arteries, as yours will!

God moves in mysterious ways, and He often uses people as instruments of His will. So if you look around and wonder about what folks are doing, ask yourself what God's hidden agenda is with them. You've surely noticed that a wave of interest is welling up around the subject of vampires—in books, films, television series. We cannot get away from them! The TV series *True Blood* shows us a world in which vampires walk among us as our brothers and sisters. I want you to think about this question: Is God inspiring scriptwriters to prepare us for what may come next?

Think back to the time when Jesus walked among us. For the twelve disciples of Jesus, what was the most challenging commandment? It was not "Love your neighbor as yourself" or "Turn the other cheek"—hard though those were, as human passions weigh against them. No, the most challenging was "Eat my flesh, drink my blood." The disciples did not even understand what He meant by this, let alone how they should do it. Even His followers said unto Him, "This teaching is difficult, who can accept it?", to which Jesus retorted, "Does this offend you?" Was it a parable, or some esoteric symbolism? The poor guys just couldn't get their heads around it.

How should we follow this command that Christ gave us? For two thousand years, the Church answered that simple question by referring to the supernatural transformation of communion wine into the blood of Christ, and of the communion wafer into his flesh. Christian denominations that split off from the mother church, that lost their way and strayed from the high road of Rome—they somehow lost the simple, literal trust in Christ's commandment. In the churches of the Baptists and the Episcopals, they make the wine merely symbolic of Christ's blood. But that symbolism is of human devising. It is not of God. In the true and apostolic church of Rome, we drink Jesus' blood in absolute literal truth. The wine is—by a miracle understood only by God—transubstantiated into the actual blood of Jesus Christ. And we drink it—we drink and swallow the blood of our Savior who died on the cross and who conquered death in the resurrection.

As we all know, Jesus was God's Son. But the Bible makes it quite plain that we faithful are all Sons and Daughters of God. The Gospel of Matthew tells us, "Blessed are the peacemakers: for they shall be called the children of God" (5:9). This was confirmed in Paul's letters to the Romans: "For as many as are led by the Spirit of God, they are the sons of God" (8:14). And the letters to the Galatians, too: "For ye are all the children of God by faith in Christ Jesus" (3:26).

How could it be otherwise? For our bodies are made of clay, and it is only the divine breath of life that separates us from the earth and the beasts. That breath of God that is in everyone—*that* is what makes us human and also makes us children of God.

And that divine breath is carried in the blood—not just the blood of Jesus Christ, but in everyone's blood. Indeed, in all living things, the life-force flows through the bloodstream. "For the life of the flesh is in the blood" (Leviticus 17:11). The writers of *True Blood* know about this. In the TV series, the astonishing healing powers of vampire blood are truly evident. Even the power to re-animate the dead is transmitted through blood. When a new vampire is made, all the old blood is drained out of a person's body, and new vampire blood is fed in, to fill the veins with immortality. And the dead person rises again after three days of burial in the ground.

What divine message might be coming to us through the TV screen? Remember, God reaches out to us wherever we may be, even sitting on the couch watching television shows. You cannot avoid Him! When He wants to reach millions of people, what better way than to inspire TV scriptwriters to put out a certain message? I'm not here to speak on God's behalf, and I'm not going to put words into His mouth—like "Drink thy neighbor's blood, just as you drink mine"—but just think about it!

Vampires have been maligned for generations, but perhaps they were actually expressing the will of Jesus in a subtle way that nobody really understood. Now, as the End Times draw near and the days of the Rapture approach, we should ask ourselves: Does the Lord Jesus wish to prepare us for the final battle against Satan by enhancing our power and health? In *True*

Blood, vampires gain tremendous physical strength, speed, and resistance to bodily harm. Of course, this is fiction. But what message does God want us to pick up from it? Perhaps that we should gain strength as a community, as the collective body of the church, by drinking our neighbors' blood? Who are we to second-guess God's intentions?

Many will be too stiff-necked to think that Jesus could ever send such a commandment, and will say it is not in the Good Book. But Jesus does not do things by the book. He *is* the book. He is the Word of God made flesh and blood. And our duty is to read the Word of God and let the true meaning enter into us and become lodged there. Even if that true meaning is something as shocking as letting your neighbor drink your blood.

It is true that the Bible is divinely inspired, written and edited by holy men under the direction of the Holy Ghost. But reading the Bible takes inspiration, too. We are all but infants in our understanding, compared to the limitless wisdom of God. And when we try to understand the Bible using merely human intelligence, we may go astray. The correct way to read the Bible is to study the text, ingest the words, savor the texture of the writing, digest the grammar and the semantics, and then . . . close your eyes and go within. Bestill the babbling brook of voices in your head. Push aside the stream of images from the day. Make a space in your mind and, by prayer, invite the God-head into your thoughts. Then, and only then, can you attempt to grapple with the true meaning of the scriptures.

There have been impetuous men in the past who would not wait to hear the quiet voice of God within them. They brushed past the courtesies and observances that should be made to invite God to infuse one's reading. And they construed the holy words after their own prejudices and ignorance. Infamous among such ignoramuses were two Dominican priests, Heinrich

Kramer and James Sprenger, who in 1486 wrote a treatise entitled *The Malleus Maleficarum* (which is Latin for *The Witches' Hammer*). Oh, rue the day when this wordy virus entered our literature! Kramer and Sprenger contaminated the body politic with a diseased distortion of the truth, and it spread like a virus, infecting one person after another, twisting their minds. Thousands of good and innocent people were falsely accused of witchcraft and vampirism, and many were tortured, hanged, or burned for following the ancient traditions of Wicca.

The prohibition on the drinking of blood—*any* blood—runs deep in the Judaic religion, in which Christianity is historically rooted. Like other traditions, such as circumcision, this ban on drinking blood arose for the pragmatic well-being of a nomadic desert people, and over time it became embedded in the distinguishing traditions that made up what it is to be a Jew. And when God sent his begotten Son among the Jews, and brought forth the new Gospel, many ancient laws were kept, which is why the Holy Book of Christianity still to this day contains the Old Testament. It was this prohibition on drinking blood that Kramer and Sprenger chose to twist into a grotesque distortion. Sit back and read what is written in chapter 17 of the book of Leviticus (verses 10 to 13):

> And whatsoever man there be of the house of Israel, or of the strangers that sojourn among them, that eateth any manner of blood, I will set My face against that soul that eateth blood, and will cut him off from among his people. For the life of the flesh is in the blood; and I have given it to you upon the altar to make atonement for your souls; for it is the blood that maketh atonement by reason of the life. Therefore I said unto the children of Israel: No soul of you shall eat blood, neither shall any stranger that sojourneth

among you eat blood. And whatsoever man there be of the children of Israel, or of the strangers that sojourn among them, *that taketh in hunting any beast or fowl that may be eaten, he shall pour out the blood thereof, and cover it with dust.*

What the final verse makes clear is that the prohibition is an expression of a *dietary* custom. It is referring to the blood of animals, not the sacred blood of the Sons and Daughters of God. It is only by the self-serving selective reading of those two wrong-headed priests, Sprenger and Kramer, that the simple, true, and pragmatic meaning of this passage was smothered in folly.

The proper reading of this Old Testament rule is reinforced in the New Testament, where we find written in the Acts of the Apostles, "For it seemed good to the Holy Ghost, and to us, to lay upon you no greater burden than these necessary things; That ye abstain from meats offered to idols, and from blood, and from things strangled, and from fornication: from which if ye keep yourselves, ye shall do well" (15:28–29).

Given the long-standing Jewish abhorrence of drinking blood, some scholars have argued that Jesus Himself could never have invited his followers to drink His blood, and that this part of the Gospels was inserted after the events, perhaps by Paul. They suggest that Paul was influenced by Hellenic Mystery Cults, where drinking the blood of a god—or being sprinkled with, or immersed in, said blood—was a way to absorb the qualities of the god. But Paul was born and brought up as Saul, a Jew, who would have had the ban on drinking blood ingrained in him from his religious practice. It is true that the idea of drinking divine blood was in circulation from other religions in Paul's time—for example, one magical text described Osiris giving Isis and Horus his blood to drink in a cup of wine, so that after his death they would not forget him. But to suggest that people who were steeped in Judaic lore could suddenly choose to adopt blood-drinking in their communal meal would strain credulity—unless they were specifically told to do so by Lord Jesus Himself. Our Savior alone would have had the authority to overcome the ancient prohibition.

The Jews did not abhor blood itself; this was not a taboo, like those found in primitive religions. The blood that was taken from animals in kosher sacrifices would be preserved carefully and offered to God Almighty, and only the bloodless meat could be eaten afterward by mortals. And blood could also be used as a medicine. But it could not be drunk!

So, not only the Holy Bible itself, but also the social norms of the day, clearly show that it was Jesus Himself who commanded us to imbibe His blood.

Was it so hard for Kramer and Sprenger to leaf forward through their copy of the Bible and compare and contrast Leviticus with the sacred words of our Savior in the Gospel of Saint John? Christ in person instructs His followers to drink His blood! How, then, can Leviticus be construed as a ban on the drinking of human blood? Their infamous declamation against vampirism rests on a staggeringly selective misreading of the scriptures. In fact, the Good Book makes it plain what is required of us: to refrain from drinking the blood of animals, and specifically to drink the blood of the Son of God. And, as stated previously, all truly believing Christians are the Sons and Daughters of God, so, far from being *pro*scribed by the Bible, the drinking of human blood is specifically *pre*scribed.

As everyone who is close to nature knows, and as Jesus Himself affirmed, "By their fruits ye shall know them" (Matthew 7: 20). As I mentioned earlier, in the fictional world of *True Blood*, the benefits of vampiric blood are manifold. Any individual who has been injured and then fed the blood of a vampire will rejoice in the healing potency of the blood as if Christ's own blood were the balm. Even wounds that ought to be fatal can be completely healed by vampire blood. What greater confirmation could there be that being a vampire is good, and true to the teachings of the Christ? These are only stories, of course, but what is their significance? Are they modern-day parables? Is the Almighty talking to us through the TV, telling us to love our neighbors in the most direct way we can? Only you can tell! Find the true meaning by prayerfully listening to God's voice, asking Him to guide you as you seek to interpret *True Blood* in accordance with the Holy Ghost's intentions.

We were told by Jesus to "Heal the sick" (Matthew 10:8). If we were vampires with the powers seen in *True Blood*, we could indeed do so! By allowing the sick to feed upon our vampiric blood, we could discharge our great debt to Jesus in the most direct manner. As Jesus hung on the cross, His sacred blood was collected in the Holy Grail and venerated. But we all have that same divine spark of life circulating in our bloodstreams. It's as if humanity is, collectively, the Holy Grail! What healing we can do, if we have faith and are willing to give of our very essence! O brothers and sisters, the glory of God is upon us when we give what is valuable to us to cure the sick! What greater grace could we hope for but the power to heal the sick with our own blood? If only the amazing world of *True Blood* were true! If only we could live as Christian vampires! But even as metaphor, what benevolence the TV series inspires us to! Not only would we rise in grace as God's healers, but we would have eternal life! In the realm of *True Blood*, when the biological body dies in the process of being made a vampire, the miraculous new body gains the ability to exist forever. O sisters and brothers, what greater reward could we ask for but eternal life to serve God as His healing corps on Earth, with the strength that comes from perfect health?

Why would it take two millennia for a new gospel to come to us? Why would God allow the vampires to be persecuted for centuries? Believe me, such trials are all part of the divine plan—which we can't see in its entirety, and probably wouldn't grasp anyway. But one part of the plan is clear: the End Days will soon be upon us, and the Lord is making His preparations now. By bringing forth a great army of vampires—or, at least, mortals who think like vampires—He is preparing for the final battle with Satan, when the Great Beast will try to drag everyone to Hell. With His legions of powerful and invulnerable healers, bonded by the sharing of the life-force, He will batter the forces of evil with the battalions of life!

Making someone a vampire wouldn't automatically change their personality. In *True Blood*, we see a broad range of psychological types—from vampires who care about the well-being of both humans and fellow blood-drinkers, to individuals who callously kill innocent people and drink all their blood. We also see William Compton, who repents and refrains from killing people for their juices. Just as a human has free will and may be good or bad, so a vampire is also a free agent who must choose which path to follow. Because of the centuries of secrecy and oppression, any vampires that may exist in this world would have had a poor moral education. Let me stress that murder is *not* a necessary part of vampirism. Many mortal humans murder and rob for material gain, yet humanity as a whole is not condemned for the actions of this small minority. Indeed, ever since Cain's bloody sin, men have killed their brothers for gain. People cannot become saints just because they are made vampires! No, they bring with them into vampirehood whatever values they had as humans. But, over the long span of years for which a vampire exists, he would have the opportunity to raise his moral stature, to purify his soul, to broaden the horizons of his empathy—just as William Compton urges his fellow vampires to do in *True Blood*. In short, the eternal life of the vampire would be an opportunity to grow into a more devout follower of Christ!

Although there may not truly be any vampirism in this mundane world of ours, I want you to *think* like a true Christian vampire, to reflect on what vital essence you can share with your fellow inhabitants of the world, and how our community is strengthened and made whole by sharing—if not by giving your blood to your neighbor to drink, then by giving whatever you can share.

———

PETER B. LLOYD has, for more than two decades, been a vegetarian on philosophical grounds, and even when he was a carnivore was repulsed by bloody meat, let alone the disturbing culinary phenomenon of black pudding. Nevertheless, he is intrigued by how the kinky tantric glamour of sucking fresh blood out of somebody interacts with the spiritual notion of the potency of blood as a carrier of life-force, as held in many ancient religions. Peter is a freelance writer with a philosophical bent, based in London, England—which is probably why he also obsesses over maps of underground tunnels.

PURE BLOOD

From Transylvania to Bon Temps

JOSEPH McCABE

A lot has been written about why vampires appeal to us, and about why *certain* vampires—and certain vampire stories—capture our interest at certain times. Joseph McCabe looks at *Dracula*, the father of modern vampire stories, and uses what scholars have had to say about Dracula's appeal to uncover some unexpected insights about our interest in *True Blood* and Sookie's interest in Bill Compton.

Life—or rather, death—can be lonely for a vampire. An endless existence spent lurking in the shadows, seducing hapless humans, feeding off of throbbing jugulars . . . It doesn't allow much room to socialize, at least not in the conventional sense. No wonder, then, that in the world of *True Blood* so much import is placed on a vampire's relationship with their maker, on observance of their lineage. This is the only way these creatures of the night may find some semblance of community, as they attempt to fill the emptiness of their undead lives, replacing the family and friends they once knew with whatever companion providence allows.

Lineage is also important to vampire fiction. Nearly all tales of the undead, across all types of media, must contend with *their* maker, the story from which the modern vampire was born into pop culture—Bram Stoker's *Dracula*. First published in 1897, *Dracula* continues to shape our perception of vampires and their storytelling potential, having yielded books and movies as disparate as *I Am Legend*, *Salem's Lot*, *The Lost Boys*, *Twilight*, and *True Blood*.

It's especially worthwhile to consider that last title, since doing so reveals intriguing parallels and contrasts between the England of Bram Stoker and his eponymous Transylvanian Count, and the twenty-first-century America of Alan Ball, Charlaine Harris, and *True Blood*'s main vampire, Bill Compton. Despite their many differences, each story is successful because it preys on the fears and desires of its audience.

Class status aligns Dracula and Bill Compton. Stoker's vampire is a count, and, as he was of Romanian blood, a descendant of ancient Rome. This stratum extends to Bill, whose ownership of land in the mid-1800s marks him as an aristocrat. Furthermore, Bill's origins stem from Southern Antebellum (pre–Civil War) society, in which manners and etiquette were highly valued, as they defined one's place in society, and the goal of becoming a proper gentleman was shared by many men.

Another similarity between Dracula and Bill is their ties to their homelands. Dracula fills his coffin with the soil of his Transylvania home, to which he races for safe haven from the vampire hunters in the novel's climax; and Bill, who also rests in his native soil (though, admittedly, by choice), returned to Bon Temps to claim his estate.

Though these trappings define the characters, the most significant parallel is that both Dracula and Bill are invaders.

Stoker tapped into the anxieties and desires of Victorian England with the invasion of his savage titular character. More than a century later, Harris and Ball draw on the fears and wants of *True Blood*'s audience, but in a subverted way—with an invasion not of savagery, but civility.

Dracula was first published in 1897, when England was celebrating the Diamond Jubilee Year of Queen Victoria, honoring sixty years of Her Majesty's reign. It was a yearlong celebration, but throughout the festivities, an unease permeated the nation; there was a mounting concern in England that the British Empire had passed its peak. As the historian Jean-Jacques Lecercle argues (according to David Glover in *Vampires, Mummies, and Liberals*), "*Dracula* belonged to a difficult historical moment in which the beginning of Britain's decline was signaled politically by setbacks during the First Boer War (1880–81), economically by the Great Depression between 1873 and 1896, and culturally by a pervasive sense that the high point of the Victorian era was now past and the signs of decadence were plainly visible for anyone to see." Coupled with this was the rise of Germany and the United States as world powers, and mounting discomfort with the morality of England's imperialism.

In "The Occidental Tourist: *Dracula* and the Anxiety of Reverse Colonialization," Stephen D. Arata argues, "*Dracula* enacts the period's most important and pervasive narrative of decline, a narrative of reverse colonization . . . This narrative expresses both fear and guilt. The fear is that what has been presented as the 'civilized' world is on the point of being colonized by 'primitive' forces." Such fantasies were all the rage in Victorian England (as evidenced in everything from H. Rider Haggard's *She* to H.G. Wells' *War of the Worlds*). Arata claims that in the invading Other, British culture at the time saw its geopolitical fears made manifest and "its own imperial practices mirrored back in monstrous forms . . . As fantasies, these narratives provide an opportunity to atone for imperial sins, since reverse colonization is often represented as deserved punishment."

Under these circumstances, *Dracula* presented the Victorian male's worst kind of nightmare—one in which a foreign invader, from the supposedly less civilized East, would take advantage of Britain's weakened state, invade his country, and take his women from him. It's not surprising that *Dracula* appealed so strongly to a Victorian audience; the story showed the triumph of the Englishman over an Eastern European invader, symbolically reasserting England's dominance in the world.

True Blood presents a similar scenario for today's audiences, albeit one both nightmare *and* dream, in which modern American society has weakened to the point that invaders—not from other countries, but from other times—can infiltrate and capture those for whom we care deepest. There are a number of such invaders in *True Blood*—Eric Northman, Maryann Forrester, even Amy Burley (a twisted parody of a flower child, albeit one born several decades late). Of all *True Blood*'s characters, however, it's Bill who is most reflective of Stoker's Count—but who is also, paradoxically, the most antithetical.

Throughout *True Blood*'s first two seasons (particularly in season one, when he was introduced), Bill often functioned as the inverse of Count Dracula, invading Bon Temps and rivaling its men for Sookie's affections, yet doing so in a manner far less obvious or diabolical than that employed by the Count. Bill did this so well, in fact, that even Jason Stackhouse and Sam Merlotte had begrudgingly accepted him by the end of season two.

It's clear that Bill is successful in his invasion not by being—like Dracula—less civilized than the men he challenges, but by being *more* so. Dracula is a four-hundred-year-old creature who comes from a far-off country to the center of Western civilization to feed, while Bill *returned* to his home, from a far-off era (the nineteenth century), to settle down. In order to do so, Bill had to learn new rules and customs. In essence, he had to become modernized.

Bill's deliberate, mannered speech reflects the Antebellum era, as does his persistent politeness, with which Sookie—though she teases him about it—appears particularly taken. An example of her appreciation for Bill's manners can be seen in season two of *True Blood*. As he threatened Hoyt Fortenberry for touching his ward Jessica, Bill threw him up against a wall. Sookie's initial reaction wasn't so much of concern for Hoyt's safety as it was a surprised, "Bill, that's rude!" when she saw Bill, for just a moment, abandon his civility. After all, Bill's propriety delineates him from the "rednecks" Sookie routinely encounters as a waitress at Merlotte's. At one point, Sookie even offered to wear petticoats for Bill, reminding him of the decorum to which he was once accustomed. It's hard for any modern man to compete with Bill in this regard.

Bill comes to Bon Temps from a time many Southerners look back on with longing, as demonstrated by the rapt attention he received when speaking to the Descendants of the Glorious Dead. Bill not only values his own heritage, but helped Sookie and her Gran further appreciate their own, as he told them the story of their ancestor Jonas Stackhouse (Bill's contemporary), and how he came to build the Stackhouse family home.

The fact that Bill still acts and thinks like an Antebellum gentleman, and returned to his family's home, reveals the value he places on the past. And it's this value that puts him in direct contrast to season one's villain, the murderous, vampire-hating Rene Lenier, who falsified his persona and heritage, thereby erasing his own history and roots.

Bill doesn't just bring Antebellum etiquette to twenty-first-century Louisiana, he also reopens the era's now uncomfortable racial, social, and class politics. And in so doing, he presents a double threat to the men of Bon Temps, reminding them of their brutal past even as he bests them in manners. In this regard, Bill echoes Stoker's Count as he reminds one of a time when America's savagery, in its purest form of slavery, lurked just below the country's supposed refinements. Bill's penance for his sins as a slave-owner comes not so much from being made a vampire, but by becoming a member of a new minority race, one victimized by a new form of bigotry. His body, like an African slave's, has become a commodity, and hate groups persecute his people. The most prevalent such group in *True Blood* is the Fellowship of the Sun, which completes a curious cycle of oppression in Bill's story, enslaving vampires and working toward an undead genocide. As Bill once believed his race superior to another, so now others would strip him of his vestiges of humanity.

Arata argues that racism lies at the center of *Dracula*'s reverse colonization. That "the 'anticipated apprehension' of deracination—of seeing Britons 'ultimately dissolving into Roumanians' or vampires or savages—is at the heart of the reverse colonization narrative." It's also worth noting that Stoker, a transplanted Irishman with conflicting allegiances, was especially sensitive to issues of racial and imperial dominance.

Not only does racism make its way into Stoker's story, but feminism does as well. In the 1880s and 1890s, a phenomenon was taking place in England known as the New Woman. Essentially the Victorian equivalent of modern feminism, the term was first coined by Sarah Grand in her 1894 essay "The New Aspect of the Woman Question." According to Jimmie E. Cain, Jr., in *Bram Stoker and Russophobia*, the New Woman "sought equal legal standing—female adultery was considered legally worse than male adultery at that time—greater economic opportunities 'in professions such as nursing and in the civil service,' political equality, and 'sexual emancipation.'" Florence Nightingale, who served in the English army during the Crimean War, came to epitomize the New Woman, as she "challenged the authority of the male-dominated medical community and army command" in her crusade to reform healthcare practices. (Her efforts, up until her death in 1910, earned her both praise and scorn.)

In the years that preceded the publication of *Dracula*, the "image of the New Woman," writes Barrie, "was the subject of popular controversy in England." Recall that Dracula aroused the dormant passions of unmarried nineteenth-century English women, who subjugated their own needs and yearnings to the propriety of their time. "That Dracula propagates his race solely through the bodies of women," writes Arata, "suggests an affinity, or even an identity, between vampiric sexuality and female sexuality. Both are represented as primitive and voracious, and both threaten patriarchal hegemony." The novel not-too-subtly implies that the Count's worst sin is not merely to render women capable of enjoying sex, but to transform them into sexual aggressors. This can be seen in the book's portrayal of its two female protagonists: Mina, the proper, hard-working assistant schoolmistress engaged to Jonathan Harker, and Lucy, her privileged, morally uninhibited, and sexually liberated friend, who cannot decide between her three suitors and so wants them all. It's Lucy who, over the course of the book, succumbs to Dracula's influence, becomes a vampire, and must be destroyed by the very men who profess to love her.

Dracula, claims Cain, satisfies a yearning for "an imagined loss of male control in both the artistic and domestic spheres. In an era when the emergence of what came to be known as the

New Woman threatened the status quo, fiction offered a soothing balm. The fates of the principal female characters in *Dracula*
and [Stoker's] *The Lady and the Shroud* attest to Stoker's personal
anxieties about this emerging threat to male hegemony."

This is where *True Blood* parts ways with *Dracula*, treating
its female characters with at least as much sympathy as its male
characters, though some of its men do take a decidedly nineteenth-century view of women. Jason Stackhouse, for example,
in season one was sexually promiscuous, yet derided Sookie for
entering a monogamous relationship with a vampire. For his
part, Bill has become a more dynamic, virile character as his
relationship with Sookie has grown, while Jason has become
more anxiety-ridden—a trait he shares with most of the male
human characters in *True Blood*, who are largely portrayed as
weak and ineffectual as compared to the male vampire characters, who are depicted as robust, healthy, and confident.
The undead in *Dracula* are similarly depicted, and are ironically "healthier" than the novel's human characters. As Jason
becomes more nervous as his story progresses, so too does Jonathan Harker, *Dracula*'s protagonist, while the Count himself
is invigorated. Arata further points out that the human characters in *Dracula* appear unable to reproduce, and that there's a
peculiar dearth of fathers in the novel; this is yet another trait it
shares with *True Blood*.

The New Woman in Victorian England paved the way for
Sookie as a sexually liberated young woman. The fact that
Sookie maintained her virginity long enough to offer it to Bill
wasn't due to an oppressive patriarchal society, but because
of her "gift" for reading minds. Apparently the thoughts of the
men around her are so offensive that reading the thoughts of a
sexual partner in the midst of lovemaking would be unbearable.
Sookie's ability further presents *True Blood* as a negative image

of *Dracula*. Whereas the Count makes himself present in the minds of the novel's women in order to prey on them, Sookie *cannot* feel Bill's mind in hers. (However, she, after drinking his blood, is now always present in *his* mind, which proves convenient considering the frequency with which he must come to her rescue.)

Bill, invader though he may be, functions as a sexual liberator. He has freed Sookie not only from the repression she's placed under by her telepathy, but also from a more insidious form of repression—psychological. In *True Blood*'s first season, after Sookie and Bill first made love, she revealed to him that her Uncle Bartlett molested her as a child. Indirectly, and with nary a trace of preaching, the series implied that women are as repressed in today's society as they were in Victorian England. It's merely the form of the repression that's changed. It may be better hidden, but it's as destructive as ever.

It's been said that *Dracula* ends on a note of cynicism, that despite the destruction of the vampire Count, and the presumed triumph of Victorian society, Dracula achieves a kind of victory by the standards of that society. The Count's blood has mixed with Mina's, and so it flows in the veins of the son she bears Jonathan Harker, a son born on the one-year anniversary of Dracula's death. According to Arata, this can be read to imply that, in order for the English "race" to survive, it must take on "those racial qualities needed to reverse its own decline."

True Blood takes a more sympathetic view of vampire invasion, and its first season ended on a more optimistic note, at least regarding Bill. Even though he was almost destroyed in his attempt to save Sookie from Rene, Bill did achieve a victory through Sam Merlotte and Sookie, in that their shared defeat of Rene is a victory for all benevolent supernatural beings in Bon Temps. Sam distracted Rene long enough for Sookie to kill him, and since Sam—like Bill—had been revealed as a supernatural creature (a shapeshifter), and so is just as much an "Other" as Bill and Sookie, his heroism and Sookie's indicated that human beings can survive the twenty-first century, despite all the violence and still-savage hatred that lies below its surface civility, if they accept those they perceive as invaders and outsiders, learn from them, and, as in *Dracula*, take on some of their qualities.

If *Dracula* is really about the displacement of ineffectual races by virile and vigorous ones, then one can argue that *True Blood* is about how civilized people displace savages, like the kind epitomized by Rene. And so if Dracula's destruction symbolizes a triumph of Old England, Bill's survival can be read as the victory of that noble surviving part of the Old South.

JOSEPH McCABE is the associate editor of *FEARnet.com*, the West Coast editor of *SFX* (for which he's written numerous articles on vampires in pop culture), and the author of the Bram Stoker and International Horror Guild Award-nominated *Hanging Out with the Dream King: Conversations with Neil Gaiman and His Collaborators*. He's contributed to the Smart Pop anthologies *The Man from Krypton: A Closer Look at Superman* and *Webslinger: SF and Comic Writers on Your Friendly Neighborhood Spider-Man*. And he's married to the photographer Sophia Quach. He dedicates this essay to his editor Leah Wilson—as insightful as Sookie, as tolerant as Bill, and as cunning as Dracula himself.

TRUE STUD

Jason Stackhouse in Search of Masculinity

KIRSTY WALKER

Poor Jason Stackhouse. The people of Bon Temps don't take him seriously and, for the most part, neither do we. Both Jason and his storylines are usually played for laughs. But the driving force behind those storylines—Jason's search for masculinity in a world where many of the usual markers of masculinity (physical strength, sexual prowess) are being redefined by the appearance of vampires—is a serious one. Kirsty Walker explains.

With every push for equality there comes a panic from those whose freedoms and privileges others are looking to enjoy. The feminist movement, the race equality movement, and lately the equal rights movement for gays and lesbians have all faced aggression and conflict from those whose power those movements threaten to dissipate. *True Blood* shows us a society in a unique state of change—vampires are "coming out of the coffin," and they are demanding rights akin to those of humans. In the equality movements we have experienced in the real world, reasons for limiting others' rights have often been spurious and based on prejudices surrounding genetic inferiority. In retrospect there has been no reason for different genders, sexualities, and racial groups to fear one another. Vampires, however, have more than the weight of folklore and superstition on their shoulders—they need human blood to survive. This fact alone is enough of a threat to make humans wish to limit the freedoms and social acceptance of the vampire race. But the vampire race is also threatening to humans, and human men in particular, by virtue of their raw and often violent sexuality, and *True Blood* offers the viewer a window into this threat, primarily through Jason Stackhouse.

In *True Blood*, parallels are drawn between vampires and many real-world marginalized groups, but in discussing sexuality, those between vampires and black men are particularly instructive. Stereotypical views of black men—large genitals, physical strength, and the always seductive pull of that which is different or mysterious—led to their white counterparts seeing them increasingly as rivals for white female affection, particularly in the first half of the twentieth century (though as recently as 2009 a Louisiana Justice of the Peace, Keith Bardwell, refused to marry an interracial couple). Similarly, tales are told of the increased libido and sexual energy of vampires, and their very blood is known to be a powerful aphrodisiac. The mainstream media is telling humans that they should sleep with a vampire at least once, and vampire bars are hives of rampant sexuality— a sexuality of dominance and submission, pain and pleasure.

Arguably, the most stereotypically masculine men in *True Blood* are all supernatural—the vampires Bill and Eric, and Sam the shifter. These are also the three men with whom the main character Sookie[1] has some form of romantic attachment. Her

---

[1] In Sookie, television has a female character who is at once alluring and threatening to her male counterparts, while also evoking the protective

"relationship" with Eric may be based on nothing more than a forced physical link, but by the end of season two it was causing her (along with the similarly afflicted Lafayette) some discomfort as her resistance to his sexuality and influence was compromised. When we first met Eric he sat on a throne in Fangtasia, surveying his kingdom. His power and his eagerness to display and protect it are typically masculine traits not diluted by his metrosexuality. He straddles a primal dominance and a modern gender ambiguity best depicted in the scene in "Nothing But The Blood" (2-1), where he ripped a man to pieces and then worried about the blood in his hair bleaching foils. Rather than emasculating Eric, the moments where he shows vulnerability or vanity only serve to underline his confidence. He thinks little of sobbing uncontrollably in front of Sookie as Godric faces death, nor of being caught in a candlelit bubble bath at Bill's house. The "rules" of a gendered society do not apply to him, as there are no consequences to his breaking of them. He faces neither violence nor emasculation, as unlike the majority of human men he can both aggressively defend himself and, if necessary, force a sexual attraction through blood sharing.

Bill can similarly choose to opt out of the gendered society but his role as a former soldier, husband, and father define his masculinity even decades after those titles have stopped applying to him. He attempts to dominate both Sookie and Jessica, playing the role of the protector and provider, but not without

---

instinct of almost every male character she comes across. Her telepathy is female intuition writ large, and those men who know about her gift find themselves immediately on the back foot, trying to keep their thoughts clean and pure even as Sookie's innocent sensuality means they are anything but. The fact that vampires, especially Bill, are immune to this ability is just another reason for human men to resent them.

obstacles. Sookie enjoys his sexual aggression while chastising him for attempting to tell her what to do. Her contrary nature confuses him and despite the fact that he is a vampire he finds himself saddled with the very human problem of figuring out what she wants from him as a man. Whether Sookie approved or not, however, Bill protected and provided by killing first the two humans who attacked her in Merlotte's parking lot, and then the man who abused her as a child—two acts a human male might want to perform but would be less likely to get away with and thus less likely to commit.

Sam's masculinity is best represented by the respect he receives as a business owner, and a self-made man. As Tara told him in "Mine" (1-3), "You're hot, you have a job, you're not a serial killer," a résumé that puts him ahead of most men in Bon Temps by a significant margin. His sexuality is also well served by his position as employer—in two seasons he has managed to become romantically involved with three of his employees (Daphne, Tara, and arguably Sookie). Sam steadily developed from hopeless romantic, rejected by Sookie and concerned by Tara's self-destruction, to confident hero as his supernatural abilities were revealed. He was closely involved in the climactic moments of both seasons, but in very different ways. In season one he risked his life to save Sookie, but like Bill was injured, leaving her to ultimately save herself. In season two however, he was the only man in Bon Temps who could defeat Maryann by virtue of his shifter ability. His human counterparts—Andy Bellefleur and Jason, who in another show might have been the heroes—were just the mostly bumbling supporting players.

Jason, a white heterosexual male, has been brought up in a patriarchal, heteronormative society where those in positions of governmental power are other white males. He should be part of the dominant group in society, but this is a society in flux, and thanks to the emergence of vampires, his status is no longer assured. Compared to Bill, Eric, and Sam, he loses out in the masculinity stakes. However, as a highly sexualized man—one who would like to rival the supernatural creatures around him for female affection—Jason is the perfect yardstick by which to measure the impact of vampires "coming out" on human males.

Our introduction to Jason was also our first contact with vampire sexuality. In our first shot of Jason, he was naked, on his knees giving Maudette oral sex. The scene depicted Jason as a sexual creature but added a note of submission, as well as a suggestion of inexperience when he was shocked by the bite marks on Maudette's body. In the vampire sex tape she showed him, the male was dominant, aggressive, and violent, and Maudette was screaming. Vampires, we learned, were sexually aggressive and deviant, and the rapid head-shaking visual effect reminded us that they could flip from human to monster in seconds.

In those first episodes, Jason, in contrast, could not seem to gain the respect of the female characters. The women he slept with variously called him a "moron," "a horn dog," and a "loser," and Dawn was particularly vicious in her evaluation of his masculinity when she threw him out of her house and shot at him because he failed to maintain his erection. The fact that she had recently been sexually active with a vampire only exacerbated Jason's frustration, because he couldn't handle being second best.

Masculinity and maleness are often difficult to define, but there is one thing that clearly says, "This is male"—the penis. For Jason, at least in early episodes, his penis did more than just represent his virility and his "manhood"; it helped define him as a person.[2] Having Dawn and Maudette compare him unfavorably, sexually, to vampires threatened his self-confidence and his sense of identity. He needed a way to re-assert his masculinity, gain respect, and be able to call himself a man—and this search for masculinity is, at least in *True Blood*'s first two seasons, Jason's primary journey. So far we have seen Jason attempt to "man up" in two ways—through sex (and love) in season one, and through power and violence in season two, both times largely through imitation of overtly masculine male role models.

When the potency of vampire sexuality threatened Jason's ability to define himself as a man through this model of masculinity, his initial solution was to emulate the threat. He twice copied the vampire Maudette showed him on film, once with her, and later with Dawn after she left him tied to the bed. This

---

[2] At every significant juncture in his arc Jason has either been motivated by or undone by his penis. He was accused of four murders, got hooked on aphrodisiac vampire blood, was implicit in the killing of a vampire, and had an affair with the wife of someone offering him salvation, all because his sexuality was his prime motivator. Even when he did not intend any wrongdoing, the promise of sex and the power that women hold over him could persuade him down the wrong path. His desperation to be the best lover he could be and his addiction to sex via V also stripped him of his dignity, as we saw in this exchange from "Burning House of Love" (1-7):

JASON: Look. I'll pay however you want. I'll even show my
           wiener. On your website.
LAFAYETTE: You can take your little stumpy white dick and get the
           fuck up out my joint. That's what I want.

When Jason overdosed on V we saw that his penis could easily become his undoing. When the V kicked in after he was arrested for murder, giving him an insistent and painful erection, he was unable to concentrate despite the severity of the situation, and Tara had to come to his rescue.

impersonation of the vampire took place after two instances of subjugation by women, and images of the vampire also flashed into Jason's head during sex at later points in the season.

Jason's use of V is also a form of copying. Jason believed that by drinking V he could tap into vampire sexuality as a tourist, taking that stamina, energy, and lust and wrapping it up in a nicely tanned package with none of the negative side effects of actually living like a vampire. When he overdosed and got the hard-on to end all hard-ons, however, the message was clear: Jason could not handle vampire sexuality. We knew, even if he did not yet, that he would need to find another way to reclaim his masculinity.

The search for masculinity is not an easy one. Since the women's liberation movement, which picked up speed in the 1960s, and the rise of the metrosexual in the early 2000s, our understanding of what a "man" is has changed. Slowly but surely, almost every facet of traditional masculinity has been deconstructed. Even statements like "men don't wear make-up" are nonsense when we have the word "guyliner" in our vocabulary. In 2008 Thomas Beatie became the first person legally identified as a male to give birth. We assume these things are true in *True Blood*'s world as well. With masculinity in such a state of uncertainty, is it any wonder that Jason displays issues with self-esteem and self-actualization? In "Scratches" he prayed to the God he had only just begun a dialogue with, saying, "Please, please give me another sign. 'Cause I'm lost. I'm so fucking lost."

In most cases a boy's first male role model—the person who shows him what it is to be, and to become, a man—is his father. When a father is absent there can be consequences for a boy's behavioral and emotional development as well as to his self-esteem, especially if there is no comparative male relationship to take its place. Jason lost his father at the age of eleven, and the negative effects of his father's death are especially evident in his sexual development. His relationships with women can certainly be seen as unhealthy: a string of one-night stands and shallow attachments based on both parties' desire to scratch an itch. (No woman Jason slept with told him she loved or even cared about him until Amy, and he had difficulty admitting love for her in return.)

In season one, Jason found an unlikely substitute father figure in Eddie. Eddie had been forced to abandon his own son because he was turned, and regretted it; "A boy needs a man in his life," Eddie said ("Plaisir D'Amour," 1-9). Jason had been unable to stand up to Amy about her ill-conceived kidnapping plan, yet another instance of his subjugation by stronger women, but despite her aggressive stance he went against her wishes in order to provide comfort, company, and sustenance to his new friend, and later, it is clear that the memory of Eddie's violent death at Amy's hands has stayed with him.

Eddie's death ended Jason's use of V as an aphrodisiac, as masculinity in a vial. Perhaps this was because, as a relatively unattractive, middle-aged gay vampire, Eddie subverted the idea of vampire masculinity Jason had spent so much time pursuing. Or it could be argued that it was Jason's relationship with Eddie that made the difference, and after Jason learned to see a vampire as a person, he could no longer see V as a consequence-free commodity.

However, Jason's efforts to obtain V did actually assist him in his pursuit of masculinity, as his need for V brought him into contact with Amy, who taught him that sex could be a bonding experience.

The kind and loving parts of Jason's nature, which he displayed occasionally early on in his affection for Tara, Sookie, and Gran, were only really indulged by Amy. She was the one female character who accepted his negative attributes and reassured him that he had something to offer. When they met at Fangtasia, his weakness was already evident, as she knew he was there to get V. In not only accepting this weakness but also providing him with the V itself she did not display any of the disappointment and lecturing that he usually received from the women in his life. Amy told him he was "wise" and "special" ("The Fourth Man in the Fire," 1-8), and gave him the opportunity to open up emotionally and talk about the death of his parents, including the blame he apportioned himself for that tragedy. This was the first (and as of the end of season two the only) time we had heard Jason talk in-depth about the most traumatic episode in his life. Although she eventually became controlling and aggressive toward him, Amy also enabled Jason to find at least some semblance of peace and acceptance. Her death, apparently at his hands, was another attack on his self-worth. "There's something inside me that's just wrong," he said after his arrest, accepting that he must be the saboteur of his own happiness ("You'll Be the Death of Me," 1-12). At this point Jason abandoned the search for masculinity through sex, at least for the moment.

In season two Jason latched onto another male role model, Steve Newlin, initially impressed by his status and the respect he commanded. Newlin told us his own thoughts on masculinity in "Scratches": "If I didn't hate vampires and do everything in my power to avenge my family's death, what sort of man would I be?" Jason did not hate vampires, and his sister, not him, avenged his grandmother's death, so his answer told us all we needed to know about how he judged his masculinity at this point: "A pretty bad one."

Without any real thought as to what his actions meant he set about trying to impress Newlin with his physical abilities, most notably in the game of capture the flag. Their trip into the woods to shoot paintballs at cardboard vampires had all the hallmarks of a bonding exercise, two men yelling and waving around their phallic symbols, showing their aggression. The day even ended like a stereotypical male fantasy, with meat and beer while Newlin's comely wife gyrated in front of the grill. Jason's need for a male role model was only superseded by his libido, and in effect he managed to take some of Newlin's status by screwing his wife within the walls of his domain—the church.

Newlin was not, however, the source of Jason's initial interest in the Fellowship of the Sun. Sociologists attempting to explain young men's membership in terrorist groups have pinpointed inadequacy and alienation arising from lack of positive male role models. The Fellowship of the Sun can certainly be seen as a terrorist group, from its process of indoctrination, targeting of the young and directionless, to its stockpiling of arms for the glorious revolution. Jason was visited by the Fellowship of the Sun when he was at his lowest point and was given the opportunity to be part of a group with a noble cause, serving the ultimate father—God. Recruited as a repentant sinner, it was his flaws and inadequacies that make him the perfect candidate. Rather than being reasons for him to be rejected they were his chief selling points to the Fellowship.

Just as Jason tried to emulate vampires sexually, he initially bought into the Fellowship's ideals of matching the violence of vampires in order to destroy them. When he was brought up on stage to role play on the opening night of the boot camp, his expression of violence and loss of self-control were applauded, and he was quickly identified as one of the best new recruits. But his inner conflict was evident as he flashed on Eddie's death. He later saw Eddie's face in a weird sex dream—his subconscious connecting his pursuit of sex and his pursuit of power.

Newlin thought the sight of an obliterated vampire would be "awesome" ("Let's Take A Trip Together," 2-4), but to Jason it was an image he found traumatic. As a route to masculinity, violence against vampires was confusingly blocked by his affection for and grief over one, and a male one at that. Jason's reluctance to fully commit into the ideals of the Fellowship was the beginning of his journey to self-awareness. He had reason to fear and resent vampires, but his views on them were no longer black and white. When he was forced to pick sides, he chose his sister and Bill over Newlin and the Fellowship, and even found it within himself to apologize to Bill over the way he had treated him. Seeing the vampires as equals, he no longer felt the need to emulate them in pursuit of masculinity.

Both sex and violence ultimately failed as ideologies by which Jason could become self-actualized, because they encouraged him to be selfish and to objectify others as things to be conquered. However, there were moments in both seasons where Jason began to develop and grow as a person, and thus took steps in the right direction. By the end of season one, he had learned to enjoy sex as a bonding experience rather than just a way for him to be physically satisfied. The way he gazed at Amy and focused on her pleasure was a stark contrast to the sex he had with Dawn in "The First Taste" (1-2), where he pointed at himself in the mirror as if cheering himself on. By realizing that sex could be fulfilling emotionally as well as physically, albeit through use of V as a hallucinogen, he had begun to use his masculinity to complement femininity, rather than dominate it.

Likewise, in taking the ideology of power and violence to extremes with the Fellowship of the Sun, he realized that judging the vampires as a group was flawed and that the path to righteousness and redemption lay in strength of character instead. He told Sookie that he would support her relationship with Bill, admitted he was wrong, and joined in the fight to save Bon Temps from Maryann, using his brain to distract the cult members from killing Sam. He was a very different Jason from the one we met in episode one, and though his character development consisted mostly of learning from very bad mistakes, he *did* learn from them.

In an interview with About.com, actor Ryan Kwanten stated that it "was important for [Jason] to have a sense of vulnerability and for the audience to be able to sympathize with him, and to not see him as . . . a piece of meat or just a dumb redneck, that there really is some soul and some hurt deep inside." Jason's search for self through masculinity allows him to become more than "just a dumb redneck." Jason questioned his motivations and tried to better himself, and by the end of season two had reached a point where he actually sounded self-aware. "The whole point in being a hero," he said in "Beyond Here Lies Nothin'" (2-12), "is to do something bigger than yourself."

Jason's last act of the season, however, was to shoot Eggs in defense of Andy. Burdened with Eggs' death, Tara's grief, and his own guilt, Jason will have more challenges to overcome and it remains to be seen whether his search for self can lead him any closer to an ideal as elusive and mythical as anything seen on *True Blood*—a real man.

———

KIRSTY WALKER turned an obsession with screens into a patchy and unsuccessful media career. A Manchester University graduate in TV Production, she was employed variously as a runner, corporate video director, and radio station manager before she turned to teaching. She is the content editor for endofshow.com and travels from Cannes to Comic-Con using her press pass to score free drinks and easily impress men. She lives in Runcorn, in the northwest of England.

A KINDER, GENTLER VAMPIRE

VERA NAZARIAN

There are two kinds of vampires television allows to live for more than an episode or two: broody, guilt-laden good-guy vamps, and amoral, charming bad-boy vamps (unbeating heart of gold *possibly* included). Which category do we put Bill Compton in? The first, obviously . . . right? Not so fast, Vera Nazarian says. There's a little more to Vampire Bill than meets the eye.

It seems like vampire leading men are all the same.

Whether it's "vegetarian" vampire Edward from *Twilight*, brooding champion of the innocent Angel from *Buffy*, righteous detective Nick Knight from *Forever Knight*, sweet vermineating weakling Stefan from *The Vampire Diaries*, or remorseful and compassionate Louis from Anne Rice's *The Vampire Chronicles*—they've all got a certain *something*.

Really, think about it.

It's as if a committee of all-powerful creative types got together for a super-sekrit brainstorming session and assembled a very special "vampire romantic hero prototype" package.

First they went, "Hmmm. What is it that women (or queer men; let's be inclusive here) want in their sexy XY chromosome bloodsucker? Oh, we know! A very heavy forehead! A broody heavy forehead, with almost Neanderthal brow ridges. Very manly, almost Klingon. You know what they say about forehead size and—"

After much unseemly tittering, they continued. "Okay, what next? Kind of bulky, well-ripped, with rock-hard abs. Must have darkish hair, short-trimmed, manly."

"Yes, yes, manly," they all muttered. "The opposite of metro-sexual, very clean-cut. We cannot have metrosexual."

"Wait—I kind of *want* metrosexual!" called a lonely voice from the back. "With pretty flowing locks?" But the speaker was immediately football-tackled and shackled to his chair. As his mouth was being viciously duct-taped, another creative type whispered in his ear, "Quiet! Don't you know that metrosexual is only for the villain bad-boy and ambiguous love interest? No flowing locks, especially not platinum blond!"

The super-sekrit committee of creative types continued. "Hmm, heavy brow ridges—check. Clean-cut and bulky—check. Now, he must be excessively tortured in soul (if he happens to have one) and spirit, barely able to live with himself and his sordid, bloody past. Think of all those historical kills he committed, all that rampaging and mayhem! That is, before someone threw the morality switch in his head and he went all 'Tree of Knowledge' and good-guy. No wonder he's brooding 24/7, liable to go off the deep end—maybe even stake himself, or decide to watch the sunrise (or both, simultaneously). So, yeah, personal hell, with precarious mental state—check.

He must display a permanent frown (supported by those heavy-duty brow ridges, since no normal forehead can handle that kind of pressure without cracking). Consequently, he must be fundamentally allergic to superfluous facial movement—in particular, smiling—and absolutely lacking in a sense of humor."

"Yes, yes!" the committee clamored, "Eradicate humor—check. Also, remove all irony, wit, sarcasm, smart-alecky repartee, and wiseass 'tude."

And they all chanted for at least five minutes: "No 'tude! No 'tude! Only constipation!"

"But wait!" someone else piped up. "How can he be brooding, handsome, and vampire-heroic without at least *some* kind of attitude? At least give him a black leather jacket, for gosh sakes! Or even a crummy trench coat!"

And so they decided to let our special vamp keep his angry 'tude—really, a kind of eternally suppressed rage. "Since, you know, that's sexy and dangerous. Can't have a non-dangerous vampire hero. Without an edge, what is he, an undead Chihuahua? Edge and humor are not peanut butter and chocolate. No one can have both in one heroic place. He must always look like stormy skies. He must gaze into your eyes with grim tragedy. Even when he cannot roll/turn/hypnotize you ('cause the hero, as a rule, can never mind-fuck the leading lady), he can still make you melt.

"Because, face it," they concluded, "he's one of a kind, a noble, *nice*-guy vampire, with a Scary Dangerous Façade. But underneath, he's *controlling himself*—unlike all those other amoral crazy vamps. Okay, maybe he's a bit on edge. Maybe his psycho brakes need new pads and drums and rotors. But—just look at all that sexy willpower!

"Furthermore, he *loves*—truly, madly, deeply. But his love is always problematic. Even when our heroine is willing (as a rule, the leading lady fantasizes about jumping his undead bones even while putting up her own Scary Dangerous Façade), he absolutely must deny himself any pleasure. Because what better way to torture a hero than to introduce sexual repression, or even insist on abstinence?"

And so, the super-sekrit committee put their final stamp on the whole thing. The prototype was launched into common imagination on mysterious wings (the flapping of trendy black leather outerwear) from an undisclosed location.

And that's how we got broody Angel from *Buffy*, mopey stalker Edward from *Twilight*, and puppy-dog Stefan from *The Vampire Chronicles*—all with that same Forehead of Doom. Along with the forehead, they got all the rest of the baggage and special-snowflake moral uniqueness. And if we dig around deeper and wider in the vampire and urban paranormal genre, we find that almost *all* leading males fit this prototype, with only minor deviations.

Then along came *True Blood*.

Bill Compton, our leading man hero and Sookie Stackhouse's "true bloody" love interest, is an all-around broody good guy, a Southern gentleman at heart. He's carrying ancient guilt baggage (not to mention all of the horrors of the Civil War) crowded into the backrooms of his cranium. And he's trying to do the right thing, despite his vampire past. Granted, his brow ridge is not so prominent, but he still has that grim glare down pat. At first glance, this makes him yet another sterling example of the "vampire nice guy" prototype, version 1.0. Plus, in the world of *True Blood*, he seems to be the *only* one of his moral kind . . .

The kinder, gentler vampire.

One might ask—why is there typically *one* and *only one* vampire per story milieu who can keep his beastly demon nature under control and pass for "socially adjusted human" in all sincerity? And why is it that all the rest of his fellow vamps are either incapable of it, or have to jump through metaphysical hoops to even approach anything remotely civilized?

The pat answer is: that's because all these nice guys are prototype v. 1.0. And the rest of the vamps are . . . not.

So, then, what's up with vampire Bill? Didn't we just demonstrate that he easily fits the mold?

Or . . . does he?

I'd like to propose the curious notion that Bill truly is a different case. Even among the so-called morally civilized, Bill is *not* just an archetypal "uniquely moral vampire" example of everybody's favorite genre-trope-leading hero.

In fact, let's call him version 1.1.

Allow me to illustrate how Bill is a *new and different* kinder, gentler vampire.

That Unique Personal Touch

Bill may be traditional, but he always does things with a personal twist. In the presence of other vampires (such as the wild bunch of old friends who invaded his house early in season one), he claims Sookie as his own by the traditional vampire designation, saying "She is mine" in order to protect her, but it quickly becomes obvious that he will not take advantage of her. Nor does he attempt to use the incident as a sneaky way of impressing her with his chivalry (Eric is a bit guilty of this kind of behavior).

Indeed, unlike other good vamps who might put on a power show in the presence of their vampire peers (followed by just a teeny bit of preenage and posturing in private), he doesn't even particularly pretend to be rougher and "meaner" than he really is, or hide his gentlemanly behavior toward Sookie from his fellow vampires by artifice, smoke and mirrors, or chameleon deception (think Jean-Claude, master of power staging, from *Anita Blake*). Bill is just Bill—he allows himself to be himself in every situation, which sometimes makes him a little awkward and off-kilter. This becomes rather amusing when other vamps start having certain expectations about his honest, predictable, but oddball reactions and get a kick out of messing with his composure on purpose.

Non-Aggressive, to a Human Degree

For a vampire, Bill is fairly passive. When, in the first episode, local vampire-hunters captured Bill and bound him with silver chains, he acted more like a human victim of a crime would, and Sookie had to rescue him. Almost made one think of poor Bill as a kind of innocent wild creature caught in a human-laid trap. It's somehow doubtful that another hero-vamp would have been caught so easily.

It makes Bill a little bit awkward, almost human in his vulnerability. Definitely an interesting "first" in a vampire hero, and possibly an empowering turn-on for Sookie, to have him at her mercy, with the victim-predator tables being turned.

To further the mellow image, Bill's home is stocked with bottled Tru Blood—that amazing artificial construct made in Japan—and he is on a strict non-violent diet. This is absolutely not for show.

Bill is not a typical alpha male (as all the other moral vampire heroes seem to be, except for Stefan Salvatore from *The Vampire Diaries*, who is a full-blown beta). But neither is he a complete wimp.

Rather, he is something in between (not in the Lafayette sense), which makes him unconventional—strong but able to be guided, emotionally accessible, kind, and responsive without being spineless. Bill may not start fights, but he always *tries* to finish them. When he had to face Maryann the maenad in season two, he went at it knowing full well he was not likely to succeed. Poor Bill! A mouthful of that evil black stuff that runs in her veins put him temporarily out of commission, but he does get an A for effort.

Indeed, Bill's more of a gamma independent type, that elusive *something else*.

Flexible in Social Mindset

Some vampires seem to get stuck in their ways over the years, their mindset frozen in the historical time period of their death, and their habits from that point forward dictated strictly by vampire custom. Bill may be rigid in his moral convictions, and about as humorless as a Puritan granny, but he is generally flexible in other unexpected ways. Throughout the series, he fully embraces his vampire heritage as though it were an ethnicity, making no excuses for it. But he is also willing to step outside his "ethnic identity" and live in the greater society that is the human world.

He showed up at Merlotte's Bar and politely ordered Tru Blood. Then he allowed himself to be seen all over town in Bon Temps, making no particular effort to keep himself away from humans. He fraternized with his neighbors. He started openly dating Sookie.

And despite his personal shyness and the reserve left over from his human days, Bill *the vampire* revealed a talent as a PR man and diplomat. He even gave a Civil War presentation lecture to the old ladies of the town—in a church, of all places—graciously answering pointed questions and showing no fear of the cross.

What Bill seems to do best is adapt, both as a time-transplanted person and as a vampire living in new times.

Dutiful Son, Ethnic Traditionalist, Supports the Status Quo

Like many of his version 1.0 brothers, Bill has a strong sense of duty. What's different is who Bill feels he owes that duty to.

As a human being, he was loyal to his wife and family and to his military cause. As a vampire, this translates to loyalty to his own vampire kind, and to others in general. He submits himself, of his own free will, to punishment by vampire law. When ordered by the vampire tribunal to drink the blood of a helpless human victim and "make" a daughter (Jessica), he did the dark deed, even though he understood the implications and felt terrible regret on a personal level. And then he became a typical human dad in the kind of helplessness and responsibility he exhibited when dealing with rebellious teen vamp Jessica from there on.

Other fictional good vamps might obey the vampire laws nominally, and eventually break with tradition (Edward from *Twilight*, Angel from *Buffy*) or become complete loners (Blade, Nicholas Knight from *Forever Knight*, John Mitchell from *Being Human*). But Bill really does obey sincerely (and not because he is ordered to by Eric or the vampire queen), and does not for a moment question the rightness of doing so, even though he might be screaming inside.

Bill is not a rebel (possibly because the last time he had a real cause was during the Civil War), and he sees the expediency of not going against the status quo. Obeying authority is just something that comes naturally to him. It doesn't compromise his personal convictions.

As an ex-soldier, Bill knows his place in the chain of command, and always obeys Eric, the local vampire chapter boss.

Recognizing the traditional hierarchy of vampire power, Bill carries out his various unsavory orders, despite personal tension with Eric. Boy, does he hate the fact that Eric has his eyes on Sookie! And yet, Eric is his sheriff and his ranking superior, so if Eric says he wants to see Sookie, Bill brings her over to Fangtasia himself (even as he stands seething in silence while Eric checks her out). Now *that's* loyalty.

Law-Abiding Dual Citizen

Possibly the most startling new and different thing about Bill is that he's willing to abide by the laws, rules, and social conventions of *both* vampires and humans, with *equal* conviction. He is a model denizen of two worlds, human and vampire, living not outside and beyond the scope of each, but *inside* both, able to somehow blend and reconcile the two together. From what we've seen so far, he is honorable and law-abiding by nature—and treats his situation not as segregation or an exile, but as a kind of dual citizenship with full voting privileges.

This doesn't mean he never breaks the laws of either community. A dark, violent past with guilt, regret, and bloody kills—and a present with the occasional abuse of power in the name of doing good—is every vamp hero's burden. But Bill doesn't brood or rail in futility, or even try to redeem himself by overcompensating in the champion-for-the-innocent department (Angel, I'm looking at you, you hunk o' broody love). Bill simply does what needs to be done *in the moment*, consequences be damned, and then stands by his actions and takes his lawful punishment.

Bill was turned into a vampire very much against his will, and he has not forgotten it. He harbors a serious grudge against his maker Lorena—more excessively than other vampire-maker relationships seem to warrant. Other vamps mellow out over the years, and some, like Eric Northman, display such fierce loyalty to their makers that it goes beyond the realm of supernatural compulsion into true emotional attachment and friendship.

But not Bill. He remembers his companionable years with Lorena with sadness and disgust. And yet he obeys the maker's compulsion and the laws of vampire society—up to the point when the vampire laws (within the scope of your power hierarchy, take justice into your own hands) start to conflict with the human ones (don't be a vigilante; call the cops), and human conventions (protect your loved ones) clash with vampire ones (love is irrelevant; the vampire power hierarchy is everything). In season two, when Lorena tried holding Bill in the Dallas hotel room as a delaying tactic to prevent him from running in all-out vampire-vigilante fashion to save Sookie from the fanatical goons of the Fellowship of the Sun, he obeyed for as long as he could bear it, and then fought her with all his force, to the full extent of his abilities. In season one, when Bill killed traitorous vamp Longshadow, also to protect Sookie, he stood before the Magister and obeyed the gruesome vampire law, breaking a human one in the process—which suggests that this whole thing is still very much a juggling act of allegiances for Bill. Yes, he's learning as he goes, but he's learning fast. After first trying to get Eric to take Jessica off his hands (and off his conscience) and being told firmly (and sarcastically) that she was "all his," Bill was faced with the acknowledgment of this gruesome new responsibility. He cannot make up for murder (to satisfy the human law), but he *can* punish himself by accepting the burden of his own making. And so he turned things around and tried to "raise" new vamp Jessica as a humane vampire. Indeed, there will always be some fundamental conflicts between vampire and human laws and conventions, and Bill cannot always give both sides equal and simultaneous allegiance, but he does an admirable job of balancing things out in the long run.

And then there are those basic human social conventions that vampires mostly disdain. Bill did not just pick a casual vampire sex partner. Sookie is not merely an accessory or object to be used and discarded—to be given "marks" or bound by occult fluid exchange. Instead, he did the very "proper" and legal thing by asking Sookie to marry him in the traditional human sense—starting with a romantic dinner and proposal, and a diamond engagement ring. Had things not ended with his mysterious disappearance from the restaurant while Sookie vacillated in the ladies' room, Bill and Sookie *might* have been safely hitched by the end of season two.

THIS LAST ITEM IS THE key to the new kinder, gentler vampire.

The whole milieu of *True Blood*, with its open, socially "accepted" vampires, has made William Compton into a kind of cultural and social pioneer of his own kind. More so than any previous vampire hero of film or literature, he has to be *both* a model vampire *and* a model human citizen in order to straddle both societies successfully.

At its heart, *True Blood* is a supernatural-meets-natural culture clash. And Bill's the guy who has chosen to embrace both cultures, though their values are drastically different—one might even say incompatible.

Now, in order to reconcile both, you have to be a little bit crazy. Or, maybe, a whole lot of flexible. Or maybe you just have to love someone very much?

Whatever it is, Bill's the new breed, bridging the cultural gap between human and vampire. He drinks only synthetic blood, obeys both sets of laws, and has to tread a very fine line to be true to himself. And in that balancing act, he is truly unique. It's a tough job, tougher than anyone can imagine. No wonder he has that frowny forehead.

You Are What You Eat

It is said, "You are what you eat."

Bill genuinely sustains himself neither on human blood nor on a faux "vegetarian" menu of lesser creatures, like many of his broodier brethren, but on the artificial construct Tru Blood.

Tru Blood, the amazing laboratory elixir, is the blood substitute that actually works to quench the vampire hunger (kinda like MREs for vampires, and supposedly just as unpalatable as army rations, even though it does the nutritional trick). By consuming this stuff exclusively and on a regular basis, Bill is ultimately on the road to becoming a new kind of vampire (possibly even chemically; who knows what kind of magical mystery chemicals are in that stuff?). He's on that road whether he likes it or not. Whether he plans for it, or even thinks about it. And it's bound to happen to all the rest of the vampires who might choose to embrace the new way and to co-exist in human society.

Now, this doesn't mean Bill is taking the same evolutionary fork in the road as that ancient vampire "saint" Godric, Eric's maker, who, after his two thousand years, is more of a deity than a demon—a kind of Vampire Gandhi.

By the end of his unimaginably long undead existence, Godric chose to reject his dark vampire nature completely. His final act of self-immolation was a kind of martyrdom and redemption that Bill is not quite ready for, no matter how much he might hate his undead predicament.

That's because Bill might be a good guy, but he is far from a saint, and is definitely a pragmatist. His own road to redemption lies not so much in self-denial and the perfect rejection of his dark side, but in embracing *a new way of being a vampire.*

And in this new day and age of technology and innovation, he's got it easy. He can drink Tru Blood and remain cruelty free. None of that old-school angst and baggage need follow him along into the brave new undead world.

He's a new, modern, civilized, and sanitized vampire. A hero vampire with a new lease on existence, on love, and on everything else that matters.

And with civilization comes personal quirks. A reawakening of the self. The ability, in some ways, to go back to his human personality roots. To become a decent person again, with some hope for the future. The will to change and grow, and to choose his own path that does *not* include self-destruction.

It was far too late for Godric. He had put himself through two thousand years of self-inflicted purgatory, and was infinitely weary—dead in spirit, long before Tru Blood came along with its hopeful promise of justification for redeemed existence. (Here Tru Blood might be the vampire analog of the Industrial Revolution.)

But it doesn't have to be this way for Bill, or for any of the others who take this kinder, gentler path. Because the key word for all of them is *hope.*

Hope's the other fork in the evolutionary redemption road.

And this hope, with all its alien new promise, lies in Tru Blood.

———

THE SUPER-SEKRIT CREATIVE COMMITTEE PROBABLY didn't see this coming. They might still think of Bill as the original version prototype, but we know better.

Enough with the despair and the rubber-stamped personality. Enough with the angst and the anvil forehead. Time to crack open the archetype, and crack a smile, even. And just maybe, someday, time to find a vampire-safe way to watch the dawn.

It's time for the kinder, gentler, *liberated* vampire.

———

VERA NAZARIAN immigrated to the United States from the former USSR as a kid. She sold her first story when she was seventeen, has been published in numerous anthologies and magazines, was seen on the Nebula Awards ballots, was honorably mentioned in *Year's Best* volumes, and has been translated into eight languages.

A member of Science Fiction and Fantasy Writers of America, Vera made her novelist debut with the critically acclaimed *Dreams of the Compass Rose* (Wildside Press, 2002), followed by *Lords of Rainbow* (Betancourt & Company, 2003). Her novella "The Clock King and the Queen of the Hourglass" (PS Publishing, UK) made the 2005 Locus Recommended Reading List. Her debut collection, *Salt of the Air* (Prime Books, 2006, expanded and reissued by Norilana Books, 2009), contains the 2007 Nebula Award–nominated "The Story of Love." Recent works include the 2008 Nebula Finalist novella "The Duke in His Castle," and two Jane Austen parodies, *Mansfield Park and Mummies* (2009) and *Northanger Abbey and Angels and Dragons* (2010).

Vera lives in Los Angeles. In addition to being a writer and an award-winning artist, she is also the publisher of Norilana Books.

Visit her website: www.veranazarian.com.

WHAT A STRANGE LOVE

Or How I Learned to Stop Worrying and Love the Shifters

PHILIPPA BALLANTINE

These days it seems like vampires get all the love. It's easy to forget that they aren't the only option when it comes to romancing the supernatural. Luckily, Phillipa Ballantine is here to remind us. Sookie may not fully appreciate Sam's charms, but that doesn't mean we can't.

Sam Merlotte. Bill Compton.

The competition for our supernatural affections has never been stronger. Indeed it seems that we've broken down into the usual two camps—shapeshifters and vampires—like we are in some sort of primitive tribal ritual where fangs or fur are the only options.

Vampires appear to have a strong lead, with a wealth of history and literature to back them up. Certainly the movies haven't helped us shake our love affair with vampires—in fact, they are positively enabling it. Vampires are everywhere: casting covetous eyes on teenage girls, writing maudlin diaries about their eternal pain, and even getting themselves assistants like some Hollywood starlet.

The arrival of the vampire-centric series *True Blood* seems to be just another dish served up cold and sexy for those of the fangbanger persuasion, with such delicious main courses as Bill Compton and Eric Northman.

Maybe we can understand why Sookie Stackhouse is always running across her lawn to leap into bed with brooding vampire Bill Compton. Yet there is always the other side of the coin: the warm embrace of Sam Merlotte, the shapeshifter.

For long enough shapeshifters have been the also-rans, the silver medal to the vampires' gold. As full as *True Blood* is packed with vampires working their sexy charm, the show has also brought us something warmer and cuddlier, something that has the call of the wild stamped deeply on it.

Bon Temps resident shifter, Sam Merlotte, is a fine example of why shapeshifters deserve a second look. Unlike your average vampire, Sam has a regular life. He's owner of the bar where all the locals hang out, vampires come to play, and the resident telepath serves you Southern hospitality. Sam and his bar are an institution in Bon Temps, and his charm and good looks are part of the reason it is a success. You get the feeling that while the men come for the beer and the cooking, the women might be there for other, just as primal reasons. Even if he were just the simple owner of Merlotte's there would be plenty of people walking through Sam's door.

But we know he's far from anything simple. From the moment that mysterious collie turned up, we wondered about Sam and how he fit into the supernatural landscape of *True Blood*. He didn't exactly act like a totally normal human being, and when Sookie tried to get a glimpse inside his head we all worked out that he wasn't. But what was he? Was he some kind of werewolf? Or something far more complicated? While vampires are way out in the public gaze (they even have their own media representative, for goodness' sake), Sam Merlotte is playing it low-key. That just adds to his mystery and intrigue.

His physical attractions are obvious—as Coralee observed in her own special way, "God bless who ever made those jeans! I'd wear that man as a scrunchie!" ("Beyond Here Lies Nothin'," 2-12). While we boggle at the physical difficulty involved in that particular statement, we find ourselves kind of agreeing with her. Even if we feel it might be more subtly put.

We found it charming when we discovered that Sam Merlotte's favorite form is a shaggy dog. Sure, that form is the safest, since people are far less likely to shoot at a dog than, say, a mountain lion or a bear, but we also imagine that it is a reflection on Sam's personality.

Like a dog he is amazingly loyal to those he cares about. He showed how good he was with children when he looked after Arlene's kids, after Arlene fell under Maryann's spell. Like a good puppy he knows all about the importance of bringing gifts. Tara didn't like it when he bought her flowers, but that reflects badly on her, not on our dear sweet Sam. He keeps the dog around not just so he can copy his shape, but also, we guess, because he genuinely likes dogs. (Another thing the shifter has to his advantage—after all, animals don't seem to take kindly to vampires.)

He also loves running through the woods, enjoys swimming, and is incredibly brave. How many people do you know who will take a knife just to help out their friends, as Sam did for Sookie and the rest of the townsfolk at the end of season two? Unlike a vampire, who might be able to take a couple of knife wounds and still kept his dinner reservations, Sam could have died.

But Sam isn't appealing in spite of being a shifter—he is appealing because he is a shifter. Shifters are closer to nature than we are, and we all yearn to get a bit of the wild back into our lives, though our ancestors were only too glad to leave it behind. We want the wild even as we are terrified of it. It sets our pulse racing, and as every teenage boy who has taken his date to a scary movie will tell you, once you get someone's pulse racing you're halfway there. Fear is just another form of arousal. And that fear of and attraction to the wild is what makes the pull of the shifter every bit as powerful and primitive as what we feel for the vampire.

Shapeshifter legends have been around just as long as vampire stories and appear in cultures around the world. From the werewolves of Europe to the skin-walkers of North America, all of them hold a certain fascination for us.

The legend of the werewolf was born around the fire, when everything else was dark mysterious woods and the wolves howled out there somewhere in the dark and cold, sending shivers up our ancestors' spines.

Werewolves used to be people but how you became one was up for some debate. In European legend there were many different explanations: sleeping under the full moon, putting on a wolfskin, or consorting with the devil. However it happened, you were reduced to base animal nature, and no one—not even your family and friends—was safe.

In the tiny villages in the rural backwaters of Europe, being trapped with a neighbor turned werewolf was a terrifying prospect. Take, for example, Peter Stumpp. Stumpp was the most famous reported werewolf in history. He lived in Germany in the late sixteenth century, where he was convicted of being a serial killer and making a pact with the devil. Using a magical belt the devil gave him, he inflicted panic and terror on his community in the form of a wolf, earning the title "the Were-wolf of Bedburg." Among the numerous people he was said to have killed was his own son.

Werewolves were traditionally unattractive. Customary physical traits included a mono-brow, long curved fingernails, and elongated ears. (Even Tara with her self-esteem issues might think twice before jumping into bed with an old-time werewolf.)

Yet werewolves are not the only form of shapeshifters we see in mythology. Many cultures had their own half-human, half-animal werepredators: hyenas in Africa, tigers in India, and jaguars in South America. And in other cultures, shapeshifters did not begin as human at all: while some were people who made bargains to gain the powers of an animal, others were said to be animals that chose to walk among us and torment us with their beauty and cleverness. These shapeshifters were often devastatingly attractive to us mere mortals.

In Japanese mythology, foxes would take on the shape of beautiful women—often at dusk—to lure the unsuspecting and foolish. These Japanese fox spirits, kitsune, were cunning and enjoyed outwitting and tormenting humans by using their ability to create illusions and become invisible. Rumor had it they did have a bit of trouble with their fox tails, however, which sometimes refused to shift.

In Scotland, the selkie would often cast off their seal forms by shedding their skin and go for a walk on land. Selkie men were so beautiful and seductive that they could pretty much have their pick of mates but, generously, would go looking for unsatisfied women (something that the female residents of Bon Temps might want to suggest to Sam). Selkies did have one important vulnerability: if you stole their skin, they couldn't return to seal form.

The Native Americans' vision of shapeshifters, skin-walkers, were a little more disturbing. There are many legends from various tribes, but generally skin-walkers were people who gained the power to become an animal through evil. Unlike European werewolves, the skin-walkers could take any shape that they needed and use the powers of that animal to further their own aims.

Sam doesn't fit easily into any one of these shapeshifter traditions. Instead, in creating Sam and his shifter kinfolk, *True Blood* (and Charlaine Harris, who wrote the books the show is based on) seems to have mixed and matched a variety of powers and weaknesses from shapeshifters all over the world.

He is not limited to a single shape like the European werewolf, though he does have some features in common with them. The most obvious one is the importance of the moon. In myths it holds sway over werewolves, and in *True Blood* it calls to Sam and his kin as well, exerting a pull on him that can lead to embarrassing situations, such as his early-morning sprint through the woods wearing nothing but a look of concern in season one.

However, Sam does seem able to control the darker parts of his animal nature that mythological weres are unable to. Unlike his European werewolf brethren, Sam isn't evil. Shifter actions in the seasons we have had so far have been no worse than things done by men (or vampires). Sam is just a man who had to look after himself—after all, stealing from a maenad hardly counts. The second shifter we met, Daphne Landry, made some bad choices, but we can't judge her too harshly either, as she was pretty much living in fear for her life working for Maryann. Though we are not entirely sure we can ever forgive her for trying to drag Sam off to be sacrificed!

Like the skin-walker, Sam can pick and choose which animal he wants to take the form of, and when—so there's no need to lurk about the fringes of society like the poor old European werewolf. Sam can stalk through the woods as a wolf if he likes, and the next minute take the shape of a silent white owl and soar above the treetops. Maybe turning into a fly is not the most attractive choice, but it certainly got Sam out of a rather difficult situation with Maryann!

The *True Blood* shifter's abilities are not limitless, of course. And their chief limitation, the need for a template to copy, echoes the selkie's need to always have his or her seal skin. Some stories claim similarly that skin-walkers require the pelt of the animal they want to change into. Luckily Sam lives pretty close to nature and can usually find a useful creature nearby—and unlike a selkie he doesn't need to worry about someone stealing his skin and holding it ransom (though Coralee would love that!).

However, in much the same way that skin-walkers have animals they prefer to copy (usually the coyote, crow, wolf, or owl), so do the *True Blood* shifters—though their choices seem to be more individual. Sam has his shaggy dog and Daphne had her pig (though why she chose a pig is a bit of a mystery).

One difference *True Blood* shifters have from skin-walkers or werewolves is that they are born, not made. Sam had the good fortune, though he might say otherwise, to be born one.

After all, being a shapeshifter seems like a pretty good deal. Compare being a shifter to being a vampire. Sure, they're hurt more easily than vampires (damn them and their regenerative blood), and since they age, they may not share vampires' extended life span. But maybe that's a good thing. It means shifters still have real human emotions, untainted by the passing of so many years. In fact, immortality seems to bring out the melancholy in some vampires (Bill Compton, we're looking at you). When Sookie asked Sam, "Are you lonely?" and he honestly replied, "Yes, I am. I am very, very lonely" ("Mine," 1-3), women all over the world wanted to rush in and find a way to comfort him. It's the kind of melancholy we can understand, rather than the angst of "Gosh it's a drag to be smoking hot and live forever." Shifters are just more emotionally accessible.

However, unlike vampires, who are out of the coffin, shifters have to hide their true selves from normal folk. Sure, they don't have to worry about avoiding the sun and sleeping in the dirt, but it still can't be easy. Sam's struggles to maintain a normal life mean that he has pushed people away lest they discover his secret. Sookie pleaded with Sam to reveal himself to people, open up a little, because, "You're kind and brave. There's nothing there not to love" ("You'll Be the Death of Me," 1-12). However, he's finding it hard to trust. One woman he revealed his secret to prefers vampires, and the other tried to have him sacrificed to a bull god. And given our history with killing or dissecting the unfamiliar, we can understand his choice.

So as attractive as shifters are in *True Blood,* you still might want to think twice before dating one. Sookie Stackhouse may be the only woman in Bon Temps able to resist Sam's charms, but maybe she's onto something. Sure, we can question her horrified screaming when she woke to find a naked Sam at the end of her bed, but maybe she was thinking more long-term.

Dating a shifter might present some real problems.

Having your local vampires around for a party would probably be out. We've seen that Sam and vampires, for example, have about the same chances of getting along as alligators and rattlesnakes. It took a long time and a lot of perilous situations before Sam and Bill trusted each other enough to team up to save Bon Temps from Maryann and the residents she'd turned into black-eyed hedonists. And back when the vampire trio of Malcolm, Diane, and Liam invaded Merlotte's, you could practically see Sam's fur standing on end. So be careful not to mix your supernatural creatures if you don't want a throwdown to occur.

Sleepovers . . . yeah, they might also be tricky. Everyone wants something warm to snuggle up to, and yes, Sam is both warm and snuggly. However, we know from Tara that Sam makes strange noises in his sleep—and we're not talking about snoring. Being woken up by a barking, whimpering Sam might be fine the first couple of times, but if you are looking for a longer term commitment he might have to sleep on the mat by the door now and then. If you've ever seen a dog twitch and run in its sleep you can imagine what sharing a bed with the human-sized version could do to your beauty rest.

Also, the sensitive senses thing could get a little odd on occasion—when Sam started rolling around in Dawn's bed, the bed she'd died in, it was a little disturbing. You know when your dog rolls around in something stinky in the park? We could only hope that was what Sam was doing. And even then, it's less than attractive behavior in a boyfriend.

Still, a shifter like Sam, he'd be like the Swiss Army Knife of boyfriends. Maybe you'd have to put up with a few eccentricities if you dated one, but no one can deny that the shifters of *True Blood* are a fascinating and alluring creation. Sam and his kin are the perfect blend of genuine humanity and the call of the wild, with all of the benefits of his mythological forebearers and few of the downsides.

So while running with wolves may be as dangerous an activity as running with vampires, running with shifters . . . that opens up a whole new world of possibilities.

———

New Zealand author **PHILIPPA BALLANTINE** is a writer, podcaster, and librarian. Her fantasy novels include *Chasing the Bard*, *Digital Magic*, and the upcoming *Geist*. She is currently residing in Wellington, where her two Siberian cats keep her well under control.

A FEW BLOWN FUSES BEFORE THE NIGHT IS OVER

Alan Ball and the Circuit of Abandon

JACOB CLIFTON

Adapting a book, or a series of books, is never as simple as just putting the plot onscreen (just read Ginjer Buchanan's essay). Choices need to be made—what gets cut, what gets added—and these choices reflect the vision of the person making them. What, in their view, is the story really *about*? Jacob Clifton takes a broader look at Alan Ball's television and film oeuvre, and uses it to help us better understand the storylines that *don't* appear in Charlaine Harris' books—in particular, Tara Thornton's and Jason Stackhouse's.

> "Don't think of it as a clog. Think of it as some sort of magical circuit board, a motherboard, filled with desire, that travels all over the world. That touches you, that touches me. That connects everybody. You just have to find the right connection, the right circuitry. Look at all these people out there: They're trying to find the right connection. And I personally expect a few blown fuses before the night is over. And maybe one of them will be yours."
>
> —*Shortbus* (2006)

In every fairytale—which is to say, *every* tale—the Hero meets a Guide, someone wiser and often older, somebody touched by magic, somebody who knows the Thing and has been sent by the Powers That Be to teach him or her the Thing. Sometimes it's a wizard, like Gandalf or Dumbledore. Sometimes it's Doctor Who. Often, these days, it's a psychologist—Jennifer Melfi, Robin Williams—who leads us into the forest of ourselves and out again. In the heterosexual coming-of-age tales we're so fond of, it's usually an older and more confident guy who knows how to fix cars, but occasionally—like Clementine in *Eternal Sunshine*, or the mysterious Bacall and Novak *femmes de noir*—it's a wonderful woman who opens new doors in us. In Alan Ball's fictional worlds, it's invariably a drug dealer.

American Beauty's Lester Burnham has only taken a few steps off the well-lit path before he meets young pot dealer Ricky Fitts, and falls in love with Ricky's consequence-free approach to life. Nate Fisher's accidental ingestion of a tab of E in *Six Feet Under* leads him to a dreamy poker game underworld where his father introduces him to spirits of Life and Death, and he sees their raucous and hilarious lovemaking for himself. And then there's *True Blood*, where the drug of choice is vampire blood.

Because there is something revolutionary about letting ourselves fall that deeply into our own chaotic worlds—a little bit unruly and a whole lot terrifying—the "illicit drug dealer" metaphor continues to carry weight. It's a given in Ball's world that the divisions between and within us are created and enforced by society at large: How better to dramatically enact the wildness, the suspect freedom, of tossing all that shame and appropriate behavior than under cover of darkness? The drug deal—the contract with the fairytale Guide—is only ever the first step in a journey that takes our Hero out of the world of polite men and women altogether. It is terrifying, for us as viewers and for the characters at hand, because it represents succumbing, on some level, to temptation. Stepping out into Crazy and seeing what you can find.

But the trick, and the monster at the end of this essay, is that there's always a price. The Hero has to return to the World, and learn to be normal again, once he's learned the magical Thing. Otherwise, there's no point: You have arrived at Crazy, and decided to stay there.

Now, classically, the wizards, the Guides, are the ones that can and do come and go at will. But Ball's subversion adds another layer, where even the Guide is unreliable. Lafayette, staunch and strong defender of sexual and gender freedoms we don't even have names for, is eventually brought low by his involvement with V. Kidnapped, nearly murdered, Lafayette spends most of *True Blood*'s second season in a post-traumatic nightmare and is eventually enthralled as Eric's latest acquisition, selling V for the Queen of Louisiana. What was once his gift to offer, as Jason's Guide to the underworld, has become his *raison d'etre*.

Or take poor Amy Burley, who serves as Jason's Guide to the possibility of real, human, nonsexual connection with another person. Her love affair with V goes even more sour, as she becomes enthralled by its possibilities and beauty to the point that she loses all perspective on kindness or compassion, lost in her own need.

Other *True Blood* Guides and their drugs of choice? Well, there's Miss Jeanette, whose hedge-witch magic brings Tara's mother to a wonderfully healing place . . . but also brings about her own death, when she and Tara unleash the chthonic, destructive Maryann on Bon Temps. There's beautiful Godric, who played Eric's Guide thousands of years ago, and whose disappointed dreams of parity between vampires and humans eventually leave him so exhausted that he extinguishes himself.

There are the Newlins, Sarah and Steve, who guide Jason toward his own healing reconciliation while they slowly and quietly fall apart. And there's Maryann herself, who leads Tara into great beauty and strength, before dissolving her altogether.

> "It's a great thing, when you realize you still have the ability to surprise yourself. Makes you wonder what else you can do that you've forgotten about."
>
> —*American Beauty* (1999)

The subversive power—and I would say, a bit of the popularity—of each of Ball's stories is that the Guides presented are never eternal, never reliable, because nothing is eternal, and nothing is reliable. There is no Answer that is always going to be the Answer. In fact, a good rule of thumb for all three narratives is that once something becomes the Answer, it stops *being* the Answer. Whether it's Ruth Fisher's "personal development seminars" or Lester Burnham's free-flying midlife breakdown, the Answer immediately begins to rot around you the second that you find it. Brenda Chenowith's sexual awakening becomes too dark to look at; Sookie and Bill's immediate mutual obsession falls into domestic disagreements about stepdaughters and "us time"; Tara's discovery of Miss Jeanette's true identity sends her into a full-on meltdown complete with gaudy prom dress. You cannot simply turn a corner in your life and become a new person. Thinking that you can is how you end up in a cult. Or lonely, or addicted.

———

BUT IF THERE'S NO PLACE to rest, no fixed answer, what's the point of these stories? Temperance. Balance. Because for each character in these stories, there is a choice to be made between abandon and repression, and it's a knife-edge we all have to walk. What makes them fictional is their resilience in falling off that edge so very often, because as characters they don't ever have to settle down. They can keep flipping back and forth across that line for their entire fictional lives.

Jason Stackhouse's graphic and ubiquitous sex scenes in the first season's early (pre-Amy) episodes were shocking for some viewers, repetitive for others, which I would say is the point: he's not going anywhere, serially looking for that something he's missing in the beds of every Merlotte's waitress he can meet. It's only when Lafayette gives him his first hit of V that Jason seems capable of admitting that other people exist: he finally sees the wondrous beauty of Tara, inside and out, in a vision that portrays her as an earthly goddess. But even that first night, V takes him too far. He is so taken with the wonder and interconnectedness of the world that he thinks nothing of having sex with a random woman behind Merlotte's, rubbing garbage all over her skin and his own."

Throughout the season, we see Amy—and Lafayette, until he finally gives up—trying again and again to lead Jason to a mediating place where he can bring the sensual and emotional openness of those V experiences into the daylight world of his conscious life. Where the love he feels for everything and everyone can be expressed in a way that doesn't call his masculinity into question; where he can reconnect with his sister, to whom he is always loyal but from whom he becomes increasingly distant; where his nonverbal wisdom and inner strength can find a means of expression rather than mute demonstration.

Meanwhile, Tara Thornton's first-season arc is one of tremendous and ongoing lack of control, from our first glimpse of her—setting impressive fire to her bridges at the hardware store—to the very moment of her exorcism. Tara only seems capable of being the grounded, intelligent woman that she clearly is when everything around her is going insane (a strong and insightful characterization, given her upbringing) and she seems unable to separate her own healing from that of her mother's. After Lettie Mae's successful exorcism and reintegration into Bon Temps church society, it's only a matter of time before Tara will be tempted into buying Miss Jeanette's services for herself.

But this exorcism goes very differently. Narratively, it provides explicit entrée for Maryann's character in season two, although we don't know that yet. But the starkly defined purpose of the ceremony—essentially, to slam-bang five years of therapy into a single drugged-out nightmare—is painfully characteristic for Tara, who never met a problem she couldn't shut the door on. It's just another version of her barely romantic negotiations with Sam Merlotte, in which she sought verbal confirmation of the idea that a sexual relationship would have no emotional consequences. (We get another version of this narrative from her at the first season party in which she explains her non-romantic aims to a suitor.) In both cases, her intellect and seemingly pathological fear of complications lead her to attempt the cleanest break, the most sterile circumstance possible. In both cases, it causes immediate breakdown.

Tara is defined both by her passions—her wild acting out, her fierce love for her friends—and by her fearful resistance to those passions, seeing in her own loss of control a redux of her mother's brutal path. In the end, season one's exorcism storyline provides her with a seemingly perfect solution—which requires no compromise or abandon at all.

———

BY THE SECOND SEASON, JASON'S traumatized and feeling crazy, and—in his own version of Tara's exorcism—decides to cut all ties with the increasingly (and this is key) *complex* world of Bon Temps. He sneaks away to join an anti-vampire cult with strong Christian sensibilities, and even pledges abstinence. While the Fellowship doesn't give him peace, it does give him direction, and while the positive effects on Jason's self-image—as a man of purpose, as something more than a washed-up ex-jock on a road crew—will be balanced out by the failings of the Newlins, they give him the approval and love he desperately needs . . . until he chokes on it.

Meanwhile, you have Tara, who moves in with Maryann in order to rebuild herself, retreating from the increasingly (and this is key) *complex* world of Bon Temps. She sneaks away to join a "family" with strong pagan sensibilities, and begins to rebuild herself as a woman in her own right. While her household with Maryann doesn't give her direction, it gives her peace, and while the positive effects on Tara's self-image—as a severely intelligent woman with inordinate potential, as something more than the daughter of an addict doomed to repeat the cycles of abuse in which she was raised—will be balanced out by Maryann's failings, she gives Tara the approval and love she desperately needs . . . until she chokes on it.

> "Well, we're all wounded. We carry our wounds around with us through life, and eventually they kill us. Things happen that leave a mark in space, in time. In us."
>
> —*Six Feet Under*, "The Will" (1-2)

Jason Stackhouse and Tara Thornton spend the first two seasons of the show on parallel and opposite courses: one exploring abandon as the other nears total repression, and then reversing this course in the second season. As Jason explores inner abandon through the therapeutic effects of V and emotional abandon in his devotion to Amy, Tara is pulled further and further toward a dangerous asceticism that finds its final expression in her exorcism: the horror in that image, Tara stabbing her "demon," in the form of her most vulnerable and terrified childhood self, is only outweighed by that of the terrifyingly familiar "everything's going to be perfect from now on" determination that followed it.

A more visceral demonstration of the concept of "repression" I can't imagine. Literally looking your pain, your history, your unloved self in the eye and thinking you can just stash it somewhere forever, stab it to death, walk away from it bleeding on the ground? That's hateful on a level I can barely imagine. If there were Gods of abandon, of self-love, of respect for our histories and personal stories, I imagine they'd be offended . . . or very, *very* interested.

Because only the Gods know the secret: that in their extremity, abandon, and repression are just two ways of letting go of ourselves. Sometimes it's necessary to cut loose, and go a little wild. And sometimes it's necessary to pull yourself together and go to work with your pants on. Rarely, I would wager, is it necessary to engage in orgies with your whole town, or stalk and kidnap a living creature to feed your own drug addiction, or join a paramilitary cult, or do any of the things these nuts regularly do for our entertainment. But it's not out of the question.

———

AND SO IN SEASON TWO the poles reverse. Jason heads off to forget he ever loved the vampire Eddie, or lost Amy, and tries to find his purpose as a man without the sexual and physical crutches that used to define him, while Maryann pulls Tara into her web. From the breakdown that inevitably follows "perfect from now on" resolutions like Tara's to the final ritual in Sookie's defiled front yard, Tara is on a single trajectory. It starts wonderfully, with lots of hugs and unconditional mother-love from Maryann, and moves into Tara's first true romantic relationship, but continues to move further and further into the shadows, until Tara's self disappears completely, subsumed in the Goddess just as Jason's will is subjugated to the will of the Newlins' God.

But weren't their *selves* the point of the journey? Didn't Tara set out to free herself of the chains of self-doubt and terror and fear that were the only childhood she knew? Didn't Jason want to find himself, a respectable adult and more than just a pretty face? Didn't they both want to connect to other people in ways that weren't immediately subverted by their own anger and pain? Didn't Tara just want to connect? Didn't Jason just want to be his own man?

You can't connect if you're not home, which is what begins to happen more and more often under Maryann's control; you can't be a man when they're keeping you in the dark. The Answer has stopped being the Answer. The Guides are fallible, once again. For Maryann herself, what starts as simple belief in herself and her aims—and in the potential of her protégées—becomes selfishness and addiction, and eventual self-election as the Messiah. Her abandon and passion are beautiful things, desperately needed by the sometimes-repressed people of Bon Temps, but taken too far, they become violence and dissipation.

> "This is for your own good, boy. You have no respect for other people's things and for authority . . . Can't just go around doing whatever you feel like . . . There are rules in life . . . You need structure . . . You need discipline."
>
> —*American Beauty* (1999)

And meanwhile:

> "Whatever happened to that girl who used to fake seizures at frat parties when she got bored? Who used to run up to the roof of our first apartment building to flash the traffic helicopters? Have you totally forgotten about her? Because I haven't."
>
> —*American Beauty* (1999)

Ultimately there's nothing easier than retroactively crossing Amy, or Maryann, or even the Newlins, off your personal list of "good people" and discarding any good they've brought into Tara and Jason's lives, either directly—through their own kindness and love—or through the growth that came about through the experience of loving them. Without Amy, Jason would have never met or loved Eddie, and might have stayed in the Fellowship's cult forever without the pain of Eddie's death pushing him forward. Without the constantly reinforced cultural mismatch of his love affair with Amy (upon which even Sookie saw fit to comment more than once)—not to mention the spiritual connection of their shared drug use—Jason would never have come to see women as anything other than useful puppets. His love for Amy, and broken heart at her death, have pushed him into both darker and brighter places as he continues to search for his own version of manhood.

I would argue that Jason's spirituality, always a vibrant if dormant aspect of his personality, would never have emerged into his consciousness without the Newlins' providing him with both positive and negative examples. Even more, Jason was able to play out an entire family psychodrama through his relationship with them, separately and together: from adoration of them both, to Oedipal betrayal, to the inevitable understanding of them as flawed, crazy people. When Jason returns to Bon

Temps as a classic Hero, he is operating as both a warrior and a man, two roles he never would have felt capable of assuming before the Fellowship.

Likewise, without Maryann to pick up the pieces from Tara's prom-dress flameout—and to provide the positive reinforcement and self-esteem that she never learned—her spiral would have continued, I believe, unto her death. Without her own "carnival family" relationships with Maryann and Eggs, Tara would never have allowed herself to believe in her own ability to build a life and a home for herself with Sookie. Even though Maryann went unbelievably sour, and Eggs died awfully, Tara's relationships with them, separately and together, gave her a framework for the idea of family itself.

———

BUT IN EITHER CASE, I would argue that to judge or discard the Guides—even negative ones like Amy or Maryann—misses the point entirely. People aren't "good" or "bad"; they're *people*. They're fallible. Sarah Newlin learns to verbalize her own tenuous relationship with feminist ideals through Jason's adoration and eventual respect for her—notice her final scene with Steve, in which she clearly rankles against her previously touted desire to be "the woman behind the man"—while Steve is given multiple chances at redemption by Jason, Eric, and Godric. Even the most elemental villain, Maryann, is given more and more complex emotional flavors as the Bon Temps frenzy rises in pitch. The question remains, as in all of Ball's work: Where does the Guide stop being useful? When should you hop off the train and find your next answer?

You can plot the line of Maryann's many speeches on self-worth, start to finish, according to how healthy they actually are (and, more importantly, whether they are useful to Tara's attempts at healing herself at the exact moment Maryann delivers them). There's a definite point at which they take a hard left—in "Release Me" (2-7), standing there with that poor bunny, by my estimation: "Feeling sorry for things is just an excuse not to celebrate your own happiness."

That is the point you get out of there. That's when the Guide stops being a guide past the trouble and becomes part of the problem. That's when the Answer rots. And if you don't catch it, that's how you know you stopped thinking and started following—that it's become easier to have the Answer handed to you, and you've gotten stuck once again in somebody else's stuff. You've become a character in the story where they're the protagonist: their needs, their history, their hunger.

Even Maryann's persona—mother-figure, domestic goddess, liberal social worker, free-flowing food and wine—is impossible to sustain. She's the candy-house witch in the forest, warning us against eating all that sweet stuff even as she saves us from starving altogether.

> "Lisa didn't believe in borders, and that is why I know that wherever Lisa is right now, she's everywhere! She's everywhere, and that means she's home!"
>
> —*Six Feet Under*, "Falling into Place" (4-1)

What *True Blood* has allowed Ball to do is to access and play with this abandon/repression continuum on a level that is both visceral and compelling. In a story that is literally about penetration and crossing the lines of self/other, he's made vampire fangs a working metaphor for philosophy (and of course sex!) but also works with these ideas through the multitude of metaphors available in this universe. Shapeshifting, brainwashing, psychedelic psychic lovemaking, blood-bonding, repeated insistences of humans as vampires' "Mine": all of these are just as much about the breakdown in our defenses as they are about sex.

Sometimes, there is too much of both! I don't think it's a coincidence that complaints about Jason's first-season exploits were mirrored—almost verbatim—by the complaints about the repeated Maryann orgy scenes in the second season: too repetitive, too gross, too graphic, too embarrassing. I mean, isn't that the point? Sex scenes aren't always love scenes. And no scenes have to be entirely one or the other.

It can't be that the audience is prudish—I don't see anybody changing the channel when Sookie and Bill get romantic, or when Eric takes off the clothes he seems to wear so infrequently—which means there's something else going on. It's often the case that sexual images manage to turn off our brains: that we stop thinking of sex as a part of the story, stop thinking altogether, and either get grossed out or turned on. Either way, it's no longer about the story, or the meaning of the sex in the story: it's just sex. We have identified what's happening onscreen.

> "Don't get too comfortable. It tends to get more authentic as the night wears on."
>
> —*True Blood*, "Escape From Dragon House" (1-4)

This mental short-circuit is why I opened with the quote from *Shortbus*, which is often described as "porn for people who think they need plot." (I've heard the same of *True Blood*.) But as the film's writer-director John Cameron Mitchell pointed out, in Hitchcock's day there were tons of metaphors for sex. (Almost as many as there are for drug use. I remember taking an entire film narrative class that seemed to be entirely about those old Hays Code workarounds.) Now that we can, as a culture, accept the existence of sex onscreen, doesn't it follow that sex itself could be used as a metaphor in storytelling? "They don't ask whether I could've done *Hedwig* without the songs," he said. I think our short-circuit is just part of our natural animal response to sexual images: yes, that's sex.

We at least understand that this other sex is different from the high romance of Bill and Sookie's sex. The lighting is always so much softer and more like candlelight with them, and the cello's going, and they are clearly very much in love. So that's the kind of sex you can watch and not feel unsettled, because everybody is in on it.

Jason's first-season sex, and the increasingly deranged second-season activities of the citizens of Bon Temps, are not "good" sex. They're weird, and a little scary; they are unhinged. In a word, they represent uncontrolled *abandon*, just as Bill and Sookie's liaisons represent a much more human and understandable, and directed, *passion*.

The narrative has tricked us into doing precisely what the narrative is telling us *not* to do (what all of Ball's narratives are telling us not to do): repress, look away, pretend it's not happening, pretend not to be tempted. Don't take the V, don't put it on your tongue. Don't find out what happens next. I think it's the show's smartest, and grandest, trick: illustrating Ball's message by demonstrating it both in the story and in the effects of the story. Flannery O'Connor used to do that all the time: her protagonist would marvel at his mother's racism, completely overlooking his own, inviting the reader to complete the circuit by considering their own areas of blindness.

> "That's the day I realized that there was this entire life behind things, and this incredibly benevolent force that wanted me to know that there was no reason to be afraid. Ever."
>
> —*American Beauty* (1999)

"What if I don't need to be protected? What if wanting to be protected makes me feel like the helpless little girl I used to be all over again?"

—*True Blood*, "Plaisir D'Amour" (1-9)

BILL: Sookie, you cannot be frightened of everything you don't know in this world.
SOOKIE: Well? My world's opening up mighty fast!

—*True Blood*, "Sparks Fly Out" (1-5)

In their twining dance of abandon and repression throughout the seasons, Tara and Jason play a counterpoint to Sookie's adventures that just happens to embody Ball's own narrative obsessions. Because Sookie's life is a dance between the two paths, of course, all its own, her relationship with Bill (and theirs with Eric!) is a marvelous lynchpin for the show's plot. But for pure theory—theological, sociological, philosophical, all the way to ontological—give me Tara's push and pull with her own demons, and Jason's constant shifting between extremes. I love them.

And looking at these paths in this way, I think we can make some guesses as to their future selves. Both Tara and Jason have now loved, in an authentic way, and lost those loves in horrific circumstances. Jason has put off dealing with that fact for a season, and one hopes that he will once again find something more than a sexual connection in the future. And, if the pendulum holds its rhythm, we'll see him diving into that relationship in a way that explodes his newfound masculine tranquility all over again. Tara, on the other hand, needs to rein herself in again, having lost so much—and a romance mirroring that of Sookie's with Bill might be just the ticket. If the story stays true to Tara's own bullheaded issues, perhaps a more controlling older man is on her horizon.

In the end—just as Terry is leading Lafayette and Arlene into the lighter side of Post-Traumatic Stress Disorder, or as Daphne taught Sam to love his powers and begin the search for himself—I think we've already seen the seeds of what both Tara and Jason will become. I believe Tara's balance will be found in the "natural magic" of Sookie's secret world, perhaps as a witch. She must contain and synthesize the passion of her intellectual and creative powers with the self-control she keeps abdicating, and she must do so on her terms. And Jason? I think he's already begun to become the man he always wanted to be: synthesizing his wildness, his appetites and passions, with an eventual desire to become a husband and father.

Which brings us to the end of season two, and the exquisite melancholy that defines both Alan Ball's work and this tremendously engaging, funny, erotic, sad little show. Neither Jason, nor Tara, nor even feisty Sookie, have ever allowed themselves to acknowledge their desires for simple normalcy. It's just not in the cards. Bill's proposal and immediate disappearance are, in their way, another example of the show's inability to rest on easy answers, and point to the deeper metaphor: Jason and Tara's stories as mirrors for Sookie's development as well as being engaging stories in their own right. Recognizing the fact that normal doesn't exist—that for every Team Bill member there is a Team Eric person yelling just as loud; for every repressed character finding joy in his passion there is a wild character finding peace in harmony—is the only way any of us can ever really exist. And knowing that these characters—and we—are not alone in doing it is, I would say, the highest possible truth we can seek out: to find our own Team *Sookie*, and join it forever.

———

JACOB CLIFTON is a novelist and staff writer for Television Without Pity and the Science Channel's Remote Possibilities. He spends nights revising his novels *The Urges* and *Mondegreen*, and his days wishing Team Bella were a viable alternative.

BLUE-COLLAR BACCHANALIA

ALISA KWITNEY

Previous essays have touched on Maryann Forrester in a few different ways. Nick Mamatas cast her as evil social worker, as much a hindrance as a help to working class Tara. Jacob Clifton called her an example of the Guide archetype, capable of leading her charges to greater self-understanding. Here, Alisa Kwitney offers yet another way to understand Maryann—as bohemian intellectual, come to destroy Bon Temps' small-town way of life.

Writers are fond of saying that stories are as much defined by their antagonists as they are by their protagonists. (Writers are also fond of saying that they are working on essays when they are really trawling the Internet for sexy video clips of Sookie, Bill, and Eric, but the former assertion is actually true.)

Take Maryann Forrester. Like most villains, Maryann has a master plan: in her case, to intoxicate the residents of Bon Temps and stir them into a frenzy of violent passions. She also intends to sacrifice Sam, the shape-shifting owner of Merlotte's, to bring about the return of her god. *True Blood* is billed as a show about vampires, but Maryann strolls into town, sets the agenda, and turns the second season into a blue-collar bacchanalia.

What makes Maryann a particularly intriguing antagonist is that she is a combination of two distinctly different villain archetypes. On the one hand, she's a savage maenad who worships her deity with bloody rites of celebration. On the other hand, she's a smoothly sophisticated bohemian intellectual, espousing free love, passing around the hooch and the drugs, and whipping up exotic cannibal cuisine, like braised human heart in wine sauce.

While one archetype may be savage and the other sophisticated, both posit the villain as someone who stands outside the norms and constraints of regular society, threatening the community through some essential Otherness. Yet in the final analysis, Maryann winds up challenging our preconceived notion that evil is something that comes from without. What makes Maryann so dangerous isn't what lies in her nature—it's what lies in ours.

At first glance, however, Maryann seems like the latest in a long line of predatory single women. Long before Hollywood gave us Glenn Close threatening to destroy a family with her fatal attraction, the ancient Greeks gave us the maenads—the original girls gone wild.

Maryann as Maenad

The maenads (pronounced *may*-nads) were followers of the god Dionysus. Some sources suggest that the maenads started out as nymphs, but according to Euripides, the maenads were mortals. A certain king of Thebes denied Dionysus' divinity; in retaliation, Dionysus caused the king's female relatives to go mad and rend the monarch limb from limb.

From that point on, the maenads—and their Roman counterparts, the Bacchantes—were enthusiastic participants in violent, orgiastic group-bonding exercises. These ordinary women left their homes and families to roam the countryside in bands, drinking wine, engaging in rough sex with passing strangers, and ripping apart the odd sacrificial goat. Or, occasionally, ripping apart passing strangers and engaging in rough sex with the odd goat.

Maenads put their own needs and desires first, and like the evil career women seen in classic eighties films like *Basic Instinct* and *Working Girl*, the maenads represented the dangers of unconstrained female aggression and desire. There's a saying that in order to succeed in a man's world, a woman must be twice as good. The maenads were the dark side of that coin, demonstrating that women could also be twice as ruthless and savage.

This is certainly true of Maryann, who manages to intimidate not only humans, but also shapeshifters and even vampires. Faced with Maryann's machinations, even the usually unflappable Eric Northman, vampire sheriff of Area Five, leaves town to appeal for help.

Maryann may be *True Blood*'s first maenad, but she's not the first savagely ruthless femme fatale. In the previous season, Jason Stackhouse's sociopathic college dropout girlfriend, Amy Burley, demonstrated just how dangerous a little Philosophy 101 can be.

But while Amy exerted a lot of control over Jason and the innocent vampire they held prisoner, she lost control over her own rapacious desire for sensation and pleasure. Unlike Maryann, however, Amy seemed to have no ambition other than getting her next fix. While she did manage to undermine Jason's basic, intuitive grasp of right and wrong, she rapidly devolved from smart coed sociopath to druggie chick.

Maryann, on the other hand, may say that "we need to be out of control; we crave it," but she knows how to surrender to sensation without relinquishing her sense of self or her self-control. She doesn't seem to take any sexual partners herself, although she and Sam were lovers in the past, when he was younger and more vulnerable. Maryann sets herself up as a conductor of frenzy, not a mere player, and as such she nearly manages to take down the whole town of Bon Temps.

Maryann and Amy have other similarities. Both are urbane women with East Coast accents. We are told that Amy is the product of an Ivy League education, while Maryann, with her innovative approach to social work and her penchant for creating meat sculptures, seems like she probably has a master's degree tucked away somewhere. Both are given to lofty, artsy pronouncements, and have elaborate justifications for indulging their vices.

Both, in short, are examples of the bohemian intellectual as villain.

Maryann as Bohemian Intellectual

Like the maenad, the bohemian intellectual villain is an established archetype, and a staple of Hollywood films and television shows of the fifties and sixties. In classic sixties sitcoms like *I Dream of Jeannie* and *Bewitched*, the bohemian intellectual is the black-haired, sexually aggressive sister or cousin of the blonde heroine, vamping and plotting to throw a wild party in the quiet suburban split-level ranch. In horror movies of that period, the bohemian intellectual villain is the depraved ringleader who suggests performing a satanic ritual in the graveyard—just for fun, of course—and then digs up a corpse to bring back to the old house. Reckless, feckless, and more than a little mad, the bohemian intellectual villain is the insidious influence of free love, psychedelic drugs, and Eastern philosophy, all set to infiltrate a happy American home.

Maryann may tear out someone's heart from time to time, but her real power lies in her ability to loosen the constraints that keep people from going off the rails. Under her influence, the townsfolk of Bon Temps are transformed into a frenzied mob of sensation-seeking revelers.

This is actually a classic trope of McCarthy-era science fiction and horror films, such as *Invasion of the Body Snatchers*. In post–World War II America, monsters often operated by turning individuals into a monolithic mass of bodies, all walking and thinking in lockstep. In contrast to this nightmare vision of people tightly controlled and subsumed into one gigantic organism, *True Blood* gives us terror for our post–Cold War age—a loosely organized band that seems to operate with a fair degree of autonomy.

In those McCarthy-era films, there was usually an intellectual involved, and never in a good way. Not all intellectuals were the same, of course. There were three main types: the mad scientist, whose evil plan was often the cause of the threat to humanity; the dried-up old expert, who remained oblivious to the threat; and, possibly worst of all, the debauched and degenerate bohemian intellectual, who embraced the threat by adopting the enemy's values.

The fifties and sixties may have been the heyday of the bohemian intellectual villain, but this archetype never really went away. While the Cold War provided an ideal climate for demonizing intellectuals, there are still a lot of narratives out there about untrustworthy Ivy League elitists. And as anyone who watched the last presidential election knows, these narratives still compel a wide audience.

One of the reasons that intellectuals make such effective villains is that they function as excellent foils for all-American heroes. Americans have a long tradition of prizing individuality over conformity, of valuing raw talent over training, of preferring instinct to analysis. Americans like to champion outsiders with humble beginnings, and they are particularly enthused by people who display some sort of virtuoso ability without the benefit of formal lessons.

Classic American heroes tend to possess a strong streak of individualism, go with their gut instincts, and evince natural gifts unspoiled by rigid schooling. The untrained dancer who wins a spot with a professional ballet troupe (as in *Flashdance*) is a classic American hero.

Of course, in real life, professional ballet requires years of training, which must begin by the time the dancer is ten or so. And while innate ability is always impressive, there is an argument to be made for the importance of advanced and continuing education. Furthermore, it is certainly not clear that gut instinct is superior to reasoned analysis in all situations—we all tend to hope that juries will review all the facts and the evidence presented to them, for example.

Still, Americans show a marked predilection for working class heroes with commonsense smarts, coupled with no-nonsense modesty. Sookie Stackhouse is a classic American hero. Maryann, sensing Sookie's power, asks her, "What are you?"

"I'm a waitress," Sookie replies, as forthright and unpretentious as a six-year-old child (and then follows up with the equally blunt but less innocent rejoinder, "What the fuck are you?") ("Beyond Here Lies Nothing," 2-12).

In contrast, Maryann is all guile and duplicity. On the surface, she appears to be full of kindness and charm; underneath, there is manic glee and steely determination. Maryann also wields the language of psychology and sociology to manipulate others, demonstrating the pernicious effects of higher education.

Yet while Maryann may seem like a direct descendant of the bohemian intellectual villains of old, she's actually something quite different. *True Blood* is fueled by irony as much as it is by lust and precious bodily fluids, and its writers tend to serve up the old familiar myths with an unexpected twist. Part of what made *True Blood*'s first season so original was the way it treated vampirism as a way to explore homophobia. In season two, the writers seem to be using the wild, drunken, orgiastic Bacchanalian rites as a way to examine some enduring, popular—and populist—American myths.

Maryann Forrester wasn't created to reinvent the bohemian intellectual villain. She was created to bury the classic American hero.

Small-Town Values

At the climax of *True Blood*'s second season, it's hard not to cheer when construction worker turned vigilante Jason Stackhouse announces his intention to fight Maryann because "I ain't letting weird shit take over my town!" ("Beyond Here Lies Nothing").

Jason's declaration sets up a classic situation: a small band of valiant townsfolk must defend themselves from some dangerous outsider. This is the kind of battle Republican vice presidential candidate Sarah Palin invoked when she spoke of "Joe Six-pack" fighting back against the insidious threat of foreign influence and an Ivy League education.

But in Bon Temps, things are not as simple as they appear. Bon Temps may be a small town, but its values are hardly the kind that the GOP would want to invoke at rallies.

In her acceptance speech, Sarah Palin reached back more than seventy years to quote Westbrook Pegler's line, "We grow good people in our small towns." (Pegler, a conservative commentator and foe of Eleanor Roosevelt, would have felt right at home on the Fox network.)

Palin went on to say, "I grew up with those people. They're the ones who do some of the hardest work in America, who grow our food and run our factories and fight our wars. They love their country in good times and bad, and they're always proud of America." (The implicit corollary here is that big cities are filled with bohemian intellectuals, criminals, foreigners, and bums who do not work hard, do not produce anything, and do not love their country.)

Palin's words may be stirring, but they are not accurate. Small towns have not been the hub of either farming or manufacture for generations, and many of them have been struggling with high unemployment rates for years—along with all the attendant woes unemployment brings.

There is also plenty of proof that there are, indeed, locally grown sociopaths and friendly neighborhood serial killers, but that doesn't seem to impact the myth of small-town goodness. Bad things may happen in the *real* real small towns, but those events don't count. When politicians speak of "the real America" or "Main Street," they are really invoking the alternate reality of small-town America made familiar to us in countless Hollywood movies and television shows.

In the days before videos and view-on-demand, reruns of series like *The Andy Griffith Show* and retro hits like *The Waltons* and *Little House on the Prairie* were watched by huge audiences. Day after day, the suburban version of the archetypal small American town appeared in people's living rooms. Many of the shows had a supernatural element, like *Bewitched*, *I Dream of Jeannie*, *The Addams Family*, and *The Munsters*. In the sixties paradigm, witches, genies, vampires, and other monsters might have been a little eccentric, but they were also regular folks and, in effect, Andy Griffith's spiritual neighbors.

Bon Temps, on the other hand, is a long, long way from Mayberry. Instead of one good-natured town wino, there are a fair number of bad-tempered drunks, not to mention other locals who seem to view the vampires as either walking sex toys or low-tech meth labs. Instead of homemade pie, there's homemade porn. There's no danger that the vampires are going to prey on the innocent here—there isn't enough innocence in Bon Temps to feed a mosquito.

Which explains why, at the climax of season two, *True Blood*'s mob is composed of individuals. Unlike so many classic science fiction and horror movie mobs, there is no single socialist group mind. As each person joins Maryann's madding crowd, he or she reveals some deeper layer of character, good or bad—festering resentment in the case of Boyd's mother, a talent for leadership on Terry's part, a penchant for doing it doggy style in the case of that lady who winds up chopping off her own fingers.

Maryann's power, like alcohol itself, brings people's dark desires and secret vices to the surface, so that the evil comes not from without, but from within. So much for the "small town good, big city bad" cultural meme. Sure, some of the incidents of self-mutilation and cannibalism can be chalked up to Maryann's influence, but being drunk and under the influence of a maenad does *not* explain away everything.

The Flimsy Veil

Perhaps the clearest proof that Maryann is not a purely outside evil comes near the end of the storyline, when she reveals that she didn't just arrive on the scene—she was summoned. It was "that night in the woods with that unfortunate pharmacist," Maryann explains, referring back to Tara's attempt to be exorcised of a demon she believed was possessing her. At a crucial moment during the exorcism, Tara saw an image of herself as a little girl with eyes gone entirely black—the sign we have learned to associate with people in Maryann's thrall. Tara stabbed and killed that demonic version of herself, but we later learned that the whole experience was a hallucination, because Miss Jeanette, the exorcist, turned out to be a fake.

"A ritual is a powerful thing," Maryann retorts, "and calling forth that kind of energy . . . that's god's ritual" ("Frenzy," 2-11).

This means that by refusing to acknowledge her own personal demons, small-town, hard-working, plucky blue-collar heroine Tara inadvertently wound up calling forth a *real* demon.

"The Greeks knew there was the flimsiest veil between us and the divine," says Maryann, who then proceeds to rip that veil away, revealing to everyone in Bon Temps what Sookie, the telepath, already knew: beneath the civilized façade we show the world, we all have savage impulses we ache to satisfy.

But is the savage entirely bad? A world without Dionysian impulses would be a world without the bump and grind of roadhouse blues, without chili fries and beer at midnight, without reckless, sweaty, dirty sex. Sure, you wouldn't want Maryann moving in permanently, but you don't have to be a shapeshifter to know that there's a little pig in all of us, just aching to get out and rootle around in the mud.

And that is part of *True Blood*'s hidden complexity. The vampires and monsters you meet here are certainly capable of great evil. But they are also capable of great goodness, and, most strikingly—like people—they tend to occupy the gray space between those two poles.

Given *True Blood*'s ironic and morally complex sensibility, it's probably not coincidental that Maryann's name is one that is traditionally associated with sweetness and innocence. (In the novels the show is based on, the maenad was called Callisto.) On the mythical small town of *Gilligan's Island*, Maryann was the avatar of sweet, small-town, wholesome femininity, while Ginger was her opposite—the sexually experienced big-city siren. (In the real world, the actress who played Maryann, now in her late sixties, has been busted for smoking marijuana in her car.)

As the world becomes more complex, it's tempting to cling to the old constructs. Big cities produce anonymous evils, race riots, crime. Someone screams murder and the passersby don't even bother to call for help, let alone intervene. There is safety and purity in small towns, where children can walk to school and neighbors look out for one another.

But in Eastern Europe just after the end of World War II, villagers killed people they had known since childhood. Much more recently, festering grievances have turned neighbor against neighbor in Rwanda. And the list goes on.

There is an often-used quote, originated by Walt Kelly in his *Pogo* comic strip: "We have met the enemy, and he is us." In the final analysis, there may indeed be evil all around us, but it's the evil *within* us that will open the door and let it in.

So let's drink a toast to Maryann the maenad, who reminds us that there's only the flimsiest of veils between us and the divine—and the demonic. And there are times when it doesn't take much to tear that veil away.

ALISA KWITNEY is the multi-published author of humorous women's fiction and graphic novels, including *Till the Fat Lady*

Sings, which the *New York Times* called "darkly humorous . . . imaginative and quirky." Her work has been translated into German, Russian, Japanese, Norwegian, and Indonesian. As Alisa Sheckley, she has written two paranormal romances, *The Better to Hold You* and *Moonburn*. A graduate of Columbia University's MFA program and the recipient of a scholarship of merit, Alisa was an editor at Vertigo/DC Comics for seven years and has taught a course in graphic novel writing at Fordham University.

NIGHT IS THE COLOR OF BLOOD

The Color Aesthetics of *True Blood*

PEG ALOI

In a television show, the things we see on screen, from sets to costumes to camera angles, are the result of intentional choices. Because of that, we can look to these choices to gain a deeper understanding of the story the show's creators are telling. Here, Peg Aloi gives us a primer on *True Blood*'s use of color, from Sookie's red-on-white season one costuming to Tara's ubiquitous purple eye shadow in season two.

Color is the most pervasive and prominent feature of our visual environments. Our minds and emotions often respond to it unconsciously, and we make many choices daily based on the appeal or distaste that color communicates to us: buying clothes, choosing fruits in the market, deciding which path to take while on a walk in the park. In recent years, color has taken on a special emphasis in advertising and home-improvement media. It has become a billion-dollar industry, especially in the trend-dependent worlds of fashion, interior design, and home/garden improvement. There's no denying color's considerable impact on our lives, or its ability to deeply affect our emotions and psyches. We even use it in language to describe our moods: in the pink, seeing red, or feeling blue.

Nature is the primary source of all color, and humans, being far more visually oriented creatures than, say, dogs (who have limited color vision but finely tuned senses of smell and hearing), are extremely sensitive to color. We have to be: earlier in our evolution, we relied on color to determine whether food was ripe or spoiled, to detect illness, to recognize poisonous or useful plants, to interpret weather. Though our interactions with the natural world may be lessened these days, our deeply complex interaction with color continues. Our emotional responses to different colors can be so complex and subtle that we're often unaware of it. But we only need to become aware of those responses to appreciate color's effect on our lives.

Our eyes and psyches still interpret color as our ancestors did; the sight of color invokes emotional and literal connections as old as human consciousness. Beginning with black and white, those absolute colors of darkness and light, color has for millennia signified humankind's deepest fears and desires. The sun provided light, warmth, and food; the night brought cold, loneliness, the danger of unseen animals or pitfalls. Ancient humans also paid heed to the colors of the natural world, initiating associations that remain strong today. Blues are cooling and pacifying, like water, a calm sky, or a carpet of forest bluebells. Modern humans still value blue's soothing tones: we see this in hospital gowns, tinted windows, and household cleaners. Reds signify heat, danger, lust: like fire, poisonous mushrooms, blood, engorged genitals, or ripe fruit. Today, stop signs and bright lipstick both send a strong message. Yellow cheers us and put us in mind of spring (honey, daffodils, or butterflies anyone?), but also attracts our attention (hence its importance on traffic signs and toxic label warnings). Green is perhaps the most complex color of all in terms of meaning, which makes sense for the hue that is dominant in nature. It makes us feel balanced and whole (hospital walls use green to speed healing; we eat greens to stay healthy), as well as lucky and confident (shamrocks, the crisp color of money), but also may alert us to poison or decay (a sludgy swamp, a warty toad, moldy bread, or spoiled meat).

Since humans are socialized, sophisticated beings, we have evolved to use color in symbolic ways that are drawn not just from these ancient, natural associations, but from culture as well. Purple, for example, reminds us of serious matters: royalty (who, in days of yore, were the ones who could afford the rich dyes required to make purple clothes), the occult (see classic 1960s horror films like *The Devil Rides Out* or *The Dunwich Horror*, or Kenneth Anger's shorts films). But purple's main symbolic meaning is death. Author Patti Bellantoni titled her study of color in film *If It's Purple, Someone's Gonna Die*: the cover image features a smiling Catherine Zeta-Jones in Rob Marshall's *Chicago*, bathed in lurid purple light. But purple can also be light-hearted in its pastel incarnations, and we're culturally inured to associate it with both femininity and homosexuality (see Todd Haynes' Oscar-winning *Far From Heaven*, a story of closeted homosexuality and forbidden interracial love in 1950s Connecticut).

The Many-Colored Silver Screen: Color Design in Cinema

Film and television, being perhaps our most popular visual media, use color to maximum effect in order to attract viewers, but also to lull us, incite us, and, by using our instinctive and learned responses to color, manipulate our emotions. Picture

Dorothy Gale from *The Wizard of Oz* in red and yellow polka dots instead of pale-blue-and-white gingham, or the Wicked Witch of the West in Glinda the Good Witch's sugary pink—it would drastically change our emotional response to the characters. Color in film provides a shortcut to express and reinforce everything from character to tone.

Color's introduction to cinema changed everything. Audience-pleasing genre films that showcased dramatic use of color were the popular result of this new technology: grand musicals like *Singin' in the Rain*, *Meet Me in Saint Louis*, or *Oklahoma!*; swashbuckling adventures like *The Adventures of Robin Hood* or *The Adventures of Don Juan*; horror classics like *Rosemary's Baby* or *The Wicker Man*. Now that color's use in film is not as novel as it once was, it's being used in more complex, subtle, and meaningful ways, adding layers of meaning that make films more memorable and storytelling more dynamic—even when viewers are not consciously aware of it.

Although the blockbuster films made in the golden era of Hollywood and the fledgling days of Technicolor were huge collaborative affairs, often without a single guiding vision, in more recent years the use of color in cinema has become something that can be uniquely used by individual directors, cinematographers, and designers. The symbolic use of color in visual narrative is largely concentrated in costume and set design, with costumes in particular allowing subtle—and sometimes explicit—commentary on character behaviors and motivations.

These days, film genres that are defined by visual spectacle (such as musicals, fantasy, or horror) are more likely to have color palettes that are intense and laden with meaning. Horror, as a genre that is slightly larger than life, is able to use color in especially dramatic ways, and vampire films often have their own unique color palettes. The description of color is a powerful literary device even in the original gothic novels featuring vampires (such as Bram Stoker's *Dracula*), and has traditionally defined many cinematic expressions of stories of the undead. The motifs of vampire stories necessitate communing with color: blood, of course, along with rosy cheeks or ghostly pallor, and many other visual signposts, such as the moon, the night sky, the dark forest, the pale golden sun. When I think of those wonderful Hammer Productions films of the '70s, I can see the ghost-pale female victims running through graveyards in their diaphanous white gowns, Christopher Lee's pale face and blood-red lips, and the bouquets of red roses and rich jewel-toned velvet fabrics in the luxurious castles. Many contemporary directors utilize similar palettes to create depth of meaning in their horror-tinged storytelling: Joss Whedon, creator of *Buffy the Vampire Slayer*, is one notable example. *True Blood* creator Alan Ball is another.

Alan Ball, A Colorful Storyteller

Alan Ball's work is notable for its heavily symbolic use of color: the film *American Beauty*, written by Ball and directed by Sam Mendes, had a very strong red, white, and blue color palette, befitting its topic. In the film, these colors are not merely patriotic expressions of America, but portray specific emotions and qualities of various characters. White stands for innocence, inviolability, and, perhaps most of all, the pristine sterility of the main characters' home. Red is all about lust and passion: we see Kevin Spacey's teenage temptation drenched in red rose petals, and the roses tended by Annette Bening convey the anger beneath her cold exterior.

Six Feet Under, Ball's acclaimed series for HBO, featured a color palette that defined and linked all of the major characters

(Nate, David, Claire, Ruth, and Brenda were brown, red, purple, green, and blue, respectively). The characters' specific colors were sometimes apparent in their costumes (Brenda's pale blue shirts were ubiquitous, mirroring her involvement in yoga and massage, the soothing balms to her frenetic intellect and sexual addiction; Nate's brown tones reflected his interest in making the funeral industry more natural and grounded in simple tradition), sometimes in settings (Ruth spent a lot of time in that green kitchen, and among the flower arrangements at Nikolai's shop), and sometimes took their time becoming apparent (David's red motif didn't become prominent until he was abducted and tortured by the thug wearing a red hoodie). Claire's costumes and bedroom were full of muted shades of lavender and purple; even the hybrid car she drove off in at the end of the series was a pale mauve. As Claire was modeled after Ball himself, and since Ball has said that the show was inspired by his own feelings about death and dying, it made sense for her main color to be one associated with death. But the colors were never deep or intense, hinting perhaps that her self-destructive behavior and brushes with mortality would nevertheless put her death far off; indeed, she is going to be the last to die, as the finale's artful flash-forward sequence told us, at the fine old age of 102.

In *True Blood*, Ball's color sensibility is also on lavish display in every episode. Its rural Louisiana location is sensual and evocative; the back roads are often dark and mysterious, and the deep green tones of the swamps and forests have a menacing primeval feel. But the series' main protagonist, young telepathic waitress Sookie Stackhouse, is the primary canvas on which the show's color symbolism is painted: her pristine white costumes with carefully placed accents of color, especially in season one, are symbolic of her journey toward self-awareness and sexual maturity. But there are many other consistent, meaningful uses of colors in the show's first two seasons. *True Blood*'s symbolic use of color is an artistic approach that often echoes the most memorable films of the modern horror genre, while creating its own distinctive visual language.

Red (Blood, Lust, and Excess) and White (Innocence, Purity, and Light)

Perhaps no color combination works on a more mythic narrative level than red and white. It is, for example, the primary color duo in fairy tales: Snow White's pale skin and dark hair form a clear light–dark dichotomy that communicates innocence and evil, but it is her red lips, the red blood from her white finger that is pricked by a needle, and the red apple that poisons her that imbue the story with complex layers of emotion and danger. So-called "fairy tales" are usually thinly veiled coming-of-age stories of sexual initiation; the Brothers Grimm barely hid this fact, though later iterations of the tales, and especially the family-friendly Disney versions, tend to downplay the sexual nature of such stories. On some level, vampire stories, those classic tales of the corruption of innocence, are merely darker, more adult versions of these fairy tales.

True Blood's fairy-tale figure is sweet-natured Sookie Stackhouse. In the show's first season, Sookie wears white costumes almost exclusively. White is a color that signifies innocence, purity, youth, a "blank slate" or beginning. However, her costumes are rarely totally white; from the beginning, her white clothing is frequently patterned with red. Every time she is seen with Bill Compton, outside of her working hours at Merlotte's, she is in a white dress or top with a small dark pattern on it (usually flowers). The morning after she meets Bill and saves his life, she sunbathes in a white bikini top covered with bright red strawberries. When she accompanies him to Fangtasia for the first time, she wears a white dress dotted with small red flowers. Red can symbolize sexuality, passion, maturity, violence, and varying emotions, from rage to lust. Sookie's loss of virginity (and the events leading up to it) is clearly telegraphed by her white-and-red clothing, the red splotches representing, obviously, the resultant blood. In addition, red is symbolic and representative of the vampires that dwell in Bon Temps; since Sookie loses her virginity to a vampire, the red-on-white symbolism is doubly significant. Her entry to womanhood is both sexual and supernatural.

Once Sookie loses her virginity to Bill (after donning a white gown and running through the misty forest in a clear homage to those wonderful Hammer films), we begin to see an increased presence of red in her wardrobe, which symbolizes her deepening involvement with Bill, and her immersion in the vampire culture. When Bill kills the vampire bartender Longshadow to protect Sookie, she is literally drenched in blood, turning her white dress completely red. This powerful image contains multiple meanings: the danger of her association with Bill, and the intensity of his devotion to her, but also the irrevocable nature of her decision to immerse herself in the vampire culture. Also, Eric, the local vampire "sheriff," is associated with the color red—it's the color of the lights that surround him at Fangtasia the first time his character appears—and the drenching of Sookie's dress in blood points to her increasing closeness to Eric, who demands access to Sookie as payment from Bill for his infraction. In "Scratches" (2-3), Eric sees Sookie in a red t-shirt from Fangtasia, which she slept in, and remarks, "May I say, that color suits you very well?"

Red is worn by other characters, too, and though it may seem so ubiquitous as to be almost devoid of meaning, it nearly always holds significance. For example, the uniform worn by the grounds crew that includes Hoyt, Rene, and Jason is a burgundy color, and we frequently see Jason and Rene in their shirts even when they're not working. Jason's wearing of red signifies his active sex life and attractiveness to women, as well as his hot-headedness, his lack of control, and, later, his addiction to vampire blood. Rene is wearing a blood-red shirt when he accompanies Sookie to her house and she has a vision of him killing her grandmother. When Sookie reads Rene's thoughts, we see them, and they have a red tinge—Rene, who is obsessed with his hatred for women who have had sex with vampires, literally "sees red" when he is about to kill them.

Tara is not normally seen in red, but she wears this color during one of the most significant periods of transition she experiences in the show. She dons her red prom dress for a singular occasion: Arlene and Rene's engagement party, where she gets drunk, tries to seduce Sam inside Merlotte's, and then has a car accident when she swerves to avoid hitting Maryann Forrester. Tara is still wearing red when her mother Lettie Mae comes to see her in the county jail the next morning, when Lettie Mae lets Tara know she can't come home because she has "the devil" in her, whereas Lettie Mae claims to be on a path toward salvation. Tara becomes angry at this, befitting the hot color of her dress. And she's still in red when Maryann shows up to pay her bail and invite her home with her. For Tara, the color red foreshadows her involvement in Maryann's cult. And, lest we have any doubt about Maryann, her car is bright red, as is the front door of her palatial mansion. As we later find out, Maryann feeds off her followers' lust, anger, and violence—emotions closely associated with the color red.

Interestingly, at the bacchanalian orgies where her followers gather to pay her homage, Maryann wears white, the color of purity. White is also said to have been the color worn by virginal devotees of cults in antiquity, so this emphasizes Maryann's ancient origins, as well as foreshadowing her ultimate goal: marriage, in a white wedding dress, to her white bull-god.

White and Red Make Pink (Romance, Innocence, Love, Femininity, Sexuality, Emasculation)

One intriguing aspect of the white and red that dominate Sookie's costumes is that the two colors mixed together make pink. This is obvious, of course, but considering pink's powerful meaning in visual storytelling, it provides us with another layer of meaning.

Pink combines Sookie's two most prominent color motifs: the white of her innocence, the white that makes her a primed canvas for all occurrences, the blank slate of experience; and the red of her daring and of her connection to the vampires, as well as her links to violence, sex, and death. But instead of seeing Sookie's loss of innocence as a purely negative outcome, the combination of red and white to make pink encourages us to view her growth in experience in season one as healthy and positive. Pink signifies unconditional love, a gentle nature, beauty, femininity, and health. It is the color of the heart chakra, the one associated with love and emotional balance. Nearly every culture in the world associates pink with romance and youth. In season two, when Sookie witnesses the death of Rodric, she wears a red-and-white gingham frock (similar, perhaps intentionally, to what Dorothy wears in The Wizard of Oz), and at a distance the dress looks like a rosy pink. This scene is an important one in establishing Sookie's deepening connection to Eric, as well as her sexual attraction to him as a consequence of being tricked into drinking his blood.

Pink is seen frequently in paler shades that signify the inno-cence of young women who later become victims. We see Tara in pink several times: she wears a warm pink tank top when she propositions Sam, signifying a romantic attachment between them, however brief. Tara also wears pink in season two, just before the sacrificial ceremony performed for Maryann; here, pink suggests Tara's victim status as Maryann uses her to try to kill Sam, and reminds us of Tara and Sam's affair. Tara also wears a silky pink robe at Maryann's home, the place where her love for Eggs is born. Arlene is wearing a bright pink tank top when she discovers that her fiancé is not what he seems. Here, the color is used ironically, and the candy-brightness of her shirt hints that the love she feels for Rene is based on a false understanding of who he really is.

Perhaps surprisingly, pink is a very common color theme in *True Blood*, and its presence sometimes lulls us with its pleasant associations. But within the context of the show, it may also be warning us against feeling too safe: a perfect blend of red and white, it reminds us that blood (and the actions associated with blood: violence, corruption, lust, seduction) is a primal force that can transform every pure or innocent being in its path.

Green (Nature, Balance, Decay, Poison, and the Outsider)

Green is in the exact middle of the color spectrum, and because of this, its presence helps an image feel richer and more com-plete. Green has very diverse meanings when displayed in cin-ema, including harmony, balance, nature, and innocence, along with the more negative qualities of jealousy, decay, corruption, greed, poison, and a sense of alienation, often depending on the shade. Generally, the more "sickly," muted, or yellowish shades of green have more negative connotations, whereas brighter shades of green represent the health and dynamism of nature. In addition, green is often worn by characters who are outsiders or transformative presences, and at such times is usually the only green visible in the frame.

In *True Blood*, green is associated primarily with Merlotte's, and therefore with Sam: the uniform logo and neon sign are both green, and the building itself is located on the edge of a forest. Green also defines the realm of the outdoors and the natural world. Sam's dual nature as a shapeshifter, as well as his tendency to run naked in the woods when he is shifting to or from his animal form, makes his connection to green especially appropriate: it emphasizes his deep connection to the natural world as well as his alienation from humans. He is both more and less than human, a state exemplified by green's associations with both balance and alienation. Interestingly, Sam's costumes tend to consist of blue jeans and drab plaid shirts that rarely include the color green; these seem to act as a form of camouflage for his secret identity.

The only time we see Sookie in green is when there is something being communicated about her relationship to Sam. When Sookie goes on a date with Sam to attend the talk that Bill gives for the Civil War society, Sookie wears a floral-print dress, a white background suffused with shades of green, yellow, and purple, signifying the complex, confusing nature of their relationship. Prior to this scene, Sookie has not been seen in patterned clothes or bright colors, so this dress stands out sharply. After losing her virginity to Bill, Sookie covers the fang marks he left behind with a green-and-white scarf. The scarf accents her waitress uniform, but also signifies her complicated involvement with Sam and his jealousy about Bill.

Tara is also seen in green, but only twice, which makes those instances significant. When she asks Sam for the money to get an exorcism from Miss Jeanette, she is wearing a pale spring-green top. This might hint at new beginnings and renewal, but during the ceremony, Tara drinks the potion Miss Jeanette offers, becomes violently ill, and imagines a young version of herself, whom she kills with a knife—a moment that is later revealed to be the catalyst for Maryann's arrival. This underscores green's association with poison and corruption. When Tara vomits up the "snake juice," the color's association with nature and renewal shifts to an association with illness and poison. This dual meaning works well, since Tara soon finds out that Miss Jeanette is a fraud, and the renewal and rebirth Tara experienced is spoiled.

Tara also wears a bright lime-green camisole on the night of her birthday party. The intensity of the color hints at an exaggerated and surreal connection with nature; this is the night when Maryann's ability to enslave Tara, Eggs, and the townspeople is first demonstrated, and we see Tara's eyes go black.

Like Sam, Maryann is an outsider, both because she is new to town and because she is something other than human. Her true identity is also closely tied to nature. Appropriately, Maryann wears bright green a number of times, usually in robes or lounging wear at her home. Significantly, she never wears green when she is outside of her living area, indicating that she is an outsider even in the places she should feel at home.

Gold and Yellow: The Sunshine Colors

Gold is a signifier of wealth, and its association in *True Blood* with Lafayette—through his gold clothing and jewelry, and even the gold eye shadow he wears on occasion (at least during season one)—is appropriate for such a resourceful, entrepreneurial character, one who works two jobs in addition to running his own porn website and selling vampire blood. Gold is also the precious metal most sacred to solar gods, a group that includes Christ, and Lafayette's reappearance and apparent "rebirth" after being imprisoned and fed on by the vamps in the dark dungeon is a powerful image of Christ-like resurrection.

Yellow, a close relative of gold, is a color with many meanings, depending on its hue or intensity. Pale yellow is associated with children, innocence, new beginnings, and springtime, and we see this color worn frequently by Sarah Newlin, one of the leaders of the Fellowship of the Sun. (Solar symbolism is very important in vampire narratives: the sun's movement both awakens and destroys a vampire's vitality, at sunset and sunrise.) After Jason Stackhouse joins the Fellowship, he is seen wearing a pale yellow t-shirt.

Notably, while Sarah often wears yellow, her husband Steve often wears purple. Color opposites used in costume design are almost always a sign of relationship conflicts. The contrast in the Newlins' colors indicates not only their marital problems, but also their differing approaches to their goal of eradicating vampires: Sarah is focused on the Bible and forgiveness, while Steve wants to stockpile weapons and help plan terrorist attacks for maximum casualties. Sarah's color, yellow, is associated with innocence and new beginnings, with life; Steve's purple clothing carries the association of death and the occult, a powerful color we see used frequently throughout the show and which we will examine in a moment.

Chartreuse, or bright yellow-green, is not often seen in costume design, so its use in *True Blood* stands out sharply. We see this color in a dress worn briefly by Sookie in season one, but later that same dress is borrowed by newly made vampire Jessica and worn to Merlotte's, where she catches Hoyt's eye. The green tones of the dress might signify the innocence of youth and new beginnings, but bright yellow is also associated with danger and warning: Jessica, intentionally or not, poses a serious threat.

Turquoise (Transformation, Healing, and Mysticism) and Purple (Death, Magic, and the Occult)

While most of the colors in *True Blood*'s palette are strong primary shades, there are two exotic colors that are also significant: turquoise and purple. Both colors are associated with mysticism and the occult, and Tara, a character with troubled relationships who experiences a number of mystical transformative events, wears a great deal of both.

Turquoise combines blue and green; it is the color of water, a feminine element and one that represents the emotions. It's associated with the planet Neptune (which represents occult knowledge, dreams, and altered states), and with healing, transformation, the unconscious, intuition, and love. Tara's painful upbringing and her difficult relationships with her mother and with men are obviously allied with these issues, and she engages with them directly through her experiences with Miss Jeanette and Maryann. Tara's first meeting with Eggs, a kind man with a rough past who treats her with compassion, occurs next to Maryann's turquoise swimming pool, itself a symbol of baptism and rebirth.

Especially in season two, Tara appears frequently in purple, the color of royalty, wealth, sensuality, luxury, and hedonism, but also of altered states of consciousness, the occult, magic, spirituality, and death. Also known as violet, this is the last color in the spectrum, and is associated with many metaphysical concepts, including the number seven in numerology, which is the number of the occult and spiritual seeking. Violet is also associated with the night sky and the powers of darkness. Tara's involvement with Maryann is marked by a new tendency to wear not only purple clothing, but also bright purple eye shadow on a daily basis, suggesting that she is experiencing some sort of transformation associated with the occult. She starts wearing purple at the end of season one, when she discovers a dead body in Andy Bellefleur's car, and is still wearing the same purple top and eye shadow at the beginning of season two. Purple maintains a very notable presence in season two, as we move closer to the season finale.

Fittingly, Maryann also wears purple frequently. When she arrives to pick up Tara after Sookie's encounter with Rene, Maryann is wearing an eggplant-colored silk shirt. She also wears the color purple when she comes to Merlotte's and orders huge amounts of food for herself, and at Tara's birthday party/bacchanal. Maryann's association with purple underscores not only her connection to the occult, but her (apparent) wealth, her power, and the altered-state hedonism she encourages in her followers.

Pale purple, or lavender, is also associated with homosexuality, and it is telling that Tara begins wearing it just before the season one cliffhanger ending: that dead body in the car with red toenail polish, which we are led (incorrectly) to believe just might be the missing Lafayette. We see Lafayette wear lavender on a number of occasions, most notably when he goes to speak publicly to the state senator, who has been secretly seeing Lafayette on the side: a man who has recently spoken out publicly against vampires, equating their immorality with that of homosexuals. Lafayette's lavender shirt speaks volumes as he intimates to the senator that he will expose him if he doesn't change his views. The walls in Lafayette's living room are deep purple, and his car also has purple animal-print décor. Lafayette also memorably pulls out a pair of handcuffs lined in purple fur to subdue Tara late in season two.

The season two finale is full of the color purple, even down to the trash bags Jason and Sam use to clean up in Merlotte's. (Have you ever seen lavender trash bags for sale? I haven't!) Bill buys Sookie a dress to wear to their dinner at a fancy French restaurant: lavender silk chiffon, a color we have never seen her wear before. We know this color must be significant in some way, but how? Of course, it may just be a pretty, feminine color (associated with Easter finery, flowers, candy, etc.) that brings out Sookie's eyes, but after Bill proposes marriage and Sookie returns from a trip to the ladies' room to consider her answer, she finds that Bill has disappeared and there are signs of a violent struggle. This end-of-season cliffhanger is, like season one's, punctuated by the color purple: a harbinger of death—or, perhaps, a hint of further occult overtones in the developing plot.

———

SO WHAT DOES ALL THIS add up to for viewers of the show? Quality cinematic television like *True Blood* is layered and complex, which is at least one reason viewers find it satisfying. Color is one more layer in which we can immerse ourselves. Alan Ball is a master of color aesthetics, and watching *True Blood* with an understanding and appreciation for the depths of meaning found in the show's use of color allows us to find even deeper satisfaction in an already rich viewing experience.

———

PEG ALOI is a freelance film critic, cinema scholar, and teacher of media studies. She also works as a freelance editor and landscape designer. Her anthology *Bloodlust and Dust: Essays on*

Carnivale (co-edited with Hannah Johnston) is forthcoming in 2010 from McFarland. Her poems have been published in the online magazine *Goblin Fruit*. Her hobbies include singing traditional music, trash-picking, gardening, baking, and covering old furniture with pre-Raphaelite images.

FANGS AND FAME

The Vampire as Celebrity

JULES WILKINSON

Vampires are a pretty fluid metaphor in *True Blood*. The show sets up a number of clear parallels to the gay community, but vampires can be read, to some degree, as representative of almost any disadvantaged minority group. But really—how disadvantaged *are* vampires? Jules Wilkinson suggests a different metaphor for vampires—one that explains our recent obsession with them eerily well.

True Blood's moody, Southern gothic opening montage sets up vampires as a marginalized social group. Gay or black, take your pick. There's footage of civil rights protests from the '60s and a sign proclaiming "God hates fangs," a pun on the anti-gay slogan.

This gives us a familiar framework in which to place vampires. There is a "vampire rights" movement, and vampires talk about "mainstreaming," that is, passing as human. In this world, vampires have recently come out—of the coffin.

But how appropriate is it for the vampires in *True Blood*, like Eric, Bill, Jess, Pamela, and Godric? If these vampires are meant to represent minority sexual or racial groups, you'd sort of expect them to be less white, or perhaps actually have gay sex.[1]

One of the most enduring figures in folklore, vampires have been reinvented and restyled more times than an aging pop star. Vampires started out representing the basic fears of society—death and disease. In the absence of a scientific theory of infection, blaming the creepy-looking guy down the road was probably the next best thing. Skip forward a few hundred years, and vampires have been a go-to metaphor for everything from addiction to capitalism. They've been cast to represent those pushed to the edge of society because of their gender, religion, or class, their mental health or their skin color, their religion or their sexuality. They've been a site for us to explore our anxieties about our bodies, about aging and death, and about sex. *Especially* about sex—from the allure of animalistic lust to determining whether true love waits. With some rebranding, vampires even became a symbol for our fear of bloody fluids infected with HIV, and of those carrying the virus.

Now, in *True Blood*, vampires have become celebrities.

---

[1] Interestingly, while there's plenty of energetic bedroom action among mortals and vampires alike, there is a decided lack of queer sex in *True Blood*. There's only poor Eddie Gauthier, who trades his own blood for sex with Lafayette and ends up meeting a sticky end in Jason Stackhouse's basement. In fact, Lafayette—the only gay in the village of Bon Temps—gets just one chaste onscreen kiss in the first two seasons. The Yahtzee-obsessed vampire queen Sophie-Anne did seem to have at least some taste for girls—here's hoping season three will reveal some Melissa Etheridge in her music collection.

In March 2009, Forbes.com, the website of the renowned business magazine, published "Bloodsuckers: Hollywood's Most Powerful Vampires." They weren't talking about A-list actors, studio executives, or agents, but vampires and their rise to fame and fortune. Included in the list was Bon Temps resident Bill Compton.

These days, vampires sparkle at us from every facet of popular culture. Elegantly wasted, they stare with slight contempt for us mere mortals, from billboards, the covers of magazines, and on countless websites and blogs across the Internet. Certainly the vamps in *True Blood* have more in common with the famous folk featured on *Entertainment Tonight* than the sullen Cullens of *Twilight*.

The vampires in *True Blood* live like celebrities. The rules of "normal" do not apply—rather than reject them for being different, we value them for it. In *True Blood*, vampires are no longer seen as monstrous freaks—they may be exotic, but they are less strange than Lady Gaga to a Bon Temps local.

These vampires have few of the responsibilities that we mere mortals do. They're not worried about health insurance, when to find time for the vacuuming, or what laundry liquids will keep their clothes smelling like an ocean breeze. Sure, Bill recycles, carefully separating his glass Tru Blood bottles and paper, but all the best celebrities are green these days.

Vampires and celebrities don't live a 9-to-5 lifestyle. They like to stay out all night, and while a nocturnal life used to lead to suspicions of deeds unnatural and evil, these days it's more associated with partying hard (and maybe the *occasional* unnatural deed!). Unlike their predecessors, the vampires in *True Blood* are not stalking through dank moonlit forests or dingy abandoned castles; they're hanging out at Eric's hip club Fangtasia. Or, in Bill's case, doing a spot of home renovating.

For all their privilege and advantage, both celebrities and vampires seem pretty broody and ill-tempered much of the time. "I'm a vampire, I'm meant to be tormented," Bill pointed out to Sookie ("Hard-Hearted Hannah," 2-6). I blame the all-protein diet—be it blood or a South Beach diet, not eating carbohydrates will make anyone grumpy.

Even living forever has its downside, causing a weary ennui we caught a glimpse of when a woman serving as a bar snack for Eric called him "baby": "Baby?" he said. "I'm over a thousand years old. There's just not much thrill left in feeding on the willing" ("Hard-Hearted Hannah"). Later, the same weariness drove Godric to a spot of suicidal sun-baking.

Like celebrities, vampires are the subject of everyone's gaze, which props up their sense of their own importance. In contrast to other vampires, those in *True Blood* can be seen in a mirror—which is appropriate, as they are a narcissistic bunch. Eric Northman, vampire sheriff of Area 5, is almost a parody of the self-obsessed vanity we associate with celebrities. He can literally rip a man limb from limb, only to be upset over the damage it causes to the hair treatment he is undergoing. "Is there blood in my hair?" he asked a terrified Layette ("Keep This Party Going," 2-2), more concerned about his coiffure than his carnage. Fitting with the gossip surrounding any celebrity makeover, there was also much speculation from fans about whether Eric had—shock, horror!—been wearing a wig.

Vampires and celebrities always look gorgeous. Whether it's through plastic surgery, botox, or whatever magic is in the blood of vampires, they exercise a control over their bodies that those of us who struggle to save up for veneers on our teeth can only envy. Vampires heal themselves of wounds or even charcoal-inducing sunburn the way celebrities rid themselves of lines, wrinkles, saggy pecs, or post-baby cellulite. Celebrities, like vampires, seem to possess eternal youth, although that immortality, whether obtained through means supernatural or celluloid, is ultimately an illusion.

We expect celebrities to dress in a way that sets them apart, and we revel in their fashion successes and disasters. Money doesn't always buy good taste, but Pam, manager and hostess of Fangtasia, sets the fashion bar high. She can glam it up dominatrix style at the club, then transform into stylish casual in her Juicy Couture tracksuit or understated chic in a Chanelesque suit. She even sports some Jackie O.–style sunglasses—despite them being the most redundant accessory ever for a vampire. Her main tragedy in season two was the sacrifice of her blood-red Betsey Johnson pumps, which suffered catastrophic damage when she was out searching for the maenad ("Never Let Me Go," 2-5). Even Eric mourned their loss. In our world, one could easily image Pam as the fierce host of *America's Next Top Vampire Model*, or perhaps teaming up with Tim Gunn to give advice to undead fashion designers.

After a thousand years of seeing fashion trends come and go, Eric is always immaculately dressed, reinforcing the axiom that black is always the new black. Even Godric, who eschews the obvious trappings of the well-off and undead, turns out nicely in some New Age–inspired threads, while young vamp Jessica goes with the Britney-inspired slutty-schoolgirl look until the disapproving Bill takes her in hand.

Then we have sex, lies, and videotapes. Tumultuous relationships and steamy sex are the hallmarks of the intimate lives of celebrities and vampires. Romances in *True Blood* seem just as fraught as those in Hollywood. Sookie is torn between steadfast, if slightly dull, Bill, and the charismatic love rat Eric. The finale of season two certainly showed that "happily ever after" may be as elusive here as in any celebrity relationship.

The drama of vampire sex in *True Blood* is strikingly similar to the hype surrounding celebrity sex. It's advertised as being the best there is, and fangbangers—vampire groupies—are lining up for it. We were introduced to vampire sex in explicit detail in *True Blood* in an appropriately celebrity-relevant format—the sex tape.

Maudette Pickens liked to watch—and rewatch—herself. When she showed Jason Stackhouse a tape of the vampire Liam giving her a good seeing to, even Jason, no slacker between the sheets himself, was impressed: "You know, I read in *Hustler* everybody should have sex with a vampire at least once before they die" ("Strange Love," 1-1). Maudette's tape was, however, of higher production value than the average grainy recordings of celebrity sexploits. Or so I'm told.

Sex is never uncomplicated, even—or maybe especially—if you're a celebrity or vampire. Jessica Hamby, the seventeen-year-old turned into a vampire by Bill, transported from repressed suburbia to a new life full of freedom, excitement, and a bunch of vampires with rather loose morals. Like any young starlet—Britney or Lindsay Lohan or Miley Cyrus—Jessica has had to deal with a whole new set of desires and appetites, while at the same time being told that she must be restrained and well-behaved. Temptation, of course, has proved impossible to resist. However, being a vampire turns out to do what many a publicity machine can only dream of, as Jessica found her virginity literally restored after each sexual encounter.

The lives and loves, troubles and travails of the famous are better than any scripted drama. We are thrilled by rumors of sexual indiscretions, stories about the famous putting their tweets in their mouth, or blurry pictures of the latest rock star in rehab. The humans of Bon Temps are no different, and the arrival of a vampire is the talk of the town. When Sookie told her grandmother about Bill's appearance in Merlotte's bar, Adele's first question was, "Did he bite anyone?"

People love a scandal. Tabloids and blogs run on celebrity gossip, and it fuels the rumor mill in Bon Temps, too. As Bill told Sookie, "Vampires are always getting into trouble" ("Escape from Dragon House," 1-4). Perez Hilton would just *love* vampires—I can imagine he'd be vaulting the red velvet rope at Fangtasia each week if he could get past Pam!

Those media blogs and tabloids are full of sex and excitement, and we feed on them the same way *True Blood*'s human population harvests and sells vampire blood (or V) for its narcotic and aphrodisiac properties. There is a consumer relationship between the public and celebrities, and between vampires and humans, although in the latter case the consumption is literal. And like Jason and Amy, and those who would have bought the blood the Rattrays took from Bill behind Merlotte's, we rarely bother to think about the cost to the celebrity involved.

Of course, it's a mutually parasitic relationship. Likewise, Lafayette and Eddie have worked out a mutually beneficial arrangement, and Sophie-Ann makes a move to control the distribution herself. Celebrities need the media too, and they can manage it to promote their own image or products. Both celebrities and vampires have the ability to influence people— to put them seemingly under a spell. Unlike Sookie, people from besotted fans to the likes of Oprah and Letterman can be beguiled by their glamour.

All celebrities need a publicist, someone to manage their image, and the vampires of *True Blood* have their own mistress of spin in Nan Flanagan, the public face of the American Vampire League. She is not only a civil rights advocate, though— she's the Ari Gold of the vampire world. She deftly debates the likes of the Newlins of the Fellowship of the Sun, with their anti-vampire rhetoric on talk shows, and comes in to manage the "PR mess" following the conflict with the Fellowship in Dallas. Like an A-list celebrity publicist, while she doesn't have the status in the vampire hierarchy of Godric or Eric, she holds the power that all those who manage images do. When she threatens Eric's position as sheriff, he charges that she can't do that. "Hey, I'm on TV," she retorts. "Try me" ("I Will Rise Up," 2-9).

What is it that draws us to celebrities and the good folk of *True Blood* to vampires? Both celebrities and vampires have an abundance of the things that we want—life, sex, and the freedom to play outside of society's rules. When our days seem routine and ordinary, vampires and celebrities supply us with excitement.

As much as we admire and adore them, there is also a darker side to our attention, a cynical schadenfreude that delights in seeing the beautiful people fall. Something in us recognizes the dangers of the uninhibited id and the need for rules, and so we want stories that also remind us that fame, fortune, or fangs don't always equal a perfect life. Luckily, vampires fit this bill perfectly. As Bill says "I am a vampire. We're supposed to be tormented" ("Shake and Fingerpop," 2-4).

Designer fashion and sex scandals, love triangles and bizarre diets, tabloids and tragedy. Tales from tomorrow's tabloid gossip headlines or spoilers from next season of *True Blood*? Tune in and find out.

———

JULES WILKINSON is a writer of original and fan fiction, a stand-up comic, and TV addict. She is part of the team behind the Wiki site www.supernaturalwiki.com, which documents everything about *Supernatural* and its fandom. Don't tell Eric Northman, but she really prefers zombies to vampires.

I LOVE YOU, I JUST DON'T WANT TO KNOW YOU (SO MUCH)

BEV KATZ ROSENBAUM

Imagine that everyone you know has a Facebook page. (This may not be much of a stretch, actually.) Now imagine that their Facebook status updates are beamed directly into your brain, 24/7, and you'll get a little taste of what it's like to be Sookie Stackhouse. No wonder she values silence so much. Bev Katz Rosenbaum says that we'd do well to take our cues from Sookie when it comes to sharing our innermost thoughts. Sometimes a little mystery is a good thing.

I was a huge John Mayer fan . . . until he started sharing every bleeping thought that flitted through his mind with the world at large on Twitter and his blog. So I can totally understand why the heroine of HBO's *True Blood*, Sookie Stackhouse, who can hear people's thoughts, eschewed romantic relationships until Bill Compton came along. Bill, a vampire, is dead, so his mind doesn't emit signals Sookie can pick up. (In "The First Taste" [1-2], Sookie said to Bill, the delightful realization dawning upon her, "That's why I like you so much. I can't hear you at all . . . You have no idea how peaceful it is after a lifetime of blah, blah, blah.")

Couldn't we all use a little less chatter and "honesty" in our lives? Poor telepathic Sookie, in her role as a waitress at Bon Temps, Louisiana's Merlotte's Café, is regularly forced to hear her customers' endless mental monologues. The show's very first episode, "Strange Love" (1-1), opened with Sookie hearing stuff about people's sex lives and marital problems, and even their lascivious thoughts about her. Aside from the fact that it's all kind of gross, Sookie can barely hear her *own* thoughts over all this chatter. (Though bothered by this, she's not half as bothered as the similarly gifted bellboy we met in "Nothing but the Blood" [2-1], who told Sookie his so-called gift is a major pain and that his "life is shit.") If you think about it, *True Blood* can be regarded as one big critique of our oversharing culture. Thanks to our constant and total connectedness—to our computers, BlackBerries, iPhones, etc.—it's all too easy to tell too much and learn too much about everyone, from our favorite celebrities to our relatives to our neighbors and co-workers.

The stuff Sookie hears as a result of her telepathic abilities acts as a metaphor for all the stuff out there we non-TV characters hear and see way too much of—stuff people definitely shouldn't be sharing (Vanessa Hudgens' sex tape, anyone?). But the show doesn't stop there. The characters in *True Blood* who value their privacy, such as Sookie and Bill and Sookie's boss Sam, are portrayed (in a way that's almost too obvious) as archetypal strong, silent heroes.

Consider Bill. When he was asked about his family while giving a speech to Sookie's grandmother's historical club in "Sparks Fly Out" (1-5), he said, "That's not a situation I feel comfortable talking about." Interestingly, by the end of the meeting at which he presented said speech, he had the whole room eating out of his hand, treating him like the second coming of Robert E. Lee, when most of the attendees were bound and determined not to like him when they walked in. BTW, Bill's *always* spouting stuff like that. In "Burning House of Love" (1-7), he said again, "I'm not really comfortable discussing my personal business." He's also always talking about how vampires don't like to make the details of their lives public knowledge (see "Strange Love" and "The First Taste"), though one can't really imagine most of Bon Temps' other vamps—more on them further on—caring one way or another who knows what about them.

Contrast the reaction to Bill at the historical society meeting with the reception a gossipy old lady got at Sookie's grandmother's funeral in "Cold Ground" (1-6). After Sookie reamed out the biddy, her best friend Tara told her not to feel bad for losing her cool, because everybody thinks the woman's "just an old bitch." (During this episode, I couldn't help but think of my religious school lessons prohibiting an "evil tongue." I still remember that all-important biblical edict, "You shall not go about as a tale-bearer among your people," and my teacher pounding home the message that to passively listen to gossip was as bad a transgression as spreading the gossip yourself. Said lesson usually interrupted a pre-class gossip session.)

Sam, like Bill, values his privacy and isn't one for a lot of chatter and noise. His refuge is Bon Temps' rarely used swimming hole, where, as he told Daphne in "Shake and Fingerpop" (2-4), there's "never any car stereos blasting stupid music." Daphne, on the other hand, revealed as a baddie in a later episode, was always saying stuff like, "You gotta share this life with people" ("Shake and Fingerpop"), while Sam was always throwing her retorts (à la Bill) like, "I have a hard time opening up," and "Not everybody likes to lay their guts on the floor" (both pronouncements from "Mine," 1-3). In "Nothing but the Blood," he said simply, "I don't feel much like talkin'." No, he never does. Of course, in Sam's case, he's hiding the teensy little fact that he's a shapeshifter. A petty detail, IMHO. The important thing—insofar as this essay is concerned, anyway—is that he helps get the message across that privacy is a virtue.

Sookie, while not exactly the silent type (she can be downright chatty), does, nevertheless, guard her privacy fiercely. In just about every episode of the first season, she got angry when she realized people were listening in on her conversations—with Bill, in particular. It seemed as if she was always saying, "Everybody's looking at us!" or some variation thereof. The viewer applauds Sookie's decision in "Burning House of Love" to tell only Bill, the man she loves, about how her uncle molested her—as opposed to, say, writing a book or going on *Oprah*.

In contrast to *True Blood*'s extremely private heroes, the other Bon Temps inhabitants all seem to think that if you haven't experienced something publicly, well, you haven't experienced it at all. Witness Tara's mother's determination to testify about her "demon" at her church in "The Fourth Man in the Fire" (1-8), and Reverend Newlin's wife Sarah ordering Jason Stackhouse, Sookie's brother, to share his feelings in front of a group at the Church of the Sun leadership conference, in "Keep This Party Going" (2-2). (When Jason was reluctant, Sarah said firmly, "Remember, we all shared a vow of honesty. Are you wearing your honesty ring?") And let's not forget Sookie's co-worker Lafayette's dungeon mate (long story), who, in "Nothing but the Blood," insisted on telling Lafayette the story of his life. (Muttered Lafayette, "I pray you're not the last guy I talk to.")

In many cases, there's a sleazier aspect to the doing-it-all-in-public thing. Bill's nastier vampire acquaintances (and that's, um, most of them) are addicted to feeding and sex—and the more public the act, the better. In "Mine," they were hanging out at Bill's place, practically doing it on his living room chairs. When they're not at Bill's, they're at a sketchy club called Fangtasia, where they get a kick out of watching human groupies do their bidding.

When Sookie first visited Fangtasia in "Escape from Dragon House" (1-4), she met Eric, the vampire elder and club owner who seemed ever more bored by the perverted public goings-on around him. He, methinks, represents what many of us are becoming, thanks to what we're bombarded with daily on the net: voyeurs who constantly crave new and more titillating sources of stimulation. Few of us realize that if we would just live our own lives instead of watching others', we might be a lot happier. (It's a lesson Sookie's best friend Tara still has to learn. To quote her faux exorcist in "Plaisir d'Amour" [1-9], "If you can't stand your own company for ten seconds, how you gonna do it for the rest of your life?")

But it's not just vamps who are into that sleazy, everything-in-public culture. In "Mine," Sookie's brother Jason agreed to perform in one of Lafayette's pornographic videos to pay for the vampire blood he's addicted to. (Lafayette to Jason: "Do you know how much you'd make if you had your own website?")

Of course, there have always been exhibitionists, but exhibitionism has become epidemic in recent years. Back in 2007, a Redorbit.com article called "Privacy? That's Old School" quoted teen pointing out, "You've got shows like *The Hills* and *Laguna Beach*, where they're in high school, but they're letting cameras follow them around and putting their lives on TV." Today, Kim Kardashian and every member of the *Jersey Shore* gang epitomize the new, non-private person. (No less an expert than Facebook co-founder Mark Zuckerberg has said that being public, not private, is the new social norm.) The problem with living publicly is that the public livers (yeah, I know that sounds icky) continually stoop to new lows so people will watch them/listen to them/read their blogs, while their watchers/listeners/readers, like Eric the bored vampire, continually expect more, bigger, better scandals.

But have faith, privacy-loving peeps: the backlash is beginning. MSN news, of all outlets, recently ran a piece about "the stars you never hear about in the tabloids" that claimed we hear far too much (duh) about the Lohans and the Hiltons, and far too little about others—the Portmans, the Johanssons, etc. (Not coincidentally, *True Blood* features a red-haired, Lohanesque teenaged vampire named Jessica who is continually rolling her eyes at Bill's attempts to instill some old-fashioned values, such as privacy and modesty, in her.)

MSN has actually been on quite a privacy-promoting tear of late. Even more recently, it reprinted a *Cosmopolitan* article with the screaming headline, "Stop! Why Making a Sex Tape Is Never a Good Idea!" Indeed, it's a more terrible idea than ever, given the inevitability of its dissemination on the Internet, where a gazillion people will see it because of that constant connectedness thing, which, interestingly, has also seen signs of a backlash: movie theaters now run ads telling people to shut off their phones, restaurant owners print messages in their menus telling patrons they don't appreciate tableside phone calls, and the trendy slow-food movement encourages long dinners filled with lively conversation.

The backlash now continues with *True Blood*, which falls squarely in the Southern gothic tradition of storytelling, whereby, according to Wikipedia, "unusual events . . . guide the plot . . . to explore social issues and reveal the cultural character of the American South." Are *True Blood*'s creators wringing their hands over the current "cultural character of the American South," particularly its inhabitants' lack of privacy and restraint? With all their vaguely apocalyptic season finales, they at least seem to be saying that Bon Temps' inhabitants are damned. Not in a literal, Church-of-the-Sun-ish way (Church of the Sun members have been painted none too sympathetically in *True Blood*), and certainly not because of their acceptance of vampires, but in a figurative, going-to-hell-in-a-handbasket kind of way.

Or, come to think of it, maybe all those apocalyptic finales are meant to remind us of what happened to our ancestors when *they* forgot all about privacy and restraint. Noah's Ark, anyone? How about Sodom and Gomorrah? (Yes, the suggestion of total annihilation as the result of a lack of privacy and restraint is rather ironic, given Maryann the monster's decimation of Bon Temps in season two.)

It's enough to make a writer re-think her plan to start blogging—to publicize, among other things, the book this essay is appearing in. We authors live in strange times. We are instructed to tweet and blog our little hearts out to promote our works in this era of brutally slashed publishing budgets, even when tweeting and Facebooking and blogging take all-too-precious time away from novel writing, and even when there is a strong danger of boring or even totally turning off our hard-won fans with daily entries about what we're making for dinner or how many words we've written today. (We older folk who grew up before Google was a verb are much more aware of the boring/turning-off possibility than our younger, Jessica-like counterparts, for whom social networks and personal blogs offer an instant celebrity similar to that resulting from reality TV shows.)

I'll probably still blog, but judiciously, and mostly about books and writing. Thanks to *True Blood*, I've realized that people like some mystery around those they admire.

You listening, John Mayer?

——

BEV KATZ ROSENBAUM, a former fiction editor, is the author of the Penguin young adult novels *I Was a Teenage Popsicle* and *Beyond Cool*, as well as a pop culture junkie. She loves that she can use her Smart Pop essays (this is her second) to justify watching TV. Bev lives in Toronto with her husband and two teenage kids, who provide endless inspiration.

ADAPT—OR DIE!

GINJER BUCHANAN

What has been especially impressive about *True Blood* is how it has stayed true to the heart of Charlaine Harris' Southern Vampire mysteries even while establishing itself as an independent entity. And I can't think of many people more qualified than Ginjer Buchanan, the Southern Vampire Mysteries' editor, to talk about how *True Blood* has done it.

> Alan and I have a good relationship. I don't tell him how to write his series, and he doesn't tell me how to write my books.
>
> —Charlaine Harris

I *looove* the Oscars. It's the only awards show I watch. I love the dresses and the montages and the hosts' lame attempts to be funny and the presenters' cheesy dialogue and the sometimes-actually-moving winners' speeches.

Beforehand, I read all the pre-ceremony coverage in *Entertainment Weekly* and *People* and other such publications. For years I've run the Oscar Pool at work. The night of the broadcast, I sit in a comfy chair with a blank Oscar Pool form in front of me and carefully note all the winners as they're announced. From Best Supporting Actor to Best Sound Mixing, I applaud them all. And, as an editor of words, the "and the winner is" announcements that I am most interested in hearing are the ones for the writing awards—Best Original Screenplay and Best Adaptation.

Adaptation: that's the watch-word for this essay.

A few years back, novelist Larry McMurty and his writing partner Diana Ossana won in the Adaptation category for their screenplay based on the short story "Brokeback Mountain." I'm sure that many of you saw the movie (which should have won Best Picture, IMHO), but did you read the Underlying Intellectual Property? It is, as I said, a short story, by literary luminary Annie Proulx. It was originally published in the *New Yorker*, won all sorts of prizes on its own, and was the jewel in Proulx's collection *Close Range*.

In the edition that I own, it's about twenty pages long.

Spare yet lyrical, it is told in the third person, by an omniscient narrator (although much of what transpires is from the point of view of Ennis del Mar, the character played by Heath Ledger). It's a powerful piece, one in which style and content are perfectly matched.

Director Ang Lee was drawn to it, and then he faced the daunting task of finding a writer who could craft a screenplay for a full-length feature from those relatively few pages. He found, in McMurty and Osanna (writers not previously associated with film), the perfect choices.

While Lee and his cinematographer certainly did their parts to expand the material, paying attention to the gorgeous visual passages, McMurty and Ossana had to flesh out the existing characters (particularly the women), create additional characters, and give screen life to characters (and incidents) mentioned only in passing.

That they succeeded brilliantly was obvious on the screen and was recognized by their Oscar win.

And oh, by the way—the running time of the movie is well over two hours.

Now, I don't actually know when Ang Lee first read "Brokeback Mountain" and saw the potential in the material. I suppose it's possible that he found an old copy of the *New Yorker* in his dentist's office.

But I do know for a fact, since he has spoken about it often in interviews, that Alan Ball, looking for something to read while waiting for *his* dental appointment, bought a paperback book titled *Dead Until Dark* by an author named Charlaine Harris. Ball was at the time looking for a new project to develop for television, to follow his successful HBO original series *Six Feet Under.*

There were ghosts in *Six Feet Under*, one of them a major character (unless, of course, he was only a hallucination!), and Ball's Academy Award–winning *American Beauty* was narrated by a dead guy. So he clearly wasn't averse to making use of the supernatural. Picking up a book about a woman who was dating a vampire wasn't that far off the reservation for him. He was, he's said at various times, attracted by the cover art and the copy on both the front and back covers.

But what he no doubt thought would be a quick, disposable read turned into so much more.

Sookie Stackhouse, her small Southern town of Bon Temps, her blue-collar background, and her feeling of being an outsider because of a difference she had to hide, all spoke directly to

Ball—a gay man with blue-collar roots from a small Southern town.

And he really liked the vampires and shifters! As he said on the panel at the 2009 San Diego Comic-Con, after a couple of seasons, there was only so much that he as a writer/producer could do with and to the Fisher family (even with the ghosts hanging around), because *Six Feet Under* was, at bottom, a reality-based family drama. After he'd read further into the Sookie Stackhouse series, he saw that no such boundaries existed in her world. If things are too quiet at Merlotte's, no need to think of a reason why there might be a bar fight—just bring in the maenad! If Sookie's already complicated love-life needs further drama, no need to worry over what kind of guy might intrigue her, considering that her two current suitors are vampires—there's a hunky werewolf down the road who's really looking forward to meeting her!

So Ball took the almost unprecedented step of buying outright the rights to the first five Sookie novels, and then announced his intent to have each season of the show he hoped to launch (which came to be called *True Blood*) be based on one book, in the order of their publication.

(A digression: this is not the usual method of adapting a fiction series for television. For example—Showtime's *Dexter*. The first season followed the first novel, *Darkly Dreaming Dexter*, pretty faithfully, but subsequent seasons have all told original stories.)

Then Ball had to begin to write his pilot script.

This brought him up against the limitations that *do* exist in Sookie's world, as it is portrayed in the novels.

The books are told in the first person, present tense, point of view: Sookie's. All the time. Charlaine Harris, a mystery writer with some twenty-five years of experience, has always managed to tell her stories effectively within this framework.

It might not be immediately obvious how challenging an authorial choice this is. But think about it: in first person, the reader is always in the mind of the protagonist. He/she never sees or hears anything that the protagonist doesn't see or hear. He/she never knows anything that the protagonist doesn't know.

Sookie, of course, is telepathic, so she (and, by extension, the reader) does have access to a bit more information than might be available to the usual first-person narrator. But still, while she may know that her horn-dog brother Jason is planning on hooking up with one of her barmaid friends, she's not going to know exactly what they do together until after the fact, and then only if Jason spends time thinking about it in detail (which he well might) and she "eavesdrops" (which, for obvious reasons, she doesn't do).

The reader wakes up with Sookie, eats with her, sunbathes with her, does (a lot) of laundry with her, goes to work at Merlotte's with her, has access—primarily—to only her opinions of the events and people (living and undead) in her world. In *Dead Until Dark*, for example, Sookie is excited to meet her first vampire. The reader knows that others may not share her enthusiasm—but only because Sookie knows that, and expresses it, because she is present when some of the other bar patrons make it obvious or because she can read their internal dislike.

But the reader doesn't know—until Sookie finds out later—that in another part of Bon Temps, murder is being done. Sookie's not present to witness it, so it's not on the page.

The challenge for Ball, then, was how to "translate" material with this narrow perspective to the screen. And, in a sense, in stating his intent to make each season follow one book, Ball had created his own problem. *Dead Until Dark* isn't twenty pages long—but it's far from being *War and Peace*. Certainly nothing was going to have to be cut!

He had two choices: stay with the Sookie-as-camera approach (Anna Paquin in every scene), which would have required writing a *lot* of original material for the character, in order to keep the plot intact and extend the story over twelve hours. (First person–single character pov television series can be done. Often they are half-hour sitcoms/dramedies like *The Days and Nights of Molly Dodd*. Sometimes they are hour-long mysteries, a good current example being *Castle*. In either case, however, each episode is pretty much self-contained, telling a complete story, separate from whatever character-development arcs there might be. And the hour-long mystery—like *Castle*—will frequently break pov to show the viewer the crime or the perp, or perhaps a scene important to one of the other continuing characters.)

Ball's other choice was to "open up" the plot, making it a story told from the film equivalent of third-person pov, with an omniscient narrator, which is the format of most series television.

(Another digression, since not everybody is an editor:

- First person, present tense: *I see a vampire come into the bar.* The "I" in the Sookie novels is Sookie.
- Second person, present tense: *You see a vampire come into the bar.* This was perhaps most famously used in the novel *Bright Lights, Big City*.
- Third person, present tense: *A vampire, a werewolf, and the Pope come into the bar.* The omniscient narrator is telling the story.)

The possibilities for taking the third-person-omniscient approach (one that would be most likely to appeal to an experienced television writer like Ball, since it's the usual way of telling stories in that medium) were obvious. There are a wealth of things that happen in *Dead Until Dark* that Sookie knows about but doesn't witness, sometimes before the fact (like Jason's plans for the evening), sometimes after the fact (like the killings). Showing them on screen would be the natural thing to do.

And that was the choice Ball made. So in the first season of *True Blood*, for instance, viewers are privy to both sights and insights of Jason Stackhouse that his little sister would never have seen or had (unless she were really being pervy). Viewers have a clearer sense of Sam's feelings toward Sookie than she herself does. The characters of Andy Bellefleur and the Sheriff are expanded beyond Sookie's dealings with them.

All of this is made to work by expanding material drawn directly from the book.

But beyond that, Ball exercised his choice, as writer/producer of *True Blood* (rather than author of the Sookie Stackhouse novels), to bring his own vision to the material.

Thus, because he wanted to have the black men and women of Bon Temps figure more prominently in the series, the Tara of *True Blood* not only gets a lot of screen time, but also becomes completely different from the Tara of the books, who, as Sookie's longtime best friend, is only ever seen reflected in Sookie's eyes. Beyond the obvious—the change in race—she is feistier, angrier, more profane, much more sexual, and, with all due respect to the Tara of the books, more interesting in many ways. (Some people who were fans of the novels beforehand might well disagree with me. They probably found this change the hardest to accept.)

And the Lafayette of *True Blood*, a minor character in *Dead Until Dark*, has his role greatly expanded, something that brings elements to the plot that don't exist in the book—elements that fall far outside anything that Sookie would experience or even necessarily be aware of. He's not just the fry cook at Merlotte's—he's a drug dealer who specializes in V, the drug made from vamp blood. Sookie doesn't know about that part of his life—and she certainly doesn't know that Jason is one of his clients.

Finally, Ball had the brilliant idea to give vampire Bill Compton a teenage daughter, to set up situations in season two that would reveal aspects of his character that had nothing to do with his growing love for Sookie. (Charlaine has said that she wishes she had thought of this herself!)

Still, with all the expansion and changes, the core of the first season of *True Blood* remains the plot of *Dead Until Dark*. Sookie still saves Bill from the Rattrays, and is blood-bonded to him as a result. Gran still dies. Rene, who is portrayed as a strong, loyal, seemingly good man, is still revealed to be the vampire-hating murderer. Ball has kept his promise—season one is *Dead Until Dark*.

Then we come to season two, *Living Dead in Dallas*. I'm convinced that, in making his decision between staying Sookie-centric or broadening the scope of the stories, Ball was guided in part by contemplating how difficult it would be to fill twelve hours of screen time with the plot of the second book. It's pretty straightforward, and it takes place mostly away from Bon Temps, so little is seen on the page of a lot of the people in Sookie's world.

So, while season two is still arguably *Living Dead in Dallas*—the story of Eric, Bill, and Sookie travelling to Dallas to find a missing vampire—it is really, in the first episode, after the viewer finds out that (spoiler alert!) Lafayette did not die (though he does in *Dead Until Dark*), when *True Blood* began to be Alan Ball's alt-universe version of the novels.

The "meanwhile, back in Bon Temps" plot, which functions completely separately from anything Sookie is doing in Texas, becomes as important to season two as the Dallas mystery. Yes, that subplot has its roots in the book. There is a maenad who shows up and causes trouble in *Dead Until Dark*, but her name isn't Maryann (I love that Callisto is renamed something as normal as Maryann! That's a good example of Ball's sense of the absurd), and she doesn't involve the entire town in her wildness. And we don't see her at all, obviously, until toward the end of the book, when Sookie, Eric, and Bill return to Bon Temps. She also, by the by, survives.

Ball, however, takes this relatively minor subplot gloriously over the top. And because of the third-person-omniscient format, he can give screen time to those characters not in Dallas with Sookie, who are part of what is developing into an ensemble cast—Tara, Lafayette, Sam, and Ball's created character, Bill's "daughter" Jessica, who is becoming increasingly important.

It's arguable that Ball's creative choices are driven not only by the limitations of the first-person narrative in the novels, but also by the differences in how broad the appeal of a television series has to be, as contrasted with a book. As I said, he intended Tara and Lafayette to be characters who would speak to the black, and, in Lafayette's case, gay, audiences. Jessica brings youth appeal to the mix. And the growing importance of Eric (who really doesn't become much more than an antagonist in the novels until the fourth book, *Dead to the World*) reflects Ball's awareness of the Team Bill/Team Eric fan dynamic. All of this can translate to ratings, and ratings mean success, leading to future seasons. And *True Blood* has most definitely enjoyed such success.

Authors of novels and short stories like Charlaine Harris, on the other hand, while they keep the readers they are writing for in mind, write more for themselves, and hope that their visions will find an audience. Charlaine has said that she knows who Sookie's one-and-only will turn out to be—and that isn't going to change because of either Alexander Skarsgård's or Stephen Moyer's popularity!

As season three of *True Blood*, based on *Club Dead*, is shaping up, it's clear as of this writing that Ball is heading even more in his own direction. Characters related to Lafayette have been cast—characters who don't appear in the books at all, since Lafayette doesn't survive Rene's killing spree. Sam's back-story (which is not at all like his history on the page) will be pursued. And I would hazard a guess that Ball's version of the Bill/Sookie/Eric triangle will play out much differently. It will be interesting to see if the hunky werewolf I mentioned earlier, who does make his entrance in *Club Dead*, will join the geometry!

But still, based on the teaser ending of season two, it does seem that the central mystery plot of season three will reflect the central mystery plot of *Club Dead*—Bill vanishes, and Sookie reluctantly turns to Eric to help find him.

And, if Team Eric is lucky, the core plot of season four (*True Blood* has already been renewed for 2011) will follow the plot of *Dead to the World*, a.k.a. the Naked Eric Book (which begins with Sookie finding the blond vamp unclothed in the middle of the road while she's driving home from work).

Because whatever else may happen around her, in Tara's life or Lafayette's life or Sam's life or Jessica's life, Sookie does in fact remain central to *True Blood*. Ball has been faithful to her all along. He may not have chosen in his adaptations to follow the books to the letter, to give the viewers all Sookie, all the time, but he has kept the essence of the novels. They are still mysteries—and Sookie is the amateur sleuth. They are still romances—and Sookie is the central love-object. They are still stories about how it feels to be an outsider—and though Sookie is learning that she is not alone in her abilities, as she does in the books, the series continues to be about her struggle with her "gift."

That, I think, should earn Ball serious accolades. But alas, there is no Emmy for Best Adaptation! And *True Blood* is a genre series, so I suspect that Ball will not even be given the writing props he got for *Six Feet Under*.

So, for what it is worth—I say the winner for Best Television Series Adaptation of Two Novels (and counting) is—Alan Ball!

———

In the early '70s, **GINJER BUCHANAN** moved from Pittsburgh, Pennsylvania, to New York City, where she made her living as a social worker while doing freelance editorial work. In 1984, she took a job as an editor at Ace Books. She has been promoted several times. Her current title is Editor-in-Chief, Ace/Roc Books. Her first (and only) novel, a Highlander tie-in titled *White Silence*, was published in February 1999. She has also had "pop culture" essays included in the third *Buffy the Vampire Slayer* episode guide and in *Finding Serenity*, a collection about Joss Whedon's *Firefly*.

FROM CASTLE DRACULA TO MERLOTTE'S BAR & GRILL

Some Notes on the Evolution of the Modern Vampire

BRUCE AND KAREN BETHKE

This final essay is less about *True Blood* specifically than it is an effort to explain the show's breadth of appeal. Karen and Bruce Bethke's television choices usually couldn't overlap less—and yet, they both love *True Blood*. Why? What is it about the show and its angle on vampires that is so appealing? The Bethkes find half a dozen viable answers. And hopefully you'll find a few new answers of your own.

I. Preamble

We are not your usual sort of married couple. She likes cats; I prefer dogs. I'm the software engineer and science fiction writer. She's the bookstore owner, unpublished fantasy writer, and paranormal romance fan with a four-novel-a-week habit. I think *Casablanca* is the greatest movie ever made. She is the only person I know who owns a library of more than fifty vampire films, covering the entire genre from the original 1931

Universal Pictures *Dracula* to *Ankle Biters*, which is apparently the only all-midget vampire movie ever made.

As you might expect, there are some serious tradeoffs that go into making our house a happy home. Once every four years, I pretend to be interested in Olympic figure skating. Slightly less often, she pretends to care about the Minnesota Vikings' playoff chances. Recently it was her turn to suffer through every single episode of *Battlestar Galactica*, from the initial series pilot to the final credits of the final episode. Currently it's my turn to suffer through every single episode of *True Blood*.

Don't let Karen know, but actually, I am enjoying the heck out of this series.

Why? To be honest, we've been trying to sort this one out for years—decades, even—ever since we first started dating and couldn't do anything after school because she had to rush home to catch *Dark Shadows*. What is it about the vampire story in general—and Charlaine Harris' Southern Vampire Mysteries series in particular—and especially about *True Blood* that has somehow transformed what was, just a few years ago, a hideously unclean and undead creature of absolute loathing and horror into some sort of dark, brooding, sexy, romantic hero?

II. A Cursory Survey of the Existing Literature

I'll admit to being not entirely immune to the charms of a good vampire story, well told. Our library is chock-full of them, from the latest Charlaine Harris and Stephenie Meyer novels to the earliest Bram Stoker—or even further back, if you go into the folklore and mythology section. To be honest, I've even written and sold a few vampire stories myself, and one of mine made it as far as the Nebula Awards ballot, although it didn't win.

Don't look so surprised. The boundaries between science fiction, fantasy, and horror are a lot more permeable than we sci-fi types generally like to let on. In fact, I have often argued that science fiction is merely horror with an engineering degree. "Yes, my villain may look and act exactly like a classic vampire—but he's actually a *space alien!*"

Or a mutant. Or a poor bugger with a rare genetic disorder. Or an out-of-control medical-transfusion robot. Or—the one I got some good mileage out of—the victim of a genetically engineered AIDS treatment gone horribly wrong.

Hal Clement wrote vampire stories like these fifty years ago. So did Cyril Kornbluth. Fred Saberhagen is revered in science fiction circles for his hard-science stories, but it was *The Dracula Tape* and its sequels that made his career. There are vampires in *Doctor Who* and even *Star Trek*, although you might have to squint a little to recognize them. Perhaps the best example of all the attempts to make vampirism work by sci-fi rules is Richard Matheson's famous novella "I Am Legend," which is so good it's been made into a movie three times: first in 1964 as *The Last Man on Earth*, starring Vincent Price; then again in 1971 as *The Omega Man*, starring Charlton Heston; and most recently in 2007 as *I Am Legend*, starring Will Smith, albeit with a script that owed more to *28 Days Later* than to Matheson's original story. But with all these writers writing all these stories over all these years, it seems we have all missed one critically important point: *Vampires are sexy.*

Say what?

I will break the guild's Code of Silence now and let you in on a little sci-fi writer's secret: in fantastic fiction, all monsters are really either lions, bears, wolves, or snakes. It doesn't matter how the critter is packaged. It may come from Mars, sport six arms, and have ice-cold hydrofluoric acid for blood, but if it's silent, strikes from hiding without warning, and causes a lingering and painful death, it's a snake. If it hunts humans by surprise in the dark and tears them to pieces, it's a lion. If it's an unstoppable behemoth, it's a bear, and if it stalks humans openly and inexorably in the broad daylight, it's a wolf.

And then there are vampires. Vampires are different from all other monsters; their strongest roots lead back not to the ancient tribal folklore of hunting stories, but into the dark twisted tangles of medieval religion and spirituality. Vampires are *revenants*: unclean spirits, vengeful ghosts who feed on the living and bring terrible sickness and slow, wasting death. Vampires are the dead who don't have the decency to stay in their graves, and as such, their stories pack an emotional wallop entirely different from that of your more common monsters.

With a beast-type monster, your choices are simple: escape from it, kill it, or be killed by it. But vampires are *human*, or at least may remember being human. They can have human emotions and motivations, however befouled and twisted. They can have voices and speech, which make them worse. As an object of horror, they cut much closer to the quick than any inhuman beast, as there is nothing at once more horrible and more piteous than a human who has been transformed into some wily and treacherous monster—especially if "monsterness" is a communicable disease. With a vampire, it's even possible to empathize with and feel pity for the monster, and at the end of the story to regret having had to destroy it, assuming—

III. My Co-Author, As Usual, Is Completely Missing the Point

Okay, Karen here, and I have to jump in and take over right now because Bruce has completely missed so many really important and obvious points.

First off, I'm not just a fan of *True Blood*; I'm a huge fan of paranormal romances in general and of Charlaine Harris' novels in particular. I'm not just talking about her Southern Vampire Mysteries, either; I've also read all of her Aurora Teagarden, Harper Connelly, and especially her Lily Bard novels, and I've loved them all. Harris has a real genius for creating likable and empathetic characters, even when they're surrounded by pure craziness. As a narrative character, I really *like* Sookie Stackhouse. She's just a really nice, sweet, likable girl who only wants the same sorts of things that everyone else wants: to find happiness with the right man, to help others, and to keep her friends and relatives from being killed and eaten by creatures straight out of myths and nightmares.

As for what Bruce terms the "inexplicable romantic appeal" of the vampire, I think the fundamental difference here is revealed by a single word—he keeps referring to vampires as *monsters*. This suggests that while we may be *watching* the same movie in the same theater, or the same program on the TV in the family room, he and I are *seeing* different movies.

As is true of most men, Bruce watches movies through the filter of his Y chromosomes. When he reads something he can usually manage to be open-minded, but when he *sees* something, it bypasses his forebrain and goes straight into his most primitive hunter/warrior fight-or-flight reflexes: "Hmm! Og see strange thing! What me do?" And then he runs down a pretty simple decision tree: fight it, run away from it, or try to kill and eat it. "Make love with it" is probably a pretty low priority, just above "burn it to stay warm."

Which probably explains why he has the largest collection of Arnold Schwarzenegger movies I've ever seen.

Most women, on the other hand, are more curious, and more likely to react to seeing something strange by wondering,

"What *is* that? What is it doing? What does it want? Will it be my friend?"—which is probably exactly what was going through Eve's mind when she first met the serpent in the Garden of Eden. Women don't *need* to react with an instant fight-or-flight decision. That's why we keep men around—so we can afford to be more inquisitive.

And yes, sometimes being inquisitive can lead you into some pretty dark places—but again, that's okay, because unlike men, we women are not instinctively afraid of dark places.

BRUCE: Unless there are spiders.

KAREN: Yes, of course. If there are spiders, then all bets are off. Go kill all the spiders you want, Arnold.

BRUCE: Thank you. But what I don't understand is, vampires are parasites. They're leeches, ticks, tapeworms in human form. They feed on human blood. How can you not feel some sort of instinctive revulsion toward them?

KAREN RESUMES: Here we see another profoundly different response. Women, on the whole, are just a lot more relaxed around blood. If a man has blood flowing out of his body, it means that something is terribly wrong; he's been injured in an accident or wounded in battle or something like that, and he needs to staunch the flow of blood quickly or be at risk of dying. "*Medic!*"

But when a woman sees blood flowing out of her body—well, to be honest, for most of her life it means, "Hallelujah! I'm not pregnant this month!"

So to be perfectly blunt, women are a whole lot more relaxed about flowing blood than men. We see it all the time. We cope with it. It's not that big a deal. A guy wants to bite our neck and drink our blood? That's kinky, not threatening.

You'll see this gender difference most clearly with parents on the playground. Little Johnny falls off the swing-set and bites his tongue, and as soon as Dad sees the blood he's in a panic: "Call 9-1-1! We've got to get him to the Emergency Room!"

Mom, on the other hand, says, "Oh, buy the kid a popsicle. In five minutes he'll forget all about it."

We tend to pay for it on the other end, though, by being really squeamish about all other bodily fluids and excretions. Little Johnny steps in a pile of fresh dog poo and really squishes it into his sneakers, or Baby Susie has a blowout and fills her diaper? Then they're *your* kids.

IV. As I Was Saying Before I Was So Rudely Interrupted

Thank you, Karen, for that interesting and pungent insight. As I was in the process of explaining—

The classic modern vampire story, then, is an interesting hybrid: a bronze-age lion-hunting tale cross-pollinated with an empathetic human monster story. Strip most of the variations on *Dracula* down to their bare essentials and they're *Beowulf*; i.e., a good and peaceful people are bedeviled by a terrible monster, which steals into their homes under cover of darkness, kills by biting throats, and then escapes into the night. A wise and brave hero learns of these happenings and travels to the scene, first to confront the monster where it feeds and drive it off, and then to track it back to its lair and kill it. The hero of the Geats and Dr. Abraham Van Helsing of Holland may be a thousand years apart, but both are cut from the same Neolithic cloth.

What makes *True Blood* interesting to me as a writer, though, is the way it stands the classic trope on its head right from the very start. The entire series begins with the "monster"— Bill—innocently and peacefully entering the lair of the wily and dangerous *humans*, and before the first hour is out it's up to Sookie to rescue Bill from the Rattrays. In the third episode she repeats and expands on the theme, this time tracking the "monster" back to its "lair" just in time to stop Bill from biting Jerry—thereby saving Bill again, this time from contracting the Hepatitis D that Jerry knows he carries.

This role reversal is an ongoing motif throughout the first season. Time and again—when Chuck, Wayne, and Royce kill Malcolm, Liam, and Diane, or when Jason and Amy kidnap Vampire Eddie to use him as a living V dispensary—it's the *humans* that are the menace, and the "monsters" that are in jeopardy. This theme reaches its peak in the final episodes of the season with the revelation that Rene Lenier is actually Drew Marshall, and therefore both the stalker who has been pursuing Sookie and the rabidly anti-vampire serial killer responsible for more murders than all the "monsters" in the first season put together.

In the second season, of course, the entire Fellowship of the Sun subplot turns on the idea that Christian humans are the greatest threat of all, and their hatred can only be expunged by Godric's explicitly Christ-like sacrifice as he goes willingly to "meet the sun."

V. The Passion of the Vampire

It's interesting that Bruce should bring that up. Now, Reverend Newlin and his Fellowship of the Sun are simple garden-variety hate-mongers and hypocrites. Take the *n* out of the GOD HATES FANGS billboard and I think you'll see who they're patterned after.

But I've always felt Bruce missed something by growing up Methodist, and not Catholic Italian and sentenced to parochial school. We Catholics *really* get into the sacramental significance of blood. It's not just figurative; the Eucharist is the actual *source* of eternal life, and we can't get into Heaven without tasting it at least once. For us it is taking God's power directly into ourselves by literally feeding on the body and blood of Christ in what amounts to an act of ritual cannibalism, since according to the doctrine of transubstantiation, the bread and wine actually become flesh and blood when you receive communion.

And speaking now as a former Catholic who has spent four years studying for the Anglican Deaconate, you must understand that what Christianity is really all about is Easter. It's not about Christmas. The Word did not become Flesh to bring candy and toys for good little goys. The entire weight of the faith rests on Easter: on Christ's suffering, death, and—most importantly—resurrection. If you do not literally believe that about two thousand years ago there lived a man named Jesus of Nazareth, who was The Christ, who suffered death and was buried, and who on the third day rose again from the dead, and ascended into Heaven—well, you may be a terrifically nice and moral person, but you are not in any meaningful sense of the word a Christian.

Now, within Christianity there is a certain strain that fixates on the bloody suffering and death of Jesus, and seems to lose interest in the rest of the message. I think that understanding this strain is essential to understanding why the romantic vampires of today are so unlike the monstrous vampires of even twenty years ago, and also why they're currently so very popular.

So here is my question for you. Beginning with Bram Stoker's *Dracula*, and continuing on through all those old-school vampire stories and movies, right up through Anne Rice's *Interview With The Vampire*, what is the one thing that was present in all those old stories that is completely missing from the new generation of paranormal romances?

Give up?

It's guilt. Sin.

In all the old-school vampire novels, the vampires were damned souls, princes of darkness, in league with the Devil and doomed to Hell. They were cursed, suffering, and in eternal torment. In story after story, someone like Van Helsing always ends up pounding a wooden stake through the heart of some-one like Lucy, and then, after a good bit of thrashing, scream-ing, and blood-spattering, piously declaring that her soul is at last at peace.

As a parochial schoolgirl, I learned all about sin, guilt, pain, endless suffering, and eternal damnation. I was terrified of the prospect of ending up spending eternity in Hell.

But . . .

But what if it's not real? What if there is no God, no Satan, no Heaven, no Hell? What if there is no afterlife in which you are either blessed or damned?

This is not an idle philosophical question. In the new gen-eration of paranormal romances, there is—with the notable exception of *Twilight*—almost never any talk of anyone's having or not having an immortal soul, much less of their prospects for eternal damnation. In *True Blood* the argument comes to a peak: there is no God, no Satan—when Jessica asks Bill if he is a Christian, the best he can manage is, "I used to be." Miss Jeanette is a con artist, pure and simple, and while the Reverend Newlin and the Fellowship of the Sun talk about God and Christ, they have nothing real except hate to back up their rhetoric. In the world of *True Blood* there may be super-natural creatures galore, but there is a notable absence of actual divinity.

There aren't even any pre-Christian pagan gods. In a way Maryann Forrester is a profoundly pathetic creature, as she has been waiting for who knows how many thousands of years for the arrival of Dionysus, and in the meantime doing terrible things to bring about his coming. Yet in the end she dies disappointed, with the last words, "Was there no god?"

So without any actual divinity, without an afterlife, in a time when even mainstream denominations are backing away from insisting that their parishioners actually believe in anything, much less in the literal existence of Christ and the historical fact of his resurrection—what then becomes of the vampire?

Let's look at the checklist. Does he have superhuman strength? Check. Can he fly? Usually, check. Is he invulnerable to ordinary weapons? Check. Does he have incredibly heightened senses of vision, hearing, or smell? Check. Does he have one mortal weakness, which if he is not careful can destroy him? Check.

BRUCE: Omigosh. It's a superhero origin story.

KAREN: Exactly.

BRUCE: *"Bitten by a radioactive bat, he acquired the powers of the bat, and became—"*

KAREN: That one's already taken.

BRUCE: So what you're saying is, it's all because of *Blade*?

KAREN: No, Blade still had honor and morality. He hated his vampire half. But if you take away the moral angle—if there is no eternal spiritual price to be paid for becoming a vampire, if the only form of immortality you can be certain of obtaining in this world is vampiric—well, why *not* embrace the power and the darkness? How do you think most people would react?

BRUCE: Like Jessica?

KAREN: Yes, like Jessica. How does she react when Bill tells her she's been "made vampire"? With horror and despair? No, she's ecstatic: "Oh boy, now I get to kill people!" And Bill has his hands full trying to convince her that she shouldn't.

BRUCE: Ah. Because without the moral element, becoming one of the undead is simply another lifestyle choice, no more intrinsically right or wrong than any other.

KAREN: Exactly.

BRUCE: And the closest anyone ever gets to eternal damnation is being stuck forever with the body they had at the time they were made vampire. Like poor Eddie, doomed to be a tubby gay nebbish for the rest of eternity, unless someone stakes him.

KAREN: Eddie got off lucky. Personally, my sympathies are entirely with Jessica.

BRUCE: Oh?

KAREN: Getting her virginity back every time she loses it? It's a wonder she doesn't bite off Hoyt's head. Or anything else.

BRUCE: Um . . .

VI. Bad Boys, Bad Boys, Whatcha Gonna Do?

BRUCE CONTINUES: Okay, so I get part of it now. Vampires are the new superheroes, and they're attractive because they can party all night, have great fashion sense, and have awesome superpowers. As Henry Kissinger once said, power is the ultimate aphrodisiac. But how can vampires be *sexy*? I mean, they're dead, right? No heartbeat? No pulse?

KAREN: *Un*dead, actually. But yes, that's the usual take.

BRUCE: Therefore no blood pressure.

KAREN: I would suppose not.

BRUCE: Therefore how on earth does vampire erectile tissue work? I mean, I can understand how a *female* vampire could be sexy. All she has to do is be beautiful and lay there like a corpse.

KAREN: Let's leave last night out of this.

BRUCE: But as regards a male vampire—

KAREN: That's why they're called Southern Vampire *Mysteries*, dear. Let's leave it at that.

BRUCE: I'd like to. But you still haven't answered my one fundamental question. What is it about Charlaine Harris' Sookie Stackhouse novels in general, and *True Blood* in particular, that keeps you hooked on the story? I mean, I can put my answer in a single word: it's *fun*. The series is cool, and exciting, and always surprising and entertaining. But considering that you've already read all the books, what keeps *you* hooked, book after book and week after week?

KAREN RESUMES: Well, first off, it doesn't matter that I've read the books. Maybe it takes a little of the scare factor out of watching the series, because I usually have some idea of what's coming up next, but Alan Ball has made enough changes from the books to the TV series to keep it fresh and new for me. I have to say that most of the changes are improvements, too: for example, I was really disappointed when Harris killed off Lafayette in the books, so I'm glad that Ball decided to keep him alive in the series.

I think another part of the appeal of the series—and of paranormal romance in general—is the "bad boy" factor. It's that X versus Y chromosome thing again. You keep viewing *True Blood* as being like *The X-Files*, only with sex. Men in general see something strange, terrible, and wonderful, and they want to kill it, put its head on the wall, and then go have a cheeseburger and a beer with the guys. Women see something strange, terrible, and wonderful, and they want to tame it and make it their friend. So that's what makes Bill an interesting character: not so much that he's a "bad boy" who's been tamed, but the implicit power of the woman—Sookie—who was able to tame and domesticate him. Women love stories that reaffirm the idea that deep down, they have the power to tame even the wildest animal and redeem even the worst man.

That, I think, is the core appeal of the paranormal romance. We are talking here about bad boys who are so bad that even God has given up on them. But *we* have the power to save them, if we just love them enough.

When it comes to *True Blood*, though, I think what I like best are the complex relationships, and the way Harris and Ball build huge, multithreaded, intertwining storylines that take an entire season to resolve. You science fiction writers like to talk about world-building, but then you concentrate on the astronomy and biochemistry. In *True Blood* Harris and Ball have built a complex *social* world, with multiple layers and subcultures, and populated it with an ever-expanding cast of interesting, engaging, and multidimensional characters. There are good people and bad vampires—and bad people and good vampires—but most of the characters are a blend of these qualities: sometimes good, sometimes bad, sometimes honest, and sometimes devious. In short, they're just like real people, only more so. Further, I think that in continuing to focus on the vampires, were-creatures, and such, you get locked into thinking of *True Blood* as a horror series, and this prevents you from seeing that it is actually a *mystery* series, which just happens to involve a cast of vampires, shapeshifters, were-creatures, et cetera, et cetera.

I mean, think this through with me. If Fangtasia was simply a creepy Goth nightclub, if "V" was just another designer drug, if Bill was simply a traumatized war veteran who *thought* he was a vampire, if Sam was just a lovesick bartender with the personality of a border collie, if the Newlins were yet another pair of hypocritical money-grubbing televangelists, if Jason was just another Darwin Award nominee waiting to happen, if Maryann Forrester was simply some Tim Leary–like hedonist drug cult leader—

If all this was true, and if Sookie herself was not actually psychic but simply a small-town Southern waitress with remarkably keen intuition—*the series would still work*. Because Sookie is at heart an amateur detective, from the long tradition of fictional amateur detectives, and underneath the paranormal trappings, the plots and subplots are largely the stuff of detective stories, and revolve around her discovering the solutions to crimes. Who killed Maudette Pickens? Who is stealing from Fangtasia? Where is Drew Marshall? What happened to Godric? What is the Newlins' dirty secret? How is Maryann Forrester corrupting an entire town? (And I have to mention that I think Jason and Amy do a wonderful riff on *Ruthless People* when they kidnap Eddie.)

That is what you're missing when you focus too hard on trying to make sense of vampire biology. Women like stories about evolving long-term relationships between characters, and *True Blood* definitely delivers that. Men like stories about problems that can be solved, and it bothers you when that doesn't happen. That is why you want your stories to have clean and solid conclusions with all the loose ends tied up, and I'm not at all worried about that, as long as the journey was interesting.

BRUCE: And that's our ending?

KAREN: It's *your* baby. *You* deal with the diaper.

VII. Conclusions and Preliminary Findings

And with that said, the learned Professor of Vampiric Studies flounced out of the room, leaving me to tidy up the loose ends. In the end we are no closer than we were at the beginning to answering my fundamental question: Precisely *how* have vampires been transformed recently from undead objects of horror to sexy romantic heroes? Is it really just a matter of gender perceptual filters? Is it true that men instinctively fixate on the vampire's "monster" qualities, while women are able to see their human aspects? Or is this a gross over-simplification?

Perhaps the question does not need to be answered. Speaking now as a professional writer, I can only say that I have enjoyed the heck out of the first two seasons of *True Blood*. In my career I have been on all sides of this equation: I have written fiction for print, I have written scripts for stage and screen, I have had my stories optioned and made into screenplays, and I have adapted other people's screenplays for print publication. Of all these things, I think the hardest thing to do well is to adapt someone else's *good* novel into a *great* screenplay. It's actually easier to adapt a lousy novel: in that case you have no compunctions about throwing out the parts that don't work and improving the story as and where needed. But as evidenced by forty years of makes and remakes of "I Am Legend," taking what is already a good story with interesting characters and turning it into a good screenplay without doing serious damage to the original story is exceedingly difficult, because print and film are two *very* different ways of storytelling, and thus major changes are always required. Given that, the ability to take a good novel and turn it into a better TV series is rare indeed, and thus far Mr. Ball and company have done a wonderful job with *True Blood*.

I can't wait to see how they carry it forward in season three.

———

BRUCE AND KAREN BETHKE live in beautiful, alligator-free Minnesota. He's an award-winning science fiction writer; she's a bookstore owner and thus far unpublished fantasy/paranormal romance writer. This essay is their first official collaboration that has not required braces or to be driven to the mall.

Bruce and Karen can be reached through www.brucebethke.com.

TRUE BLOOD EPISODE GUIDE

SEASON ONE

Episode 1: Strange Love

(FIRST AIRED SEPTEMBER 7, 2008)

Since vampires came out of the coffin after the invention of Tru Blood, a synthetic alternative to feeding off the living, people and vamps have been struggling to coexist, including the residents of Bon Temps, Louisiana. Sookie Stackhouse, telepath and barmaid at Merlotte's Bar and Grill, has finally met the man of her dreams. Bill Compton is a polite, gorgeous Southern gentleman—who also happens to be a vampire. Consequently, Sookie cannot hear his thoughts, which may make him the most interesting and appealing man she's ever met. Attacked by the Rattrays (drainers who sell vampire blood on the black market), Bill is rescued by Sookie in Merlotte's parking lot, sealing the bond between this unusual pair. Sookie's brother Jason is a ladies' man, and he has sex with Maudette Pickens while watching a video of her getting intimate with a vampire. When Maudette turns up strangled, Jason is a prime suspect. Sookie's best friend, Tara Thornton, is head-over-heels for Jason, who is oblivious to her affection, while Sam Merlotte (the owner of Merlotte's) is carrying a secret torch for Sookie. Completing the crew at Merlotte's is Sookie's redheaded divorcée friend Arlene, and Tara's gay cousin Lafayette, who cooks for the bar.

QUOTE WITH BITE:

TARA (TO A CUSTOMER): I have a name. And that name is Tara. Isn't that funny, a black girl being named after a plantation? No, I don't think it's funny at all. In fact, it really pisses me off that my momma was either stupid or just plain mean. Which is why you better be nice if you plan on getting a drink tonight.

Episode 2: The First Taste
(FIRST AIRED SEPTEMBER 14, 2008)

The Rattrays are out for blood again, but this time it's Bill's turn to rescue Sookie. Sookie feeds from Bill in order to heal more quickly, but the vampire blood has side effects—including heightened senses and libido. The Rattrays conveniently die in a mysterious tornado, and Sookie suspects that Bill has had a hand in their deaths. Bill visits the Stackhouse family at their home and wins over Sookie's Gran, Adele. Police discover the intimate video of Jason and Maudette Pickens, the strangulation victim.

QUOTE WITH BITE:

BILL: Can I ask you a personal question?
SOOKIE: Bill, you were just licking blood out of my head. I don't think it gets much more personal than that.

Episode 3: Mine
(FIRST AIRED SEPTEMBER 21, 2008)

When she stops by Bill's home, Sookie is disgusted by the behavior of three visiting vamps. Bill saves her once again from a vampire attack, but to do so, Bill has to assert that Sookie is "his." Not having learned his lesson from the incident with Maudette Pickens, Jason sleeps with Dawn Green, who also turns up strangled. Tara finally walks out on her abusive, alcoholic mother and stays the night with Sam Merlotte.

QUOTES WITH BITE:

JASON (TO LAFAYETTE): You're wearing gold pants!

BILL: Sookie is mine.

BILL (TO SOOKIE): You think that it's not magic that keeps you alive? Just because you understand the mechanics of how something works doesn't make it any less of a miracle, which is just another word for magic. We're all kept alive by magic, Sookie. My magic's just a little different from yours, that's all.

Episode 4: Escape from Dragon House
(FIRST AIRED SEPTEMBER 28, 2008)

After the murder of Dawn Green, police suspicion falls heavily on Jason, but Tara comes to his rescue with an alibi. Trying to clear her brother's name, Sookie investigates the deaths of Maudette and Dawn, whose only similarity was their affinity for taking vampire lovers. Sookie asks Bill to escort her to the vampire bar, Fangtasia, where she meets Eric, the local vampire in charge. Sam joins the ranks of the supernatural in Bon Temps when his shapeshifting abilities are revealed. Jason overdoses on the vampire blood (V) that he buys from Lafayette, and has to go to the hospital to fix the painful—and embarrassing—effects that V has on the male anatomy.

QUOTES WITH BITE:

SOOKIE: I'm sorry if I got you into any trouble tonight.
BILL: Don't apologize. We vampires are always in some kind of trouble. I'd prefer to be in it with you.

TARA (TO JASON, ON HIS V OVERDOSE EFFECTS): Lift the rib eye. Let me see what we're dealing with.

Episode 5: Sparks Fly Out
(FIRST AIRED OCTOBER 5, 2008)

Sookie breaks up with Bill after they encounter a policeman with anti-vamp tendencies. As a favor to Sookie's Gran, Bill speaks to the Descendants of the Glorious Dead, a local history club, about his experiences in the Civil War. After a club member gives him a war-era photo, Bill flashes back to the time he became a vampire. Sam finally works up the courage to ask Sookie out, and they attend Bill's presentation together. The strangler strikes again in Bon Temps, as Sookie discovers when she finds her grandmother dead after her date. Jason buys more V from Lafayette, and moves on to a woman named Randi Sue.

QUOTES WITH BITE:

SOOKIE: Are you asking me out?

SAM: Yeah, that's pretty much how I do it. Sometimes they even say yes.

LAFAYETTE: 'Scuse me. Who ordered the hamburger with AIDS? In this restaurant, a hamburger deluxe comes with French fries, lettuce, tomato, mayo, and AIDS! Do anyone got a problem with that?

Episode 6: Cold Ground
(FIRST AIRED OCTOBER 12, 2008)

Sookie deals with the death of her grandmother, as well as the mental accusations of Bon Temps locals who blame Gran's death on Sookie's association with Bill. Passed out on V at Randi Sue's place, Jason doesn't hear about Gran's death until he goes to work. When he finds out, he slaps Sookie at her house, in front of half the town. Lafayette gives Sookie a valium so that she can sleep. At the funeral, Sookie breaks down under the emotional burden. Jason tries to apologize for his earlier violence, but she runs away from him. Tara and Sam sleep together again, but struggling with thoughts about her mother, Tara leaves him. Sookie finally finds some peace as she eats her Gran's pie and cries, and as night falls, she runs to Bill's house, where he takes her virginity.

QUOTES WITH BITE:

TARA (TO LAFAYETTE): Nothing says "I'm sorry" like a tuna-cheese casserole.

LAFAYETTE (TO TARA): What the fuck is it with white people and Jell-o? Sookie don't need no bad-ju-ju cookin'. Smell this. Smell this. You can smell the fear and nastiness coming up off that cornbread.

Episode 7: Burning House of Love
(FIRST AIRED OCTOBER 19, 2008)

Sookie finds herself deeply, and happily, attached to Bill after they sleep together, but her friends and coworkers aren't as thrilled with her blooming romance. Sookie opens up to Bill emotionally and shares her painful childhood memories about her "funny" Uncle Bartlett. Tara's mom, Lettie May, wants Tara to loan her money for an exorcism to rid her of her alcoholic demon. Tara gives her the money and they visit Miss Jeanette, who performs the exorcism at her trailer in the middle of the woods. In the hunt for more V, Jason visits Fangtasia, but instead of vampire blood, he goes home with a young woman named Amy. Sam's secret is nearly exposed when the police see him running naked through the bayou. Bill's three vampire acquaintances buy a house in Bon Temps, to the dismay of the residents, who decide to take matters into their own hands and burn out the vamps.

QUOTE WITH BITE:

PAM: Does your mama know you're here?
JASON: My mama's dead.
PAM: So am I.

Episode 8: The Fourth Man in the Fire
(FIRST AIRED OCTOBER 26, 2008)

Sookie is happy to learn that Bill isn't one of the house burn victims, and they have a very sexy reunion in the graveyard, where Bill had buried himself. Desperate for more V, Jason and Amy follow Lafayette to a vampire client's house and kidnap their own source of fresh blood. Lettie May gives up drinking and changes drastically after her exorcism, even prodding Tara to have one done as well. Arlene asks Sookie to babysit her kids but hesitates—angering Sookie—when she discovers that Bill will be babysitting as well. While Sookie and Bill are babysitting the kids, Rene proposes to Arlene and everyone is enthusiastic at the news. But the honeymoon is over for Sookie and Bill when he tells her that he agreed to lend her telepathic powers to Eric, in order to figure out who has been stealing money from Fangtasia.

QUOTE WITH BITE:

JASON (TO AMY): I just want to lick your mind!

Episode 9: Plaisir d'Amour
(FIRST AIRED NOVEMBER 2, 2008)

When Sookie discovers that Longshadow is the Fangtasia thief, Bill has to step in to prevent Longshadow from killing her. Longshadow ends up dead instead, so Bill must make arrangements to go before the vampire tribunal to pay the penalty for his crime. Amy and Jason store their vampire captive, Eddie, in Jason's basement. While Amy is away at work, Jason becomes friendly with Eddie and considers freeing him. Sam lends Tara the $800 she needs for her own exorcism, and keeps his promise to Bill to watch over Sookie. Sookie takes in a stray dog for the night, but she wakes up with a naked Sam in her bed instead.

QUOTES WITH BITE:

JASON (TO AMY): I should've known something wasn't right the second you walked into my life carrying that big bag of crazy.

'Cause any woman with a purse that big is bound to have something I don't want to know about.

PAM: You're not going anywhere. Eric and your boyfriend aren't nearly done talking just yet.
SOOKIE: Is Bill in some kind of trouble?
PAM: That's for the boys to figure out. Right now what you need to do is change out of your clothes. There's vampire in your cleavage.

Episode 10: I Don't Wanna Know
(FIRST AIRED NOVEMBER 9, 2008)

Sam finally admits to Sookie that he is a shapeshifter who often takes the form of a dog. Miss Jeanette exorcises Tara's demon, leaving her feeling great—until she discovers that Miss Jeanette is a hack who spends her days as a cashier at a local drugstore. Merlotte's hosts Arlene and Rene's engagement party, where Sookie is attacked by the strangler in the bar kitchen. Jason tries to help Eddie, but Amy kills the vampire when she thinks Jason is getting too close to him. Bill appears at the vampire tribunal to hear his punishment for killing Longshadow: for taking a life, he is sentenced to make another vampire.

QUOTE WITH BITE:

SAM: Bill asked me to look after you while he was away.
SOOKIE: Did he ask you to do it buck naked?

Episode 11: To Love Is to Bury

(FIRST AIRED NOVEMBER 16, 2008)

Jason is shaken after Amy kills Eddie. Sookie and Sam further investigate the Bon Temps killings, visiting a nearby town that had a similar murder. While Sookie is away, Bill struggles to care for his new vampire fledgling, Jessica. When Tara is arrested for drunk driving, her mother refuses to bail her out. A kind social worker, Maryann Forrester, bails Tara out instead and takes her under her wing. The strangler claims Amy as his fourth victim while Jason is sleeping next to her, and Jason is arrested for the killings.

QUOTE WITH BITE:

JESSICA (TO BILL): I want to kill people. I'm so hungry, and all you do is talk, and I'm starving. You're so mean! You're supposed to take care of me. That's what you said. And, oh, you SUCK! Haha! That's funny, because you do suck.

Episode 12: You'll Be the Death of Me

(FIRST AIRED NOVEMBER 23, 2008)

Tara gets comfortable in Maryann's mansion and makes friends with the young man living there, Eggs, so nicknamed because his real first name is Benedict. Sam remembers a sexual encounter with Maryann that took place when he was young. Jason remains in jail, but Sookie maintains his innocence. In the season's climax, Rene, formerly Drew Marshall, is revealed to be the serial killer that has been targeting young women who associate with vampires. He chases Sookie to the graveyard between the Stackhouse and Compton homes in an attempt to kill her. Both Bill and Sam come to Sookie's rescue—Bill risking death by sunlight, and Sam risking the revelation of his true nature—and Sookie kills the killer. While in jail, Jason is approached by the right-wing, anti-vampire church, the Fellowship of the Sun. Lafayette is kidnapped, Vermont legalizes vampire marriage, and, as a final cliffhanger, a body is found in Andy Bellefleur's car.

QUOTE WITH BITE:

TERRY (TO ARLENE): People disappear all the time, but they're never really gone. The good parts of them stay put . . . Your hair is like a sunset after a bomb went off. Pretty.

ANDY (TO SOOKIE AND TARA, ON FINDING A BODY IN HIS CAR): That ain't mine, I swear.

SEASON TWO

Episode 1: Nothing But the Blood

(FIRST AIRED JUNE 14, 2009)

When Detective Andy Bellefleur can't find his car in the Merlotte's parking lot, he discovers that it has been moved. Sookie, Tara, and Sam look into the backseat, where they find the brutally murdered Miss Jeanette with her heart ripped out. Sookie and Bill struggle to build trust when Sookie discovers that Bill didn't tell her about creating Jessica or killing her Uncle Bartlett. Jessica adjusts to living with Bill and learning vampire ways. While Tara is staying with Maryann, a romance begins to bloom between her and Eggs. Maryann stands up to Lettie May. Sam remembers his first meeting with Maryann, and attempts to return the money and valuables he stole from her when he was seventeen. Jason has a sunny outlook after his run-in with the Fellowship in jail, and considers going to Texas for a leadership seminar. Eric is revealed to be responsible for Lafayette's kidnapping, and is keeping him imprisoned in the Fangtasia basement for selling V.

QUOTES WITH BITE:

BILL (TO JESSICA): We also recycle in this house. Tru Blood and other glass items go in the blue container, and paper products go in the white container.

JESSICA (TO BILL): You are sooo not Eric.

BILL (TO SOOKIE): I love you, and for that I shall never feel sorry.

Episode 2: Keep this Party Going
(FIRST AIRED JUNE 21, 2009)

The reunited Bill and Sookie are happy, but struggling to deal with the difficult and feisty Jessica. Eric wants to use Sookie's telepathic skills again, but she resists helping him. Feeling sorry for Jessica and responsible for her vampiric transformation, Sookie agrees to take Jessica to her parents' home. The visit goes horribly wrong, and Bill steps in at the last second to prevent Jessica from killing her human father. Sookie asks Tara to move out of Maryann's and in with her. Feeling gung-ho about making a spiritual change, Jason attends the Fellowship of the Sun leadership seminar and becomes a fast favorite of the leaders, Steve and Sarah Newlin, despite his past indiscretions. Sam hires a new waitress, Daphne, who has trouble learning the job. Maryann visits Sam at Merlotte's, and her visit causes unusually sexy behavior between the bar patrons. Desperate to get out of Eric's dungeon, Lafayette tries to escape and gets shot in the leg. The vampires get angry, so he proposes that they make him one of them; Eric, Pam, and Chow all proceed to feed on him.

QUOTES WITH BITE:

ERIC (TO LAFAYETTE): Is there blood in my hair? . . . This is bad. Pam's gonna kill me.

SOOKIE (TO BILL ABOUT JESSICA): How is that any different from being a teenage girl? No humanity . . . check. In the grips of overwhelming transformations . . . check. Cannot control impulses . . . check.

Episode 3: Scratches

(FIRST AIRED JUNE 28, 2009)

Bill and Sookie have a fight while driving home from Jessica's parents' house, and Sookie decides to walk home through the woods. Her back is mauled by a half-man, half-bull creature, and when Bill's blood fails to heal her, he brings her to Fangtasia for Eric's help. After she is cured, Sookie discovers Lafayette, left to bleed to death by the vampires. She agrees to help Eric in exchange for Lafayette's freedom. Maryann throws a party at the mansion that quickly turns into an orgy, to Tara's discomfort; however, no one in Bon Temps can remember what happens at the party. Jessica visits Merlotte's and has a great time with Hoyt Fortenberry, until Bill comes home and finds the couple necking. Sam considers leaving town, and gets to know Daphne with a revealing nighttime swim. When Daphne strips down, she reveals scratches on her back similar to the ones inflicted upon Sookie.

QUOTES WITH BITE:

ERIC (TO BILL ABOUT FEEDING BLOOD TO SOOKIE): Be careful, you'll overcook her.

JESSICA (TO HOYT): This is so embarrassing. I'd die if I wasn't already dead!

HOYT (TO JESSICA): You should try the chicken-fried steak. It's like a chicken and a steak got together and made a baby.

Episode 4: Shake and Fingerpop
(FIRST AIRED JULY 12, 2009)

At Miss Jeanette's autopsy, the coroner shows the claw marks on the dead woman's back to the police. Bill, Sookie, and Jessica travel to the Hotel Carmilla in Dallas to help Eric with the investigation into the disappearance of the area sheriff, Godric. Sookie is attacked at the airport upon their arrival, but the sun sets just in time for Bill to save her. Tara moves into Sookie's house, and Maryann throws a wild birthday party for her there, where revelers' eyes blacken—literally—as they are consumed by lust. Sam is hesitant about dating Daphne, especially when she claims to know his secret. Despite Sookie's deal for Lafayette's freedom, Eric isn't willing to let him go home empty-handed; he appears in Bon Temps and wants to use Lafayette to keep an eye on the V market, so he feeds him his blood to create a bond, and in return Lafayette's gunshot wound is healed. While at the leadership conference, the Newlins ask Jason to move in with them. At the hotel in Dallas, Sookie meets a fellow telepath, Barry the bellhop.

QUOTES WITH BITE:

BILL (TO SOOKIE): I am a vampire. I am supposed to be tormented.

JASON (TO LUKE MACDONALD): I don't know who Lazarus was, but he sure as hell was not the first vampire. Everybody knows it was Dracula . . . Maybe Jesus was the first vampire. He rose from the dead, too! And he told people, "Hey, y'all, drink my blood. It'll give you special powers."

TARA (TO LAFAYETTE): If you die I'm going to be really pissed.

Episode 5: Never Let Me Go
(FIRST AIRED JULY 19, 2009)

Daphne shows Sam that he isn't the only shapeshifter in Bon Temps when she transforms into a deer at Tara's birthday party. In Dallas, Sookie, Eric, and Bill talk to two of Godric's lieutenants, Isabel and Stan, and formulate a plan to rescue him. Eric tells Bill that Godric is his maker, Sookie tries to learn more about Barry the telepathic bellhop, and Jason starts recruit training for the Fellowship's special vampire fighting squad at the Light of Day Institute. Back in Bon Temps, Maryann uses magic to pressure Tara into letting her move into Sookie's house. Sarah talks to Jason about her relationship with Steve, and their bath-time conversation quickly heats up. As Sookie and Bill get intimate in their room, a gorgeous vampire listens in the hall.

QUOTE WITH BITE:

BILL (TO SOOKIE): Well, here I am, responsible for you and Jessica, and yet no decisions are mine. It makes me feel . . .
SOOKIE: Like a human?
BILL: Like a waitress.
SOOKIE: You're walking in my shoes and it's giving you blisters.

Episode 6: Hard-Hearted Hannah

(FIRST AIRED JULY 26, 2009)

At the Hotel Carmilla, Eric greets Lorena, Bill's maker, who he invited to Dallas to cause a rift between Bill and Sookie. Jason has misgivings about the Fellowship's teachings after Steve asks him to build a structure upon which a vampire killing ceremony will be performed. Hoyt's mom, Maxine, gets jealous of the time he's spending with Jessica and talks about the situation at Merlotte's in front of her son. Andy questions Lafayette about his disappearance, causing him to have a mental breakdown; Terry Bellefleur finally steps in and makes Andy leave. Hoyt discovers that his mother had his phone shut off, and he angrily tells her that the reason his girlfriend calls at night is because she's a vampire. Eggs gets a feeling that prompts him to stop by the side of the highway while driving with Tara. After walking in the woods, they discover a bloody rock, but Eggs can't remember what happened there. Sookie and Hugo, Isabel's human, visit the Fellowship of the Sun to look for Godric, and they are kidnapped in the basement of the church. Bill remembers his unpleasant and violent past with Lorena. Jason and Sarah finally go all the way—inside the Fellowship church. Sam and Daphne continue to shift together—Daphne as a giant pig instead of a deer—but Sam's trust is betrayed when she lures him to Maryann's orgy to be a human sacrifice.

QUOTES WITH BITE:

FANGBANGER: Ohhh, that's it, baby.
ERIC: "Baby"? I'm over a thousand years old.
FANGBANGER: Are you not having a good time?

ERIC: Well, there's just not much thrill left in feeding on the willing.

FANGBANGER: Then should I try pretending not to want it?

ERIC: Only if you're very, very good at it.

TARA (TO MARYANN): I don't know what to tell you. I wish I had a fancier crib for you to squat in, but I don't.

Episode 7: Release Me

(FIRST AIRED AUGUST 2, 2009)

Held captive in the Fellowship of the Sun basement, Sookie realizes that Hugo is a Fellowship spy. She tries to reach Bill mentally for help, but he is also being held prisoner, by Lorena. Steve Newlin discovers that Jason and Sookie are related and assumes that Jason is a spy. Sarah and Jason lay together naked in the church, and Sarah thinks that Jason is the man God wants her to be with. When the Fellowship guard attempts to rape Sookie, Godric appears and saves her. Hoyt visits Jessica at the Dallas hotel, where they become intimate for the first time. Hearing noises in the woods after seeing a giant pig in the road, Andy finds Maryann's orgy party where Sam is about to be sacrificed. He fires his gun, allowing Sam time to shift into owl form and escape. Sam confronts Daphne with a gun about leading him to sacrifice, and Daphne reveals that Maryann is a maenad, and Daphne is her servant. Only Sam and Andy remember the events of the party.

QUOTE WITH BITE:

JESSICA: Hoyt, just take off your pants.

Episode 8: Timebomb

(FIRST AIRED AUGUST 9, 2009)

Eric appears after Godric saves Sookie (with Bill arriving much, much later), and Godric orders him to leave the church peacefully. Sarah, feeling angry and betrayed by Jason after they made love, shoots him with a paintball gun as he is walking out of the Fellowship compound, and tells him that they have his sister. Jason hits her, steals her golf cart and paintball gun, and drives to the church to help rescue Sookie. A peaceful escape for Sookie and her rescuers isn't made easy when Steve Newlin and other Fellowship members surround the vamps in the church with weapons in hand. However, Godric steps in and everyone survives the showdown. Eggs tells Tara that there are other incidents that he can't remember, and that he has been having blackouts. Someone calls Sam on his cell phone from Merlotte's, where he rushes to find Daphne's body (minus her heart) in the freezer and is arrested as the prime suspect. Maryann makes a special pie for Eggs and Tara—with Daphne's heart as the filling—that causes their lovemaking to get a little violent. Hoyt and Jessica discover that Jessica will always be a virgin. When Sookie and the gang get back to Godric's house, Godric banishes Lorena after she picks a fight with Sookie. Their celebration ends abruptly when Luke, strapped with explosives, blows up the room.

QUOTES WITH BITE:

SOOKIE (ABOUT GODRIC): He's your maker, isn't he?
ERIC: Don't use words you don't understand.
SOOKIE: You have a lot of love for him.
ERIC: Don't use words I don't understand.

JASON (TO STEVE NEWLIN): I reckon I've already been to heaven, and it's inside your wife.

Episode 9: I Will Rise Up
(FIRST AIRED AUGUST 16, 2009)

In the aftermath of the explosion, Eric tricks Sookie into drinking his blood, creating a bond between them that causes Sookie to have some sexy dreams featuring Eric. Sookie and Jason have a heart-to-heart at the hotel and finally make up. Nan Flanagan, the vampire spokesperson, chews Godric out for his carelessness in getting kidnapped. In Bon Temps, Maryann tries to bail Sam out of jail, but he escapes from her again. In desperation, she uses her powers to set the townspeople on him. Lafayette and Lettie May kidnap Tara, who is acting strangely under Maryann's influence. Hoyt and Jessica's relationship hits a speed bump when he introduces her to his over-protective mother. At the end of the episode, Godric decides that he is tired of immortality. He says farewell to Eric, and Sookie stands with him as he ends his own life and meets the sun.

QUOTE WITH BITE:

GODRIC: A human with me at the end, and human tears. Two thousand years and I can still be surprised. In this I see God.

Episode 10: New World in My View
(FIRST AIRED AUGUST 23, 2009)

When they return to Bon Temps, Sookie, Bill, and Jason find the town running amok and the house trashed. Residents are still under Maryann's spell and on the hunt for Sam, who goes to Andy for help. Sam gets a call from Arlene, who says she's being held at Merlotte's. When he goes to help her, he and Andy realize they've walked into a trap, and they escape to hide in the freezer. While waiting at Bill's mansion, Hoyt's mother provokes Jessica until she bites her in front of Hoyt. Sookie and Bill check up on Sookie's house and find a totem created by Maryann, and the house full of people going crazy. When Maryann confronts them, Bill tries to use his vampiric abilities, to no avail, but Sookie seems to be able to resist Maryann's power and even fight back. Tara remains at Lafayette's house, where he and her mother despair that Tara is in an unbreakable trance. Using their combined powers, Bill and Sookie manage to wake Tara. To learn more about maenads, Bill decides to pay a visit to the Queen of Louisiana, Sophie-Ann LeClerq. Jason puts his semimilitary Fellowship training to use and rescues Sam and Andy, then tricks the residents into thinking that he sacrificed Sam.

QUOTE WITH BITE:

LAFAYETTE (TO LETTIE MAY): Jesus and I agreed to see other people. Don't mean we still don't talk from time to time.

Episode 11: Frenzy
(FIRST AIRED AUGUST 30, 2009)

Bill asks Sophie-Ann for advice in defeating Maryann, but unfortunately, Sophie-Ann's advice is to give maenads what they want. Finding Arlene's children in the woods, Sam visits Fangtasia with the kids in tow to ask for Eric's assistance. With help from her mother, Tara escapes from Sookie and Lafayette, and runs to rescue Eggs. At the house, Maryann reveals that Tara is the one who summoned her with the exorcism and possesses her again. Hoyt breaks up with Jessica for biting his mother, who, still under Maryann's spell, reveals that Hoyt's father committed suicide. Sookie and Lafayette (who is also having steamy dreams about Eric) try to rescue the escaped Tara from Sookie's house. Sookie finds Tara and Eggs making a nest in her bed, and as she turns to leave, a black-eyed Lafayette stops her. Jason and Andy drive to Sookie's house, armed to the teeth.

QUOTE WITH BITE:

PAM (TO ARLENE'S KIDS): You make me so happy I never had any of you.
ERIC: Now come on, Pam, they're funny. They're like humans, but miniature. Teacup humans.

Episode 12: Beyond Here Lies Nothin'
(FIRST AIRED SEPTEMBER 13, 2009)

Bon Temps is out of control as the time of Maryann's sacrifice approaches. Lafayette dresses Sookie in a white toga and brings her to Maryann, who is wearing Gran's wedding dress. She chooses Sookie to be maid of honor (and bait for Sam) at the ceremony, which we learn is actually her wedding to a god. Jason and Andy rush the house, but they are quickly overcome by Maryann's power and become zombies like everyone else. Bill delivers Sam as the sacrifice, and when Eggs stabs Sam, Sookie interrupts the ceremony and distracts Maryann. A white bull appears in the road and Maryann thinks that it's her god-husband, Dionysus. It turns out that the bull is actually Sam, who gores and kills Maryann. The townspeople wake from their trances and no one can remember what has happened—with the exception of Eggs, who realizes that he is the one who killed

Miss Jeanette and Daphne. Tara wants to help him, but when Eggs tries to turn himself in to Andy with a knife in his hands, Jason thinks that he is threatening the police officer and shoots him. Jessica starts to go make up with Hoyt, but instead goes to a truck stop to find someone to feed on. The season seems like it will end happily, with an engagement between Sookie and Bill, until Bill is kidnapped by a vampire while Sookie is in the bathroom making up her mind to say yes.

QUOTE WITH BITE:

TWO WOMEN (TALKING ABOUT SAM): God bless whoever made those jeans. I'd wear that man as a scrunchie!

ACKNOWLEDGMENTS

Thanks to Heather Butterfield for her invaluable assistance, including (but definitely not limited to) putting together the episode guide and quotes.

Thanks as well to Shadaliza at *True Blood* fansite The Vault (www.trublood-online.net) for her help on a few of our essays.

Want *More* Smart Pop?

www.smartpopbooks.com

» Read a new free essay online everyday
» Plus sign up for email updates, check out our upcoming titles, and more